EAST ASIAN SOCIAL SCIENCE MONOGRAPHS

THE SOCIOLOGY OF PRODUCTION IN RURAL MALAY SOCIETY

THE SOCIOLOGY OF PRODUCTION IN RURAL MALAY SOCIETY

CONNER BAILEY

KUALA LUMPUR
OXFORD UNIVERSITY PRESS
OXFORD NEW YORK MELBOURNE
1983

Oxford University Press

Oxford London Glasgow
New York Toronto Melbourne Auckland
Kuala Lumpur Singapore Hong Kong Tokyo
Delhi Bombay Calcutta Madras Karachi
Nairobi Dar es Salaam Cape Town

and associates in
Beirut Berlin Ibadan Mexico City Nicosia

Oxford is a trademark of Oxford University Press

ISBN 0 19 582530 6 27-4-84

Printed in Singapore by Koon Wah Printing (Pte) Ltd.
Published by Oxford University Press, 3, Jalan 13/3,
Petaling Jaya, Selangor, Malaysia

Preface

THIS study is based on over five years of experience living and working in rural Malay villages. My first three years (1968–71) in Malaysia were spent as a Peace Corps Volunteer working at a rural health clinic in Sik, Kedah. In 1974 I returned to the same area for a three-month visit to collect data for a Master's thesis. From January 1977 to June 1978 I again returned to Malaysia to gather data for my doctoral dissertation. The present volume is a revision of that dissertation.

In this study I seek to elucidate a systematic source of cultural diversity within rural Malay society, one based on production processes and the social relationships these processes engender. Prior to 1977, I had travelled through various Malay villages, but I actually had lived in only one. When I compared my personal experience with the written accounts of rural Malay society available in the academic literature, I began to notice some important differences. The types of labour organization among both rice farmers and fishermen, for example, seemed to be quite different from that of the rubber tappers with whom I had lived and worked.

As this idea formed, I realized that a comparative study of rice farming, fishing, and rubber tapping would serve two personal goals. Undertaking such a comparative study would allow me to learn more about each of these three economic activities. As a social scientist concerned with the application of research to issues of rural development, this practical knowledge would be valuable.

At another, more philosophical level, it became apparent that undertaking this study would allow me to scratch a personal cerebral itch. How important is what people do to earn a living to how they live and interact with their physical and social environments? To what extent do the practical and material exigencies of life shape and influence social relationships? The importance of these issues has been and will continue to be debated by generations of scholars. Herein I offer my own small contribution. I do not accept a dogmatic position of economic determinism. Certainly there are important aspects of life which are little affected by and even transcend mere economics, but there are others which are promoted or limited by their material context. I am interested in the social consequences of production processes and relationships and I argue that not only are economic and non-economic aspects of life often inseparable, but that there are traceable links between the two.

Funding for twelve months of field research was provided by a Fulbright-Hays Doctoral Dissertation Fellowship. An additional six months of research support was provided through a grant from the Center for International Agriculture, Cornell University. The final stages of dissertation preparation were supported by a Cornell University Summer Fellowship and by a grant from the Southeast Asia Program, Cornell University. To these sources of support I am indebted.

Beyond this institutional support, a large number of individuals have provided valuable assistance. First and foremost I must thank the residents of Gong Guncil, Mangkok, and Kampung Dusun who took me in, answered endless questions, and befriended me in countless ways. A number of other Malaysians also contributed their time and energies to the furtherance of my research. Of these, Datuk Mokhzani Abdul Rahim, Dr Harun Derau, Dr Radzuan Rahman, Mr Siow Kuan Tow, Mr S. Selvadurai, and Mr Andrew Lai deserve special thanks.

Among my academic colleagues at Cornell University, my deepest debt is to Professor Milton L. Barnett, who encouraged my efforts and endeavoured to keep my attention focused on those issues critical to this work. Professors Tom Kirsch and William F. Whyte offered both encouragement and solid recommendations. Professors Norman Uphoff and John Cohen assisted me in the initial design of this research project.

The Southeast Asia Program at Cornell provided an atmosphere conducive to academic work and to the exchange of ideas among amiable and experienced colleagues. Of the many members of this Program I would like to single out one man, Professor Emeritus John M. Echols, for special thanks. Professor Echols, who recently passed away, was not directly involved in the research for or the preparation of this volume. Indirectly, however, by his example and his presence, he was (and is) an inspiration. This book is dedicated to Professor Echols.

My colleagues at the International Center for Living Aquatic Resources Management (ICLARM), by their example and their support, have encouraged my continued involvement in applied social science research. The Social Science Division of The Rockefeller Foundation, through its post-doctoral fellowship programme, has made possible my work with this exciting and innovative institution.

The final preparation of this manuscript was accomplished while working with ICLARM.

My greatest debt of gratitude, however, goes to Lisa Bailey, my wife, friend, and distraction, whose editorial skills helped to make this manuscript readable and whose personal skills made writing a pleasure.

ICLARM
Manila
September 1982

CONNER BAILEY

NOTE ON CURRENCY

All references to the dollar ($) are to the Malaysian dollar, now officially known as the *ringgit*. At the present rate of exchange, M$2.35 is approximately equivalent to US$1.00.

Contents

	Preface	v
	Tables	x
	Figures	xii
	Maps	xii
	Plates	xiii
	Abbreviations	xv
1.	BASIC QUESTIONS	1
2.	RURAL MALAY SOCIETY	9
3.	GONG GUNCIL: A RICE FARMING COMMUNITY IN TRENGGANU	20
4.	MANGKOK: A FISHING VILLAGE IN TRENGGANU	82
5.	KAMPUNG DUSUN: A SMALLHOLDER RUBBER TAPPING COMMUNITY IN KEDAH	133
6.	THE MATERIAL CONTEXT OF PRODUCTION: NATURAL AND TECHNOLOGICAL RESOURCES	169
7.	SOCIAL CONSEQUENCES OF ECONOMIC ORGANIZATION	187
	Glossary	204
	Bibliography	211
	Index	219

Tables

3.1	Population of Gong Guncil Study Area by Village and Household	27
3.2	Ownership of Rice Land by Household in Gong Guncil	31
3.3	Land Tenure Status of Households in Gong Guncil	32
3.4	Number of Households by Tenure Category for Villages in the Gong Guncil Study Area	34
3.5	Average Rice Farm Size by Tenure Category for Villages in the Gong Guncil Study Area (in acres)	34
3.6	Distribution of Rice Farm Size by Tenure Relationship	35
3.7	Labour Required per Acre per Season for Rice Production	54
3.8	Comparison of Three Rice Production Regimens for a Two-acre Owner-operated Farm per Year (in $)	70
3.9	Repayment of Production Credit (in $)	73
3.10	Ownership of Rubber Land by Household in Study Area	76
3.11	Quantity of Rubber Sold per Household at RISDA Processing Centre, 1975–1977	78
4.1	Nets Used in Mangkok	99
4.2	Catch, Distribution, and Income for Five Cases, 14 January–15 March 1978	106
4.3	1978 Prices for Commercially Important Species of Fish	110
4.4	Reasons for Preferential Relationships between Fish Buyers and Fishermen	116

4.5 Value of Fish Purchased at Mangkok, 14 January–12 May 1978 120

5.1 Comparison of Yield of Dry Rubber for Old Rubber Stands and Replanted Rubber Stands (lb./acre) 146

5.2 Distribution of Rubber Land Ownership among Families Active in the Rubber Economy (N = 35) 154

5.3 Land Tenure Status of Active Tapping Families in Kampung Dusun (N = 27) 156

Figures

3.1 Rainfall Distribution and Recommended Timing of Cultivation Stages in Besut District 45

4.1 Seasonality of Catch, 1978 (Yahya) 86

4.2 Seasonality of Catch, 1978 (Dahat) 87

4.3 Fresh Fish Landings in the Mangkok Area, 14 January–12 May 1978 105

5.1 Price Paid per *Kati* for No. 5 Unsmoked Sheet Rubber, January 1970–May 1978, Sik, Kedah 162

Maps

1. Location of Study Communities (showing political boundaries of Peninsular Malaysia) 3
2. Gong Guncil 23
3. Mangkok 83
4. Kampung Dusun 135

Plates

Between pages 80 and 81

1A Ploughing with water-buffalo
1B The traditional plough used in rice fields and pulled by water-buffalo or a team of oxen
2A Gathering bundles of rice seedlings (*unting*) in preparation for transplanting
2B Transplanting rice
3A A small *pinjam orang* work party helping to transplant rice
3B Carrying a sheaf of *padi* to be threshed during harvest
4 Winnowing rice in the breeze
5 House moving
6 Pounding the sedge known as *kercut* which is later woven into mats for fish drying
7 Cleaning a drifting gill net (*pukat hanyut*) off the stern of a fishing boat in Mangkok
8A Throwing a cast net in the surf off the beach at Mangkok. The fleet of boats on the horizon are seineing for *ikan bilis*
8B Boat captain at tiller with a non-motorized boat in tow. The two boats work together in using a small purse-seine
9A Operating a small purse-seine (*pukat jerut udang baring*). The boat on the right is motorized; the one on the left is not and is towed to the fishing grounds
9B Gathering in the purse-seine (*pukat jerut udang baring*) off the beach near Mangkok
10A Gathering in the purse-seine (*pukat jerut udang baring*) off the beach near Mangkok
10B Gathering in the purse-seine (*pukat jerut udang baring*) off the beach near Mangkok
11A Early morning activity at fish landing in Mangkok with buyers crowded on the deck of the boat in the foreground
11B Small pick-up trucks used to carry fish to market from Mangkok, and for carrying all manner of goods in and out of other rural communities
12A Drying small shrimp (*udang baring*) on the beach at Mangkok

12B Drying small shrimp (*udang baring*) in the sun
13A Carrying boxes of *ikan bilis* up the beach to the processing shed
13B Cooking *ikan bilis* prior to sun drying
14 Market scene in Penarek, near Mangkok, frequented by sellers from Gong Guncil
15A Tapping rubber
15B Collecting latex from rubber trees
16A Latex collecting in coconut shells at base of rubber tree
16B Processing ribbed sheet rubber. Note shallow tin pans for coagulating latex

Abbreviations

DID	Drainage and Irrigation Department
DRC	Dry rubber content
LPN	Lembaga Padi dan Beras Negara
MARDEC	Malaysian Rubber Development Corporation
MARDI	Malaysian Agricultural Research and Development Institute
PAS	Partai Islam Sa-Malaysia
RISDA	Rubber Industry Smallholders Development Authority
RRIM	Rubber Research Institute of Malaysia
SMR	Standard Malaysian Rubber
UMNO	United Malays National Organization

1 Basic Questions

WHAT are the social consequences of differing environmental and economic adaptations? How does the manner in which people earn a living affect patterns of social interaction in both economic and non-economic relationships? To what extent can we trace the basis of social structure through analysis of the material basis of a society's existence? Answers to these questions were sought during the course of intensive field-work in three rural Malay communities in Peninsular Malaysia (Map 1), each of which is engaged in different environmental and economic adaptations. Rice farming, rubber tapping and fishing, the three adaptations compared in this study, are the most important sources of livelihood for rural Malays.

In each of these three communities, the pace, tenor, and character of village life are closely related to the needs and timing of these differing adaptations, and the kinds of social relationships formed in the course of production are found to carry over into non-economic aspects of life. Rice farming families are dependent upon their neighbours and kinsmen during seasons of peak labour demand such as transplanting and harvest. The cultivation of rice is marked by complex reciprocal exchanges of labour. These reciprocal obligations are important both in terms of rice production and in the broader social setting in which this takes place. No comparable dependence upon exchange of labour is found among either rubber tappers or fishermen. Rubber tapping is essentially an individual activity, a daily routine unmarked by seasonal labour demands. Fishermen are more dependent on one another for cooperation in handling their nets, but this cooperation is limited in scope to a few men and in time by the constantly changing composition of crews. Unlike the larger groups of workers mobilized in rice cultivation, where reciprocal labour obligations lead to relationships between farming families which persist from season to season, the composition of the smaller fishing crews is based more clearly on economic advantage for the individuals involved.

Particular production processes dictate the type of labour organization required in each of the three cases outlined above. The relative importance of cooperation and reciprocal exchange of labour has far-reaching significance for social relations within a community, but must be seen in a broader context which includes available natural and technological resources.[1] Particular types of labour organization are determined by the manner in which these natural and technological resources are utilized, and also are influenced by the manner in which access to and control over these resources are gained and maintained.

Production processes and economic relationships which these processes engender are of central importance in the formation of broader social relationships. 'The anthropologist is interested in the structure and organization of economic activity for two reasons: most social relations have an economic coefficient; many social relations are primarily concerned with economic values' (Raymond Firth, 1952: 122). This generalization is applicable across social and cultural boundaries, but may be seen to be of special significance in a society where a majority of the population live and work at or near the margin of subsistence. To be sure, even in this situation life is much more than an unending hand-to-mouth struggle for existence. Religious worship, artistic endeavour, and local forms of entertainment all have a place in the life of rural Malays. It is unnecessary to take a position of absolute economic determinism to underscore the importance of economic aspects of social life. It is enough to recognize that 'social life is a response to the practical problems of earthly existence' (Harris, 1979: ix). In an industrial society with highly developed institutions which administer unemployment benefits, social security, and other programmes of social welfare, these 'practical problems' are complex, and include far more than simple material survival. In a society where many people live at or near a basic subsistence level, however, the practical exigencies of material life are of immediate and pressing importance, and occupy a central place in their day-to-day thoughts and actions.

The basic questions asked in this study are posed not only for their intrinsic intellectual interest, but as a means of identifying important but previously overlooked sources of variation within rural Malay society. Within any given society there are likely to be a number of differing local physical environments or habitats which require specific adaptations. The three communities included in this study are a case in point. The three adaptations of rice farming,

[1] Natural resources include land, domesticated and non-domesticated plant varieties, ground water and rainfall, fish, and fishing grounds. Technological resources are essentially tools (and the knowledge and skills to use these tools) for modifying and exploiting naturally occurring resources; these include fishing gears, ploughs, hoes, and other implements, as well as irrigation facilities, new fertilizer-responsive plant varieties, organic and inorganic fertilizers, and internal combustion engines which power tractors or propel boats.

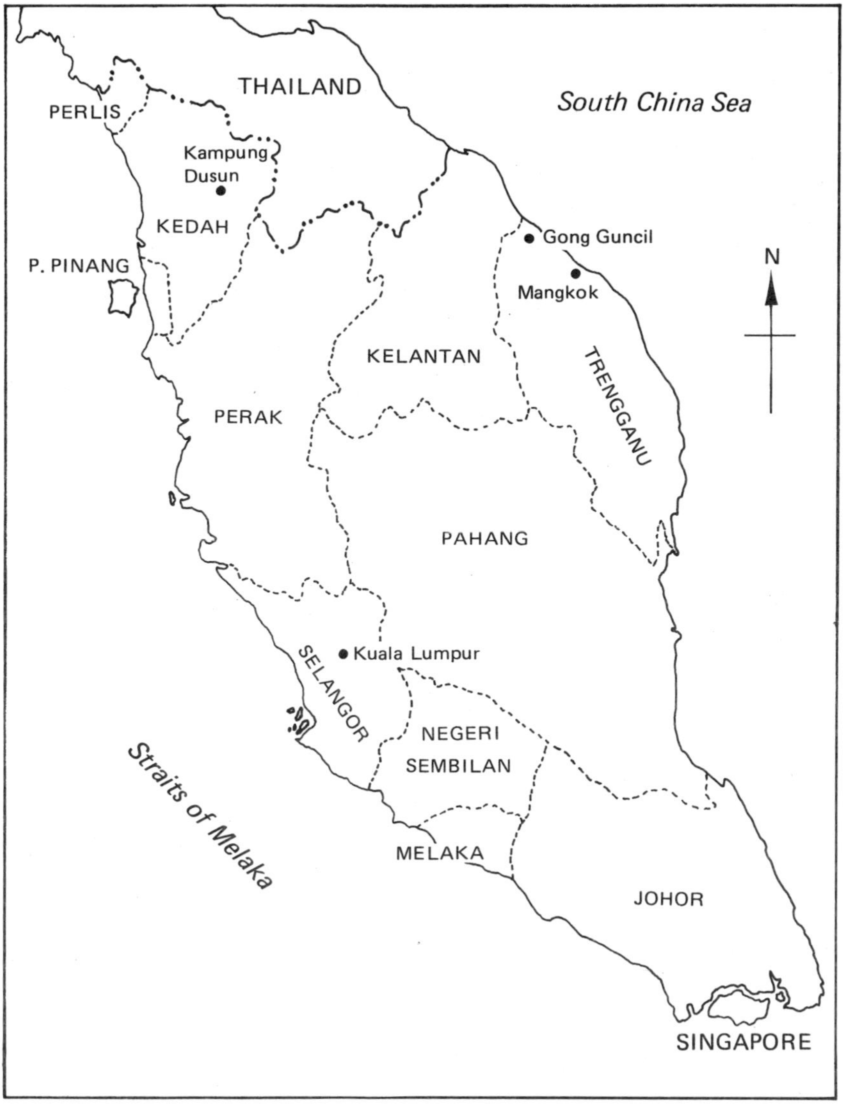

Map 1: Location of Study Communities
(showing political boundaries of Peninsular Malaysia)

rubber tapping, and fishing differ in significant respects. Previous studies comparing differing environmental and economic adaptations typically have focused attention on different ethnic groups exploiting various ecological niches within a larger environmental setting, and have described the various adaptations and symbiotic relationships involved (e.g. Forde, 1934; Barth, 1956; Bennett, 1969). Here it is argued that a similar comparative approach may be taken in the study of a single cultural grouping. Comparison of the three most important economic adaptations found among rural

Malays makes it possible to establish which features of life are linked most clearly to the material bases of their society. The basic questions initially posed can be applied to any society. This study seeks to apply these questions as a means to understanding one particular socio-cultural grouping, the rural Malays of Peninsular Malaysia. The goal is to discover important and systematic differences and similarities among rural Malays, and by so doing illuminate the essential nature of these warm and hard-working people.

THE THREE COMMUNITIES

The three communities chosen for the purpose of this study are to be found in two of the most 'Malay' states of the Peninsula—Kedah and Trengganu. Two of them, the villages of Gong Guncil and Mangkok, are in Trengganu which until recently derived its income mainly from fishing and smallholder's crops, while the third, Kampung Dusun, is situated in the rice and rubber producing state of Kedah.

GONG GUNCIL

Gong Guncil is a rice farming community situated in the middle of a broad alluvial plain formed by the Sungai Besut (*sungai* = river). Most of the land is low-lying and swampy, ideal conditions for wet rice cultivation. Gong Guncil is located within the area served by irrigation facilities controlled by the Besut Agricultural Development Project, and most of the rice land is double-cropped. Though new fertilizer-responsive varieties have been readily adopted by most farm families since irrigation was introduced 15 years ago, current cultivation practices are a mixture of the old and the new, and many families continue to plant traditional long-standing varieties on part of their land.

Where the land is unsuited to rice, rubber and fruit trees are grown and houses built. Most families also raise livestock. These and other secondary economic activities are important as sources of supplementary income, sometimes *the* major source of cash income, but it is the cultivation of rice which determines their timing and relative importance (Bailey, 1979) and provides Gong Guncil with its distinctive character.

MANGKOK

Mangkok is a fishing village located on a narrow spit of sand between the Sungai Setiu and the South China Sea. The fishermen use small diesel-powered boats, whose shallow draught allows them to pass over sand-bars as they make their way into or out of the river mouth. Currently the most common gear is a drift or gill net which is used at night. Fifteen or 20 years ago, however, diesel-powered boats had not yet appeared and fishermen depended on wind power; different types of boats and nets were used and fishing took place only during the day. Several years after the current style of boats and nets had been adopted, a major transformation in marketing relationships led to the breakup of ownership patterns which had favoured a few families. Today most boats are operated by fishermen—owners.

Secondary economic activities are important, but for the most part these are related to the processing of fish and provide employment for the women of Mangkok, who do not go to sea. Minimal organic content in the sandy environs of the village limits agricultural activities to cultivation of coconuts and provides pasture for only a small number of goats. Across the river acidic swampish soils support the *nipah* palm, used for roofing materials, *kercut*, a sedge used for weaving mats and baskets, and the *gelam* tree, used for making charcoal. Further inland is found land suitable for wet rice cultivation, on which approximately one-quarter of Mangkok's families grow a single crop of rice on land they share-crop. In rice cultivation the periods of land preparation, transplanting, and harvest coincide with seasons of poor fishing in the area. During this season, while some fishermen cease fishing to plant rice, others take their boats and nets a hundred miles or more down the coast in search of better catches.

KAMPUNG DUSUN

The people of the third community studied, Kampung Dusun, are dependent primarily upon rubber tapping for their income, which varies widely due to fluctuations in the world market price for this commodity. Kampung Dusun is situated in a hilly region where wet rice cultivation is limited to narrow valleys formed by small streams and rivers. Most of the rubber trees tapped by the villagers were originally planted 30 or more years ago and yield poorly when compared to newer varieties developed by the Rubber Research Institute of Malaysia (RRIM). Though replanting grants are available, loss of productivity for a period of at least seven years from the time of clearing the old stand until the new trees can be tapped limits participation in the government's replanting scheme.

Prior to the introduction of rubber early in the twentieth century, the population of Kampung Dusun and the surrounding area was much smaller and engaged primarily in subsistence agriculture. The predominantly hilly terrain was of limited utility, supporting hill rice, seasonal and non-seasonal fruits, and various products gathered from the jungle which were used in regional trade. Once rubber was established as a viable cash crop, subsistence agriculture declined in importance and the population of the area increased dramatically (Bailey, 1976).

In common with the other two communities studied, a wide variety of secondary economic occupations are found to exist in Kampung Dusun, and due to the volatile nature of the rubber market these alternative sources of income take on special importance. Nonetheless the character of this and the other communities studied is strongly influenced by their respective primary economic pursuits.

COMMERCIALIZATION OF THE RURAL ECONOMY

In the brief outline presented above, each of the communities is seen to have adapted to significant technological changes which affected their relationship to existing natural resources and dramatically altered pre-existing social relations. Production for subsistence needs has been replaced by increased commercialization. Rice farmers planting fertilizer-responsive varieties are beginning to produce a marketable surplus from which they must pay for purchased inputs. Fishermen in Mangkok must meet fuel and other expenses which were unnecessary before the introduction of diesel engines, and new marketing relationships have tied their economy to major urban centres hundreds of miles away. Rubber tappers are even more involved in a cash economy and dependent upon the sale of rubber for their daily food supply. This commercialization of the rural economy has altered the form of reciprocal labour obligations among rice farmers, changed the composition of fishing crews, and reduced the significance of economic cooperation among rubber tappers. Along with these basic changes have come new types of economic specialization, new divisions of labour among the sexes, and new sources of social stratification within rural Malay society.

THE COMPARATIVE APPROACH

The three communities offer the opportunity to discover commonalities and differences within rural Malay society. Adopting a comparative approach which focuses attention on differing economic and environmental adaptations enables us to understand more fully the social consequences of these adaptations than would be possible through a study of any one of them. The primary advantage of the comparative approach is to be able to compare and contrast, and in so doing illuminate the most important qualities of the subject at hand.

There have been several comparative studies of rural Malay rice farmers which have highlighted the differences between single- and double-cropping rice cultivation systems (Purcal, 1971; Ouchi *et al.*, 1977; Kuchiba *et al.*, 1979). While important differences exist among Malay rice farmers, the study of this adaptation alone provides a more limited understanding of variation in rural Malay society than is possible through the comparison of rice farmers with fishermen and rubber tappers.

Syed Husin Ali's *Malay Peasant Society and Leadership* (1975) comes close to adopting a comparative approach, though he explicitly disavowed responsibility of comparative analysis (op. cit.: 2). The focus of his attention was on patterns of local leadership in three communities, each of which was engaged in different economic adaptations. The demands of teaching made it impossible for him to undertake a careful study of production processes, which would have required extended periods of residence in each of the communities studied. As a consequence, Syed Husin Ali was unable to relate the similarities and differences he found to questions of economic and environmental adaptation, or to social relationships based on production. A more explicitly comparative approach was taken by Childs (1977). Childs's study focused on local leadership and political processes within three communities set along a rural–urban continuum in Selangor. Limits of time precluded any attempt by Childs to study in detail the specific adaptations of these three communities.

Other than the above-mentioned studies, previous students of rural Malay society have been concerned primarily with description and analysis based on case studies of single communities. This is understandable because of the great investment in time required in collecting data adequate for even a single case study. Over the years a number of case studies have been published, including those of Raymond Firth (1966) and Fraser (1960) on Malay fishermen, and those of Swift (1965) and Wilson (1967) on Malay rubber tappers.

Readers interested in drawing comparative conclusions from these studies are hampered in a number of important respects. Individual researchers have their own research agendas, and their data may not be strictly comparable. Each study asks different questions, and each student brings to the task different personalities and interests. The same no doubt is true in the case of the present study. An important difference lies in the fact that the same researcher worked in each of the three communities with an explicit comparative purpose in mind.

Adopting a comparative approach has a number of important advantages over studies of individual communities. Experience in one community raises issues and questions that can be asked during the study of another community, and that otherwise may have been overlooked. The necessity of collecting data upon which comparative statements can be made requires the focusing of attention on specific questions. For this study these questions related to processes and relationships of production. A wide range of other data was collected during the course of field-work, most of which are not included in this study since the purpose here is not to present a detailed ethnographic account of rural Malay society, but rather a framework in which systematic similarities and differences within rural Malay society can be illuminated and explained.

In this chapter it has been argued that the study of production processes and the relationships these processes engender are not only useful in their own right, but provide a fruitful means of understanding broader social processes. By focusing on production processes and relationships in a comparative context, it is hoped to present a richer portrayal of rural Malay society than has been possible through previous studies. It is further hoped that the description and analysis presented here will prove useful not only to academicians interested in Malay studies, but to planners and administrators of rural development programmes in Malaysia as well.

2 Rural Malay Society

SUBCULTURAL DIFFERENCES WITHIN RURAL MALAY SOCIETY

THE Malay population of Peninsular Malaysia comprises a mixture of indigenous Malays and various migrant groups from Indonesia, including Minangkabau, Javanese, Achinese, and Bugis, as well as migrants from Pattani on Southern Thailand's East Coast. For the most part these migrants arrived in the late nineteenth and early twentieth centuries, and their descendants appear to have retained their own diverse cultural and linguistic heritages. Even among Malays of peninsular origin significant social and cultural differences are found to exist between the East and West Coasts.

In addition to such subcultural diversity, different historical experiences have affected rural Malay society. The East Coast states were less affected by the colonial experience than were those of the West Coast. The heaviest concentration of European economic activity was on the West Coast, especially in tin mining and rubber estates. The East Coast, isolated by a spine of mountains running down the middle of the peninsula and by a lack of adequate port facilities compounded by seasonal high seas, remained an economic and political backwater. Roads, railways and other infrastructure were concentrated on the West Coast and were designed to facilitate the extractive economy of the colonial period. Non-Malay migrants, primarily Chinese who worked in tin mines and developed a dominant position in the wholesale and retail trade, and Indians who worked on British plantations and for the British administration, also were concentrated on the West Coast. On the West Coast important economic activities including the marketing of both rice and rubber came to be dominated by non-Malays, who also dominated retail trading in both large cities and small towns. Non-Malay economic penetration on the East Coast was more limited, leaving greater scope for Malay participation in local trading ventures. Even on the East Coast, however, non-Malays have come to dominate wholesale trading and much of the retail trade in the major towns.

Obviously, then, a study of differing economic adaptations cannot hope to explain all the differences found to exist in rural Malay society. The cultural tableau is too rich and varied to expect that any single factor can explain all of the variations in this society.

As far as possible, however, the factor of subcultural variation is minimized by selecting communities which are populated by Malays of peninsular origin. Two of the communities (Gong Guncil and Mangkok) are on the East Coast and separated by only 30 miles, while the third community (Kampung Dusun) is in the interior of the West Coast. Ideally all three communities should have been selected from within the same region, but due to constraints of time and energy it was necessary to include the West Coast community of Kampung Dusun, where previous field-work had been carried out (Bailey, 1976).

Though there are important subcultural differences between the Malays of the East and West Coasts, in the case of Kampung Dusun these differences are minimized in that this village originally was inhabited (during the nineteenth century) by migrants from Pattani. During the twentieth century and with the establishment of rubber as an important crop for estates and smallholders alike, Sik District (and Kampung Dusun) attracted settlers from the more densely populated coastal plains of the West Coast. Though strongly influenced by these later migrants, Sik and the neighbouring districts of Baling, Kubang Pasu, and Padang Terap maintain a distinctive character. The dialect spoken in these districts is quite close to that of Pattani and Kelantan, and frequent visits across the border into Pattani by residents of Sik serve to maintain kinship ties.

SOME UNIFYING FEATURES WITHIN MALAY SOCIETY

Despite significant subcultural diversity there are a number of features in rural Malay life which give this cultural group cohesion and a strong sense of ethnic identity. Malaysia's population comprises several distinct ethnic groups, including the Malays (who comprise about half of the total population), Chinese (about 37 per cent), Indians and Pakistanis (about 11 per cent), and a number of smaller immigrant and aboriginal groups. In this pluralistic national society, ethnic identification—a sense of 'we' versus 'they'—comes naturally and is expressed in political and economic competition. The United Malays National Organization (UMNO) and Partai Islam Sa-Malaysia (PAS), the two major political parties representing Malay interests, use the theme of ethnic identity in their political campaigns. In their own way each party strives to retain the paramount political position of the Malays in Malaysia. Malay ethnic solidarity also draws upon the brotherhood of Islam, to which all Malays belong. Islam unifies the Malay population and is the single most important factor in differentiating the Malays from the non-Malays in Malaysia.

The unifying feature of Islam provides an emotional sense of ethnic identity, but this identity must be understood in the context of political and economic friction between Malays and non-Malays. While Chinese, Indians, Pakistanis and Europeans control the nation's economy and by weight of numbers dominate urban life, the Malays of Malaysia are predominantly rural producers of primary products, the marketing of which essentially is beyond their control. The major towns of Malaysia are foreign ground to most rural Malays, and conversely rural Malay villages are foreign to most urban Malaysians. Interaction between urban and rural Malaysians essentially is limited to marketing and other economic relationships which are fraught with tension. Occasional visits to urban areas provide rural Malays with evidence of an economic vitality and wealth unknown in the rural areas. Such economic inequality has become a major campaign point of both UMNO and PAS and is reflected in the government's attempts to restructure the economy by increasing Malay participation in the essentially urban economy (*Third Malaysia Plan, 1976–1980*; see especially Chapter One on the New Economic Policy).

UMNO dominates the governing Barisan Nasional (National Front) and has dominated national politics since Independence in 1957. Under UMNO Malays have been accorded preferential treatment in government employment, university scholarships and in certain licensed occupations (e.g., taxi driver). UMNO's appeals for ethnic solidarity play on the religion of all Malays, Islam, but in this they compete with the opposition Partai Islam. Political appeals for ethnic and religious unity based on a shared religion are made by both parties, and regardless of the impact of such appeals on election day, consciousness of religious solidarity certainly is heightened. This shared religious consciousness is not simply a matter of political manipulation, however, but a pervasive influence throughout rural Malay society. Every Friday, in both rural and urban areas, Malays gather in mosques for midday prayers, uniting individuals in the common brotherhood of Islam.

Malay Muslims combine their religious orthodoxy with a number of indigenous practices and beliefs. Traditional healing practices are a blend of sophisticated herbology and supplications to unseen spirits (see Gimlette, 1971). Until recently, annual offerings were made to spirits in Gong Guncil to ensure a good rice crop; at one time a community-wide affair, now only one family performs the *semoh bendang*. Similar ceremonies were at one time regularly held in fishing villages, but are now used only by individuals whose boats have been plagued by poor catches. Whether for ensuring a good catch, a bountiful crop, or regaining health, spiritual entreaties always are made in the name of Allah, whose servants the spirits are said to be.

It is worth noting that informants in Gong Guncil and Mangkok report that the dropping of these ceremonies coincided among rice farmers with the introduction of irrigation facilities and double-cropping in the mid-1960s, and among fishermen with the introduction of diesel engines. The coincidence may be just that, and it should be noted that orthodox religious leaders for decades have attempted to purge such non-Islamic ceremonies. Yet one may speculate that technological advances have made rice farmers and fishermen less dependent on the vagaries of rain and wind, and this may have contributed to the demise of these propitiatory ceremonies.

Interestingly, no comparable propitiatory ceremony has been observed among Malay rubber tappers. Rubber tapping is a more recent adaptation than rice farming or fishing. As Wilson (1967: 94) notes, rubber tapping lacks a basis in tradition such as is found in the other two adaptations. Rubber production is a risky enterprise, but not in the sense that rice farming and fishing are. Traditional rice cultivation practices depended on adequate but not over-abundant rainfall, and the crop itself was (and is) subject to decimation by various diseases and pests. Fishermen at sea risk their lives and their equipment in pursuit of unseen prey. The risks associated with rubber tapping have less to do with pests, diseases and other natural phenomena than with the vagaries of an impersonal market—an unlikely object of propitiatory ceremonies.

Politics and religion are but two sources of socio-cultural unity in Malay society. First and foremost, the majority of Malaysia's Malay population are producers of primary products. Malay agriculturalists typically own small plots of land and the vast majority earn incomes which keep them at or near subsistence levels. Malay fishermen also are typically poor, and increasingly their small boats and simple equipment are competing disadvantageously with larger and more efficient boats controlled by urban, usually non-Malay, merchants. There is little hunger and probably no starvation among rural Malays, but their relative poverty in comparison to urban Malaysians, Malay and non-Malay alike, points to considerable inequality in income distribution (see

Hirschman, 1975; and the *Third Malaysia Plan*, pp. 159–98).

Inequality on a smaller scale is also a feature of rural life itself. While the majority of rural Malays live at or near subsistence level, a significant minority are able to generate sufficient surplus to ensure a comfortable standard of living. A wealthy rural Malay family may own 20 acres of land while average holdings are one-tenth this size. In the past, traditional redistributive obligations modified local economic inequalities and offered social prestige and respect to wealthy villagers who provided loans, gave large feasts, and were otherwise generous with their wealth. Traditionally wealth has been less important for what it may purchase than for the social uses to which it may be put (Gullick, 1965; Bailey, 1976). The traditional rural Malay egalitarian ethos requires the holding of elaborate feasts, generosity towards the poor, and other redistributive behaviour before the possession of wealth itself is accorded due respect.

Wealth alone is neither sufficient for nor the sole source of prestige, respect or influence in rural Malay society. Religious knowledge and piety also provide a Malay with considerable influence within a community. The extent of this influence may be restricted to religious affairs, or it may broaden to include such matters as mediation of local disputes within and between families. At the village level those possessed of superior religious knowledge are accorded respect and deference, as are those who make the pilgrimage (*haj*) to Mecca. Religious knowledge and piety are available to all Malays regardless of economic condition, but the expense of the *haj* means that only the wealthy can afford the honoured title of *haji* (for men) or *hajjah* (for women).

THE SETTING OF RURAL LIFE

Rural Malays live in villages (*kampung*) which may be either nucleated or linear, depending on topography and infrastructural developments such as roads and canals (Affifuddin Haji Omar, 1972). The typical Malay house is raised off the ground on stilts, is constructed of planks or locally available materials such as split bamboo, and uses either galvanized metal, clay tile, or thatch roofing materials. Being on stilts allows for improved ventilation against the tropical heat, some protection against flooding, and discourages the incursion of centipedes, snakes, or other unwanted visitors. A small house constructed entirely of locally available materials may cost only time and labour while a modest house using timber and galvanized metal roofing may cost $2,000. Larger, more elaborate houses may cost three or four times this amount. Surrounding the typical Malay house will be a number of seasonal and non-seasonal fruit trees, a small plot of vegetables and tubers, a small storage house for unmilled rice (*padi*), and perhaps a small corral for livestock.

Malay villages vary in size but except in proximity to a town rarely have a population in excess of 500 people. The definition of what constitutes a village, however, is not altogether clear. A continuous row of houses along a road may be divided into different *kampung* on the basis of a pre-existing boundary as temporary as a tree or a drainage ditch. In other cases the geographic boundary is clear but social ties (e.g., friendships and marriage patterns, reciprocal exchanges of labour) are such that two separate *kampung* may be regarded as a single community. Social boundaries may be further expanded to include those villages whose male inhabitants pray in the same mosque on Fridays, whose children attend the same local primary school, or those villages which share a common headman (*ketua kampung*).

Attendance at the same mosque or school provides a common locus of interaction for people from a number of separate villages, but because the boundaries are not likely to be the same (mosques tending to draw from a more restricted locality), the areas served by these institutions cannot always be used to delimit a community. In two cases (Gong Guncil and Kampung Dusun) it was necessary to include more than one *kampung*, as locally defined, in the communities studied. This was done in part on the basis of kinship and friendship ties, and in part on the basis of economic relationships, including share-cropping relationships and reciprocal exchanges of labour.

Defining a community on the basis of common attendance at a mosque, school, or the sharing of a single village headman is further complicated by the fact that the boundaries were established by various government agencies (the State Department of Religious Affairs, the Federal Ministry of Education, and the District Office, respectively), and not by the villagers themselves. Nonetheless, these institutions are significant in their own right. Local elementary schools have committees analogous to parent—teacher organizations in the United States of America, and mosques have committees chosen by the male members of the congregation.

The significance of these committees lies less in their activities than in their composition. The members tend to be the same, almost invariably headed by the *ketua kampung*. Where Village Development Committees (*Jawatankuasa Kemajuan Kampung*) exist, the membership is again repeated. These committees, in most villages either moribund or totally non-existent, are responsible for establishing local development priorities, carrying out local projects, and forwarding project proposals to the District Office. Lacking technical or financial resources, however, they typically do little other than request government assistance, and without immediate response wither into inactivity.

Examining the membership of the various local committees formed at the government's behest provides interesting information on local leadership patterns. Election to these committees is carried out in public, and often in the presence of a government official who has come to the village to encourage a new committee's formation. Willing to oblige, when nominations are opened the name of the *ketua kampung* typically is proferred as chairman. He may demur, citing his other committee responsibilities, but will finally accept. The position of secretary will then be filled, often with a younger man with some secondary education which will equip him with the ability to compose letters to the various government agencies. Finally, the remaining members are nominated, seconded and elected. Neither chairman, secretary, nor ordinary members are elected by means of election between competing nominees. Only one nomination is likely to be brought forward for each position and the nominee approved through informal consensus indicated by murmurs of approval and nods of agreement.

The results are predictable in advance, but the picture of consensual agreement derived from this process may be misleading. Sometimes villages are riven by factions that are not immediately apparent. These factions may coalesce around individuals who are competing for local influence, and often such factions find expression in allegiance to competing political parties. As clearly shown by Kessler (1978), who analysed political conflict in terms of economic class, political allegiances may reflect more than individual competition for local influence. Outside of Kelantan, where Kessler worked and where UMNO and PAS have been engaged in a long and acrimonious political struggle, local factions may be less clearly based upon ideological differences than upon pre-existing tensions between individuals seeking local influence. In extreme cases the formation of factions may seriously disrupt village life. During the election campaign of 1969, some villages were so divided that members of one faction would not attend wedding feasts or burial ceremonies held by members of the other. The main division, between the factions supporting UMNO and those backing PAS, was subsequently papered over by the formation in 1972 of a National Front Government which included these and other parties in a ruling coalition. (PAS was expelled from this coalition in 1977 during a controversy surrounding alleged corruption. It suffered serious losses during the State and national elections of 1978, including loss of control in Kelantan, its traditional centre of power.)

MARRIAGE

Though local factions often divide a community, ties of kinship, more lasting than the personal and political competition around which these factions form, serve as a countervailing and unifying force within rural Malay villages. Typically the residents of a given community are able to trace familial ties to most if not all of their fellow villagers, and are able to call upon their kinsmen for assistance in time of need. In so far as they are able, kinsmen are expected to help each other with emotional and material support, and to assist one another in the fields or at sea. The closer the familial bond, the stronger are these expectations, and more frequently are the obligations of kinship invoked.

Often one finds clusters of close kinsmen living in separate houses situated on a single parcel of inherited land. With the exception of the matrilocal Minangkabau, the pattern in rural Malay society is for newly married couples to live near whichever set of parents is more able to provide material support. In some cases a newly married couple will reside in the same house with one set of parents until they are able to build a house of their own, which may be located next to or near the house of these parents. The most important form of material support for a young couple is access to land, and the decision as to which set of parents to follow is often made on this basis. If land is available, the newly married couple may be allowed to share-crop the land, or title may be transferred into the name of the parents' offspring.

Marriages between Malays as closely related as first cousins are permitted, and in some cases encouraged. Though parents traditionally chose their children's marriage partners, young men and women today prefer to make their own decisions regarding when and with whom to marry. In the past women were married as early as their fourteenth year, the men being several years older. More recently the age at marriage has increased. It is now rare for women to marry before their sixteenth year, and they do so more commonly after their eighteenth year, while their husbands are likely to be in their early twenties. One major factor influencing this change in age at marriage is the increased availability and acceptance of the importance of education, for boys and girls alike, not only at the primary but also at the secondary level. Prior to Independence in 1957 facilities for secular education had been quite limited in rural areas. Since then rapid expansion of the school system has brought primary and secondary education to the previously neglected rural population.

Marriages tend to bind together families which are of approximately the same economic standing. Differences in economic standing among the majority of rural Malays are not extreme and present no obstacle in arranging a marriage. Within any given community, however, there are likely to be a few families significantly better off than their neighbours. These families typically are descendants of the original inhabitants of the area who laid effective claim to relatively large acreages of land. Through the generations they have become closely interrelated and continue to form marriage alliances among themselves. Relatively wealthy families are reluctant to conclude marriage alliances with families significantly poorer than themselves, not so much from a consciousness of themselves as a separate class but rather from concern for the material well-being of their children and grandchildren. The result, however, is the establishment of an identifiable group within rural Malay society which is isolated from the majority in terms of kinship. In recent years these families have widened the potential range of marriage alliances to include other relatively wealthy groups in society, including local teachers and government officers.

One means by which poor families are discouraged from seeking marriage alliances with more wealthy families is the requirement of paying the wife and her family a dowry, known as *mas kahwin* (literally 'wedding gold'). The sum of money demanded as *mas kahwin* varies widely: a wealthy family with an educated daughter may demand $2,000 or more. The son of a poor family will be unable to meet this expense, and will be more likely to marry the daughter of a family of roughly comparable economic standing where the *mas kahwin* may be as little as $200. While the cost of *mas kahwin* will not prevent the son of a wealthy family from marrying the daughter of a poorer family, such unions are uncommon.

The *mas kahwin*, in addition to certain other negotiated gifts, is meant primarily for the security of the wife in the event that the husband divorces her. Divorce is quite common and easily arranged. Most rural Malays appear to have been married and divorced several times, and there is little difficulty in remarrying for either men or women (Djamour, 1959).

INHERITANCE

Within rural Malay society inheritance of material assets tends to be divided equally among all children. Though the Koran favours male heirs with a larger proportion of an inheritance, Malay parents feel that both sons and daughters have equal need of and claim upon the family's property. Equal treatment of all heirs may be modified by other factors, however. For example, a parent owning 2 acres of rice land is unlikely to divide this land equally among five or six offspring: to do so would reduce the size of individual holdings to an uneconomic fragment. The distribution of an inheritance is likely to be based on the needs of the various possible heirs. Some of the children may find employment outside the village or marry a spouse who owns land sufficient for that couple's own needs. By the time a parent is ready to pass along control of land to his or her children, they already may be established economically, and their respective needs and abilities already will be manifest.

A smallholding of 2 acres of rice land, for example, may be divided between two children, and the family house and adjacent land given to a third. It is hoped that the other children will manage through marriage, migration, or other employment. There are a wide number of possible variations upon this example: each of the offspring may be given a share in the land which is then worked by one or two of the heirs, who in turn give some part of the yield to their siblings in an informal share-cropping agreement. Alternatively, the land may be sold and the proceeds divided among the heirs. This is most common if the parent dies before the land has been divided and if the various heirs cannot agree among themselves on the disposition of the land. To forestall such disagreements, parents prefer to distribute their inheritance as they reach old age, surrendering control over the land in return for material support during their remaining years.

Fragmentation of landholdings from one generation to the next occurs as the ratio of population to available land becomes increasingly unfavourable. The effect of inheritance on relatively wealthy families in the land-based economies of rice and rubber should also lead to decreased size of landholdings. It would appear, however, that fragmentation of large holdings has been delayed by selective marriage alliances which bring together families of landed wealth or unite families of landed wealth with government civil servants whose wealth is derived from a regular salary. The process of fragmentation also may be slowed down as the offspring of such families are likely to achieve above average educational attainments and enter the ranks of the civil service, in which case those siblings who stay at home stand to inherit the bulk of their family's land. Finally, it should be noted that families who already are wealthy will be able to convert their surplus income into the purchase of land which may come on to the market.

For rural Malays engaged in land-based economic activities, inheritance is the primary means of access to productive resources. Land, and especially rice land, is a limited resource which rarely is offered for sale. A family which does not inherit land is likely to remain permanently landless, because even when land is available for purchase, the price will be beyond its means.

Inheritance plays a reduced role in providing access to productive resources in a fishing economy due to the ease with which fishermen buy and sell used boats and fishing gear, and the relative impermanence of these productive resources compared to land. Boats and nets deteriorate over time and need constant repair and replacement. Moreover, the most important resource to fishermen, the sea, is freely available to all. By contrast, permanent and enforceable rights are attached to land, which may be transferred from generation to generation. Unlike land, which is in limited supply and usually privately owned, it is possible to build another boat or buy a used boat, and to add another net to the fishing grounds.

RURAL MALAY SOCIETY

Despite efforts by the government, the majority of Malaysia's Malay population will continue to live in rural areas in the foreseeable future. As agriculturalists and fishermen the majority of whom live at or near a subsistence level, their primary day-to-day concern is earning a living for themselves and attempting to ensure a decent standard of living for their heirs. Such concerns are much more immediate than questions of ethnic solidarity, which typically arise to the forefront of consciousness only during political campaigns. Daily life on the village level revolves around production processes and the social relationships which are directly influenced by these processes. In the three chapters which follow these processes and relationships are described for rice farmers, rubber tappers, and fishermen. These descriptive chapters provide the necessary background for the two concluding analytical chapters.

3 Gong Guncil: A Rice Farming Community in Trengganu

THE SETTING

GONG GUNCIL is set in the broad plain formed by the Sungai Besut, a plain rimmed by mountains reaching elevations of over 4,000 feet and set against the South China Sea. Interspersed throughout the plain are small hills, rarely over 200 feet in elevation and sometimes only a few feet higher than the rice fields themselves. In the local dialect the term '*gong*' refers to such slight elevations in the terrain, while a more substantial hill will merit the term '*bukit*'. Gong Guncil takes its name from such a minor elevation where a species of tree, locally known as a *guncil* tree, was at one time prevalent. Maps of the surrounding rice plain are dotted with the names of villages prefaced by the word '*gong*', as homes typically are located where the land is higher and consequently drier.

The Besut plain includes about 14,000 acres of rice land, including 12,600 acres which are provided with irrigation for double-cropping; further inland, the plain narrows and is succeeded by hills and mountains. The main economic activities in the interior are rubber tapping and the collection of fruits and jungle produce for sale. Limited quantities of rice also are grown for local consumption where low-lying level land is available. As one moves further up-river, the population becomes increasingly sparse and the land available for cultivation increasingly limited by the presence of a national forest reserve which protects the headwaters of the Sungai Besut and the mountains and forests which flank the rice plains.

Downstream the rice lands of the Besut plain give way to the sandy *beris* soils near the coast. Some of these sandy soils are planted with rice, but they yield poorly and more commonly are planted with coconut or tobacco. Coconut predominates along the coastal fringe, while tobacco tends to be grown towards the interior. Since the late 1960s tobacco cultivation has gained widespread acceptance due to the profitability of this crop, especially in rotation with rice.

The soils of the main rice plain are alluvial deposits brought from the surrounding mountains by the Sungai Besut. The predominant soil type is known as the Chempaka Series, a yellowish-brown friable clay. Underlying the topsoil in the rice field is a 2- to 3-inch thick plough pan created by repeated ploughing at the same depth and acts as an impervious layer through which the movement of water and nutrients is inhibited. The plough pan is the most important feature of the soil structure of a rice field and is vulnerable to damage if large, heavy tractors are used. Below the plough pan the soil becomes increasingly yellow as the organic content is reduced. The Chempaka Series is categorized as a Class II soil in Malaysia, a classification based on productivity. There are no Class I soils in Besut; the largest concentration of such soils in Malaysian rice fields is found in the state of Kedah on the West Coast. There farmers may obtain upwards of 1,000 *gantang*[1] of rice per acre per season, compared with an optimum level of perhaps 500–550 *gantang* in the Besut area. This latter yield is based on field tests conducted by the Malaysian Agricultural Research and Development Institute (MARDI) under carefully controlled conditions. Farmers in Besut report average yields of 300 to 350 *gantang* per acre per season.

THE BESUT AGRICULTURAL DEVELOPMENT PROJECT

In an effort to raise the productivity of rice farmers in Besut, the federal government has developed irrigation facilities to allow for double-cropping of wet rice. Since before Independence it has been a goal of the governing authorities to achieve national self-sufficiency in rice, the national staple. In 1961, the Sungai Angga Irrigation Scheme was built, providing irrigation to some 2,500 acres of the Besut rice plain, including the Gong Guncil area. This project supplied water by damming and diverting the flow of the Sungai Angga, a tributary of the Sungai Besut, and channelling the water to the fields through unlined canals.

In the early 1970s the Sungai Angga Irrigation Scheme was expanded to become the Besut Agricultural Development Project. A new dam diverting water from the Sungai Besut was constructed

[1] A *gantang* is a volumetric measure equivalent to one Imperial gallon; one *gantang* of unmilled rice weighs approximately 5.6 lb. The *gantang* will be the measure used for rice throughout this study; for those readers more familiar with the international measure of kilograms per hectare, the conversion formula is as follows: multiply the number of *gantang* by 2.54 (kilograms per acre) and then again by 2.471 to convert the figure to kilograms per hectare. Three hundred *gantang*, for example, equals 1 883 kilograms per hectare. The price that farmers receive is easily calculated on the basis of *gantang*, since during the period of study the price was approximately $1.00 per *gantang* of unmilled rice (*padi*).

and the irrigation canals were upgraded and lined with either concrete or prefabricated fibreglass. Paved and dirt roads were built and a rice mill constructed within the Project area. An area of 5,600 acres, including the previous Sungai Angga Irrigation Scheme, was designated Stage I of the Project; the Stage II area of some 7,000 acres, in addition to 3,100 acres of the Stage I area, had never been served by irrigation facilities and construction had to start from scratch. A South Korean firm won the international tender and construction was to begin in 1972 and be completed by 1974 or 1975. Inflation, various delays, and serious cost overruns forced the firm to abandon the Project before the basic construction was complete, and only by early 1979 was the basic infrastructure established. The Project also was plagued by unrealistic expectations.

In the light of subsequent agronomic research, the initial goal of 800 *gantang* per acre was shown to have been unattainable, and the cost–benefit calculations that were used for obtaining funds from the Asian Development Bank to carry out this Project proved unrealistic. These unrealistic goals together with construction delays led to a number of newspaper articles and political speeches which labelled the Besut Project a failure.

Despite the concern of officials in the Ministry of Agriculture, the Besut Project area had not previously attracted the attention of researchers. By contrast, the neighbouring Kemubu Agricultural Development Authority and the Muda Agricultural Development Authority in Kedah, the two largest irrigation projects in Malaysia, have been studied by foreign and Malaysian scientists in the social and agricultural fields. It was in part to remedy this situation that the Besut Project area was chosen as the site of the author's research on rice production.

THE VILLAGE

Gong Guncil is similar in many respects to other villages in the Besut plain. The village is set among rice fields interspersed with stands of rubber and fruit orchards in places where the land is unsuited for rice farming. The houses themselves are arranged in a semi-nucleated pattern on land that is higher than the surrounding rice fields (Map 2). As is the case in any Malay village, the grounds immediately surrounding the houses are kept clear of grass and other vegetation, and this area is regularly swept clean by women or young girls of the family. Beyond this little perimeter fruit trees are found, almost always including one or more coconut trees, as well as banana, *rambutan*, and others. There also may be small garden plots, though these are not as common as might be hoped.

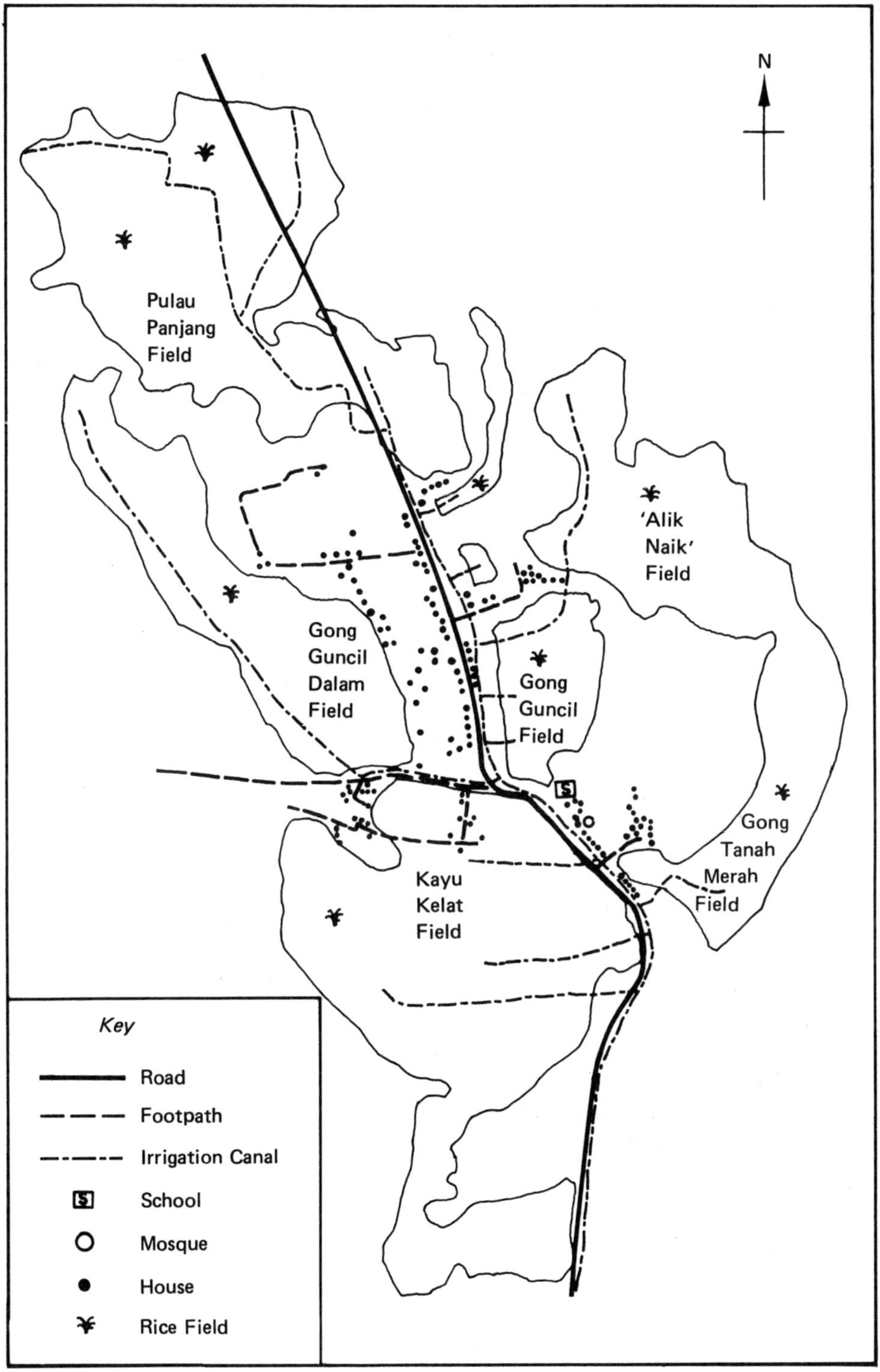

Map 2: Gong Guncil

The primary source of animal protein consumed in Gong Guncil (and by rural Malays in general) is fish, usually marine species purchased from pedlars and supplemented by fish caught in rice fields, irrigation canals, and local streams. Virtually all families raise chickens, and ducks also are common; they are valued for their meat and eggs, and may be eaten by the family or sold. The poultry live mostly by scavenging in the area surrounding the family's home but also are fed with kitchen scraps and rice bran.

Chickens and ducks are easily raised and require little capital investment. Because of the small number of such fowl raised and sold by an individual family, this is unlikely to be more than a source of pocket money, to be used for immediate expenses. The raising of goats, cattle, or water-buffalo, however, entails greater investment but also provides the opportunity for accumulating large sums of money. Inheritance often plays an important role in a family's acquisition of breeding stock, especially for cattle and water-buffalo. Buying mature reproductive stock is prohibitively expensive for most families, as the price for such animals is set by the market for meat.

A family owning no cattle or water-buffalo need not purchase an animal to start its own small herd. Often a family which already has a small herd, or which does not want the trouble of raising an animal, will turn over to another family the responsibility of rearing a young animal. This arrangement, known as *pawah*, takes a number of different forms. The family which takes over responsibility for raising the animal usually obtains ownership of the first female offspring while the owners receive the second. Alternatively, the first-born is assigned a monetary value after it has been weaned and either family may buy out the half share of the other, with first option being given to the family which raised the animal. This is especially common if the first-born is a male whose value will be limited to sale rather than reproduction.

The Veterinary Department also has a *pawah* scheme through which selected and presumably improved breeding stock is introduced into the rural areas. The family given the cow obtains full ownership of the first female offspring; after it is weaned, the mother is returned to the Veterinary Department to be given to another family. If the first-born is male, the family will usually keep the cow until a female is born.

LAND USE PATTERNS

The small parcels of land around village houses are known as *tanah kampung* (literally 'village land'). Such lands are used for many purposes, from providing for a family's needs for such important foodstuffs as coconuts and chilli peppers, to yielding cash income from the sale of fruits and vegetables. Very little *tanah kampung* is unproductive. Livestock is tethered and allowed to graze on any open land not planted to rice, rubber or other crops. Even the swampy land surrounding natural drainage channels, locally referred to as '*alor*', provides food and wallowing grounds for the water-buffalo.

Also within the village are areas referred to as *tanah dusun*, land which may appear to be undeveloped, but on closer inspection will reveal certain species of fruit trees such as the *durian*, *cempedak* and *duku*. The sale of fruits from such orchards (*dusun*) provides an important cash income to many families. Typically *tanah dusun* is full of brush and undergrowth of seemingly little value. But this vegetation serves as pasture for livestock (especially goats), provides a source of wood for cooking, and perhaps most important of all, contains a wide variety of delicious and nutritious leaves and herbs used in cooking; medicinal roots and herbs also are abundant. For many families *tanah dusun* is the single most important source of vegetables, and access is free to anyone regardless of ownership of the particular *dusun*. Only the fruit trees and their produce are jealously guarded and regarded as private property. While clearing the undergrowth from such land may allow for increased productivity of the fruit crop, it would seem that the advantages of leaving the *dusun* in a more natural state outweigh any potential increase in fruit, especially when the cost of labour necessary to keep such vegetation in check in a tropical environment is taken into account.

The difference in elevation separating *tanah padi* (rice land) from *kebun getah* (rubber stands), *tanah kampung*, and *tanah dusun* may be slight but usually is enough to preclude the latter areas from being used for rice farming. Rubber and fruit trees do not thrive in the waterlogged conditions typical of land suitable for rice cultivation, and only rarely would a house be built on such land: not only would valuable production be lost, but the site of the house would be uncomfortably wet and muddy. From November to January, the period of the north-east monsoon, much of the village is in any event a quagmire of mud, except for the paved road that runs through the village.

THE TOWN OF JERTEH

The road through Gong Guncil, paved as part of the infrastructural improvements of the Besut Project, connects the village to the main East Coast highway, only 2 miles away, and to the major town of the area, Jerteh, which is 2 miles further down the highway. Jerteh grew in importance with the construction of the highway, coming to surpass in size and commercial importance the seat of the district headquarters in Kampung Raja, and totally eclipsing Kampung Amir, which at the turn of the century was the largest town in the district but which now is indistinguishable from any other village in the area. The district's only cinema, a branch of a commercial bank, a branch of Bank Pertanian (Agricultural Bank), and the district's largest daily market are located in Jerteh. There are several eating shops, and about twenty sundry goods shops, as well as several photographers, motor-mechanics, and barbers. As is common in the urban areas of South-East Asia, the goods from these shops tend to spill out on to the sidewalks, which are occupied by petty traders—usually women—selling local fruits and sweets.

A visitor to Gong Guncil using public transport will arrive first in Jerteh and then hire a trishaw, locally known as *teksi*. For $1.40 a man will peddle his passenger or passengers the four miles to Gong Guncil, passing through villages, stands of rubber, and fields of rice. No buses serve Gong Guncil itself, but there is a bus stop at the main highway from which passengers may hail buses north to Jerteh and beyond, or south to Kuala Trengganu. The son of the *ketua kampung* operates a Mercedes-Benz taxi owned by his father, but he plies the main highway during the day, only returning at dusk. In addition to these forms of transport, there also are bicycles. Most families either own a bicycle or are able to borrow one, and the ride to Jerteh and back takes less than one hour. The *teksi* is the preferred method of travel for women, who generally travel in pairs or in groups, while the men—more easily able to travel alone—generally rely on the bicycle. In addition, within Gong Guncil there are 5 privately owned cars, 12 privately owned small motor cycles, and 2 small vans used by local traders which may be hired for various transportation needs.

The presence of privately owned cars that are not used as 'pirate taxis' is rare in rural Malay society. Due to high taxes levied on both cars and fuel, the cost of owning and operating a car is prohibitive for most. One car owner is the headmaster of a primary school, the locally born son of one of the wealthiest men in the village. The second car is owned by a couple who are both teachers. Another is owned by a man who earns a cash income as the gardener of the local primary school and has supplementary income from inherited land. The fourth is owned by a wealthy land-owner, and the fifth by a teacher married to the sister of the headmaster's wife. Each of the families owning a car is related to the others, and all five live in one area known as Gong Tanah Merah.

DELIMITING THE STUDY UNIVERSE

Gong Tanah Merah is a village in its own right, separated from Gong Guncil by a narrow strip of rice land. Gong Tanah Merah, the village of Baruh Kual, and part of the village of Pulau Panjang were included in the present study for a number of reasons. When residence was established by this writer in Gong Guncil, it became obvious that significant social relationships extended beyond the rather artificial boundaries of each village. Indeed, the dividing line between one village and another often is not discernible to the naked eye, and may not be socially significant. More important, it seemed, were such matters as friending patterns: who visited the homes of whom, who was invited for a feast, or who was asked to help in the rice fields. It also seemed significant that most of the residents of this area worshipped at the same mosque and formally, at least, were under the same headman. Consequently, data were collected across the formal though insignificant boundaries dividing several 'villages'. The study area will be referred to as Gong Guncil, the largest of the four villages. The entire study universe included 134 households with a total population of 694. The breakdown per village is shown in Table 3.1.

TABLE 3.1
POPULATION OF GONG GUNCIL
STUDY AREA BY VILLAGE AND HOUSEHOLDS

Village	*No. of Households*	*Population*	*Average*
Gong Guncil	68	353	5.2
Baruh Kual	18	87	4.8
Gong Tanah Merah	30	173	5.7
Pulau Panjang	18	81	4.5
Total	134	694	5.2

Friending patterns did not lead to the inclusion of Gong Tanah Merah in the study universe. Rather, the opposite was true. Gong Tanah Merah was atypical, an enclave of the relatively wealthy with their cars, television sets, refrigerators, electric generators, and large houses. Such conspicuous consumption seems to indicate a shift away from traditional patterns of redistribution.

TRADITIONAL AND CONTEMPORARY USES OF WEALTH

Traditionally, a wealthy family would employ its resources to establish a prestigious and influential position in society by holding elaborate feasts marking rites of passage for its children, e.g. weddings and circumcisions, materially assisting other villagers holding similar feasts, contributing generously to feasts marking religious celebrations, advancing small loans in cash or kind with little expectation of repayment, or providing land and tools to newcomers in the area and thereby assisting them to establish themselves in the community (Gullick, 1965; Bailey, 1976). Wealth was valued not for the level of consumption it could provide, but for the social advantages that followed in the wake of such redistributive largesse.

Traditional values related to the function of wealth in rural Malay society have begun to erode as more consumer goods have become available. Cars, motor cycles, television sets, refrigerators, and fancy furniture have become status symbols, but generally are limited to the use of the particular family that owns them. Television sets and cars, however, have the potential of being shared with others. Rural Malays love to watch television, and, if invited, children and adults alike will crowd before the set, especially to watch the weekly Malay or Indonesian film on one of the two national networks. Even in areas not provided with regular electricity, some shopkeepers, using generators for power, will install a television set in a window or doorway, attracting large crowds who sit, squat or stand outside and who, not incidentally, may purchase drinks or local sweets.

Whether or not television is supplanting indigenous forms of entertainment is a question worthy of more detailed inquiry. For the present study, however, it is worth noting that of the six television sets owned by residents of the Gong Guncil area, only two actually were utilized by persons other than the families who owned them. One of these was operated by a shopkeeper in the manner described above, the other by a young farmer who played his set only a few hours per week because he ran it off a used car battery which needed to be constantly recharged. The other television sets were in the homes of the wealthier villagers of Gong Tanah Merah. It is interesting to note that, despite a truly strong desire to watch television, the poorer families never intrude on the private viewing of their more wealthy neighbours; in fact, rarely do they visit these families. During the period immediately after the end of the fasting month of Ramadan, when villagers visit the homes of friends and relatives, there is little or no movement across what are essentially class lines.

The ownership of a private car places a family in a unique position to assist other families, either in times of emergency, as when an illness or accident occurs, or to give a fellow villager a lift to town. In the latter case it is notable that only when one locally born teacher drives by will villagers attempt to hitch a ride; the other drivers are said to ignore those who hail them to stop, and are described as '*sombong*' (proud), one of the harsher criticisms that a rural Malay is likely to bestow. This teacher's willingness to give lifts won him such praise as to stand as condemnation of the others. Even in cases of illness, the poorer farmers of Gong Guncil prefer to ask a friend who owns a small motor cycle to carry the sick or injured person on the back of his motor cycle 5 miles to the hospital, if it is at all physically possible.

As the author owned a motor cycle often he was pressed into such duties, and he also found himself upon occasion acting as a taxi service for non-emergency social calls (some of which turned into valuable experiences in terms of data and expanded relationships). It was obvious that he was fulfilling a role which was shared by several other motor cycle owners in the village. Among the majority of people in Gong Guncil it was held to be a reasonable expectation that such a person would help a friend and neighbour, and in this context a number of residents in Gong Tanah Merah have dis-associated themselves from the rest of the community.

By including Gong Tanah Merah in the study universe, the author became more fully aware of a fundamental and growing split along class lines, between the wealthy and the less wealthy. Focus-ing on such matters as the sharing of a ride to town or a seat in front of a television set may seem like petty details, but they are the elements upon which broader social relationships may either be built or discouraged, and they reflect current trends toward class differentiation at the village level.

The wealthy élite of Gong Tanah Merah total 9 households out of 30 in that village. Though each of these families owns above average holdings of rice land, in several cases the income from this land is less significant than income from other sources: 2 households receive their primary income from employment as teachers; while in another case a family's landed wealth is supplemented by the husband who works as the school gardener. These nine families live in close proximity at the base of the hill from which Gong Tanah Merah takes its name, and are descendants of the first migrants who opened the land to rice cultivation near the turn of the present century. Through intermarriage they have kept the size of their holdings relatively large. Although the extent of their holdings does not provide them with fabulous wealth, they and a small number of other families are able to generate sufficient surplus from their oper-ations to enjoy a locally exceptional level of comfort. The majority of farmers, on the other hand, tend to find themselves closer to the margin of subsistence.

LAND-OWNERSHIP AND TENANCY RELATIONSHIPS

PROBLEMS OF DATA COLLECTION

Obtaining clear information on the amount of land owned by these nine households proved to be exceedingly difficult. When confronted with a straightforward question, members of these families typically tried to evade the question or disclaimed extensive holdings. One man claimed that he and his wife owned only 6 acres each of rice and rubber land. When asked how they could possibly own a motor car, a generator to power their refrigerator, a television set and an electric water pump, he said that they managed through being frugal and selling as much as $1,000 worth of fruit per year. According to other informants, this man and his wife owned three times as much land as they claimed, and there is the probability that they also owned land planted to rubber further away from the village, which local informants were unlikely to know about.

It is virtually impossible to check data collected in the field against the records of the Land Office, as these are kept on the basis of Lot Number and not under the name of the owner. Even files under the name of the owner would be of limited value, since the registered owner often will be a deceased parent or grandparent. There are no surnames to go by as Malays are known only by their personal name followed by that of the father. Moreover, the formal name of the registered owner may be entirely different from the name by which he or she is known within the village. Attempting to cut through this confusion on a multi-generational basis would have been a hopeless task. As a consequence the extent of landholdings owned by an individual or family can only be discovered indirectly, especially with the wealthier villagers. Downplaying their wealth may be caused by fear that the government might levy an income tax (its lowest threshold is well above the level of most villagers), or that if the extent of their wealth were widely known they might be the object of requests for loans and gifts from their poorer neighbours.

Because of these difficulties in obtaining accurate data, the figures presented in Table 3.2 are at best educated guesses, derived from interviews with each of the households in the study universe and, where it was deemed necessary, confirmed or augmented by information supplied by certain key informants. In addition, all the rice fields in the surrounding area were mapped, and farmers working in the fields were questioned as to who owned each individual *keping* of land and, if it were farmed by a family other than the owner's, whether the operator was share-cropping or paying a straight rent. (A *keping* is the land within a bund, and there may be from two to three to as many as seven or eight *keping* per acre of land.) These maps were then checked against maps obtained from the Land Office, which were less useful for obtaining current information on land-ownership than for providing an understanding of the process of fragmentation of landholdings. The Land Office maps did not reflect changes of ownership which had occurred over the past 20 years or so. As these maps were not dated, and as changes in ownership often are not formally recorded in the Land Office, their utility was limited. Nonetheless, these maps do show that in the recent past landholdings were larger than during the period of field research. Unfortunately the extent of this difference cannot be stated with accuracy for the reasons noted above.

LAND-OWNERSHIP AND FARM SIZE

The figures in Table 3.2 refer only to those households in the study area which are actively engaged in rice cultivation or which own rice land and receive income in cash or kind from this land. Fourteen households in the study area are not included in this Table as they are not involved in the rice economy. There are 27 households which own no land and which depend on share-cropping or cash rentals to obtain access to land; among those which do own rice land, 66 out of 93 households own less than 4 acres each. Those households owning

TABLE 3.2

OWNERSHIP OF RICE LAND BY HOUSEHOLD IN GONG GUNCIL

	Number of Households				
Acres	*Gong Guncil*	*Baruh Kual*	*Pulau Panjang*	*Gong Tanah Merah*	*Total*
0	12	4	4	7	27
< 1	2	nil	2	2	6
1–1.99	15	2	2	3	22
2–2.99	13	3	5	3	24
3–3.99	10	1	1	2	14
4–4.99	5	3	1	nil	9
5–5.99	3	nil	1	2	6
6–6.99	2	nil	nil	nil	2
7–7.99	nil	2	nil	1	3
8–8.99	nil	nil	nil	nil	nil
9–9.99	nil	1	nil	1	2
> 10	nil	nil	nil	5	5
Total	62	16	16	26	120

10 acres or more are all found in Gong Tanah Merah. The best estimate of their holdings is that they are in the range of 10–15 acres, though the author has unsubstantiated information that one household owns as much as 30 acres.

The average holding of rice land owned by households in the study area is 3.3 acres, including land owned by households which do not cultivate their land. The actual farm size of households which cultivate rice is somewhat smaller. According to Yap and Dixon (1972) the average farm size for the Besut rice plain was 3.2 acres, and for that section of their survey which included the Gong Guncil area the average was 3 acres. For the research universe in which the author was working, however, the average is smaller: 2.37 acres.

The land tenure status of the 134 households of the study universe may be seen in Table 3.3.

TABLE 3.3

LAND TENURE STATUS OF HOUSEHOLDS IN GONG GUNCIL

Category	*Number of Households*
Land-owners not farming	18
Owners—operators	52
Owners—tenants	24
Tenants	25
Agricultural labourer	1
Not engaged in rice economy	14

Within the category 'land-owners not farming' are included the old and infirm who are unable to plant their typically small holdings, villagers with other occupations of a short-term or long-term nature that keep them from actual cultivation, as well as more wealthy land-owners who let others work their land. The category 'not engaged in rice economy' refers to one government midwife, one teacher, and several elderly widows and widowers who own no land and are typically dependent upon their children for their material wants. 'Owners—operators' refer to those households which farm only land that they own, while 'owners—tenants' farm what land they possess but supplement this land by renting or share-cropping land owned by others. In contrast, 'tenant' households own no rice land and depend entirely on establishing a rental or share-cropping arrangement with another family. Finally, there is one household (that of a landless widow) that is involved in the rice economy only through employment as an agricultural labourer. (This family has since moved from the area to live near relatives in another state.)

These relatively neat categories become somewhat confused in practice, as for example when a family which owns rice land finds its land unusable due to faults in the drainage system and is forced to share-crop land owned by others until the problem is rectified. (Over 50 acres of rice land in the study area were affected by such flooding during the time this study was carried out.) In other cases a family of owners—operators may own more land than it cultivates. Some owners—tenants are also in this situation. For various reasons (e.g., proximity to their home), they prefer to share-crop the land of others while renting or leasing for share-cropping to others some part of their own land. To create yet more categories, however, would tend to confuse matters without ever being able to account for the full range of possible situations—which, moreover, tend to change with each season. As the above categories are the ones most commonly in use among Malaysian social and agricultural scientists, their use here seems appropriate. It should be sufficient to note that the categories themselves are broad and do not fully represent all possible permutations.

Within the area served by the Besut Agricultural Development Project, Yap and Dixon (1972) found that the average size alloted to rice cultivation varied among tenure groups as follows:

Owners—operators	3.2 acres
Owners—tenants	4.6 acres
Tenants	3.0 acres

In the Gong Guncil area, the present writer found average farm size to be somewhat smaller, as shown below:

Owners—operators	2.28 acres
Owners—tenants	3.18 acres
Tenants	1.99 acres

In part the divergence in these figures may be attributable to the inclusion in the former of extensive areas which at the time of the survey were single-cropped. In such areas a larger farm size would be necessary to maintain a family. The figures presented by Yap and Dixon on ownership of land suggest that in these areas farm sizes are somewhat larger than in areas where double-cropping is predominant. It is also possible that the different methodologies used in collecting the data contributed to the different farm size averages. The author is aware that his figures may not be precise, but with the benefit of a smaller study universe and careful checking he believes that his figures are reasonably accurate. The data cover only approximately 250 acres. As such they should be treated with the caution due a small sample. However, on the basis of extended experience in the area the author would venture to say the figures are representative of the Stage I area as a whole.

Table 3.4 gives a breakdown of rice cultivating households by tenure category for the individual villages within the study area.

TABLE 3.4

NUMBER OF HOUSEHOLDS BY TENURE CATEGORY FOR VILLAGES IN THE GONG GUNCIL STUDY AREA

Village	*Owner—Operator*	*Owner—Tenant*	*Tenant*
Gong Guncil	29	14	11
Baruh Kual	10	2	3
Pulau Panjang	6	4	4
Gong Tanah Merah	7	4	7
Total	52	24	25

Data on farm size by tenure category for the individual villages within the study area are found in Table 3.5; they indicate that the average size of farm in Gong Tanah Merah is significantly larger than that found in the other villages studied.

TABLE 3.5

AVERAGE RICE FARM SIZE BY TENURE CATEGORY FOR VILLAGES IN THE GONG GUNCIL STUDY AREA

(in acres)

Village	*Owner—Operator*	*Owner—Tenant*	*Tenant*
Gong Guncil	2.17	3.30	2.36
Baruh Kual	2.20	2.50	1.42
Pulau Panjang	2.25	2.38	1.38
Gong Tanah Merah	2.93	3.88	2.00

Average figures are useful in drawing a general picture, but often the range from which these figures are obtained is at least equally significant: Table 3.6 indicates the distribution of farm sizes for families actively cultivating rice.

It may be seen that the majority of all rice farms (87 out of 101) are less than 4 acres. Twenty-two of these cases are tenant farmers, half of whom cultivate less than 2 acres of land. This may be due to a number of factors, including a preference for alternative employment. Nine of the 25 tenant households depend largely or even primarily on outside employment, as labourers with the Drainage

TABLE 3.6

DISTRIBUTION OF RICE FARM SIZE BY TENURE RELATIONSHIP

Size (acres)	*Owner—Operator*	*Owner—Tenant*	*Tenant*	*Total*
0—0.99	2	nil	2	4
1—1.99	16	2	9	27
2—2.99	17	4	8	29
3—3.99	11	13	3	27
4—4.99	4	3	2	9
5—5.99	nil	1	1	2
6—6.99	2	1	nil	3
Over 7	nil	nil	nil	nil
Total	52	24	25	101

and Irrigation Department (DID), trishawmen or petty traders; rice is grown by them primarily for home consumption.

Tenant households would appear to have adequate labour resources to work larger farms, with the overwhelming majority having at least two able-bodied adult workers within the age range of 30—50 years. In only one case were the adult members of the tenant household over 50 years of age. In 23 cases the tenant households were comprised of adults between the ages of 30 and 50; in only one case were the adults under 30. Only 3 tenant households had less than two able-bodied adults. (This definition of adequate labour, however, is static in that it does not take into consideration short-term incapacities due to illness, advanced pregnancy, etc.)

Twenty of the 25 tenant households have lived in Gong Guncil ten years or more, and are not newcomers who may have had difficulty in establishing working relationships with local landowners. Three of the remaining households have moved into the area within the past ten years, live in Gong Tanah Merah, and share-crop the land of the richer residents of that village. The limited size of most tenant operated farms cannot be explained by a shortage of labour available to tenant farm families, or by an inability to find owners willing to let them work what land is available for share-cropping; rather, the factor primarily responsible for their small farm size is the limited availability of such land.

The amount of land available for renting or share-cropping is variable and depends on a number of factors, most notably the labour that households which own land can mobilize. Most families in the owner—operator category usually plant all of their own land, but occasionally a short-term limit to their labour resources will necessitate renting or share-cropping some part of their holdings. This may be due to personal exigencies such as an illness in the family, the advanced pregnancy of the wife (or recent childbirth), or the husband taking temporary employment outside the village. In the case of land-owners who every season have a surplus of land beyond their own capacity or willingness to farm, tenancy relationships tend to be of longer duration and generally cease on the initiative of the tenant family.

Most tenancy arrangements are made between farmers in similar economic situations and in a bare majority of cases are concluded between kinsmen (25 out of 49 recorded cases). During the off-season of 1977 a total of 92.5 acres was either share-cropped or rented. Both tenants and owners—tenants are included in this figure, which represents 49 households. The average acreage of such tenancy arrangements is 1.9 acres; with few exceptions the range was from one to three acres of rice land.

TENANCY RELATIONSHIPS

The conditions of tenancy relationships are controlled by accepted social norms and generally are regarded as fair by all concerned. All share-cropping and rental agreements are verbal, and there is no legal guarantee that the tenant will be allowed to farm on the same plot the next season. There is in fact considerable shifting around from season to season on the part of households which depend in part or in full on the land of others. This is understandable because a large proportion of rental or share-cropping arrangements are made to take advantage of short-term changes in the labour availability of a land-owning family. The flexibility of the system allows the land-owning family still to obtain some income while ensuring continued cultivation of the land.

Only in 11 cases were the tenancy arrangements based on a straight rental, with payments averaging approximately 80 *gantang* of *padi* per season per acre. In cash terms this is the equivalent of $72—80, depending on the variety planted and the date of marketing. In fact most of the rice obtained from such rentals is consumed by the owner. Older land-owners who have small but fixed needs prefer the fixed rental system as it limits the risk element attendant upon share-cropping arrangements.

Two forms of share-cropping arrangements exist, *bagi dua* and *bagi tiga*. There were 36 cases of *bagi dua* and 6 cases of *bagi tiga* recorded during the off-season of 1977 in the Gong Guncil area; 4 cases were found where more than one tenancy arrangement had been made. Most commonly with *bagi dua* all expenses of production are shared evenly by tenant and owner, and the crop is divided evenly in the field. In cases where the tenant family does not have the cash on hand when fertilizers have to be purchased, the land-owning family may pay for this input initially and be reimbursed at harvest time. Under *bagi dua* it is the responsibility of the land-owning family to harvest its share of the crop; alternatively, the family may hire someone (more than likely the tenant family) to harvest for them at a rate of 20 *gantang* of rice for every 100 *gantang* harvested, or 25 *gantang* if the rice is delivered to the owner's store-house. The tenant family is responsible for seeding, transplanting, and maintaining the crop in the field, including water control, bund maintenance, application of fertilizer, and pest control. Variations exist, as when a tenant will prepare the land by water-buffalo and the owner will pay for the fertilizer. Share-cropping agreements are both informal and flexible and allow for the respective needs and capacities of the families involved.

In most cases of *bagi tiga*, the owner of the land supplies all inputs, prepares and seeds the nursery, and often maintains the crop once it is transplanted, while the tenant does all the trans-planting and his one-third share of the harvest (with the possibility of harvesting the owner's portion at the standard rates noted above). Tenants who lack sufficient working capital to provide their share of inputs often prefer this system. The second variation of *bagi tiga* most frequently occurs when an owner in need of cash leases a parcel of land to a fellow villager who in turn allows the owner to cultivate the land as usual. In such cases the person who leases the land takes one-third of the crop without contributing to the produc-tion costs or labour, which are borne by the legal owner.

Lease arrangements, also made verbally in most cases, cover less than 5 per cent of the total rice land in the study area. Leasing out land provides a land-owning family with a means of mobilizing quick cash while allowing those who have managed to save up a quantity of cash to increase effective farm size.

Two forms of lease agreements are recognized locally, *pajak* and *gadai*. '*Pajak*' refers to an advance of money by which use of a piece of land is gained for a stipulated period of time (i.e., one to several years). This form of agreement approximates a straight rental of the land, though the 'rent' is paid in advance rather than at the end of each season. Because payment is made in advance the rate is lower than a normal rental, often by at least 50 per cent. '*Gadai*' refers to loans for which the capital must be repaid, the leaseholder retaining rights of usage over the land until the principal is repaid.

Gadai is the most common lease arrangement in the Gong Guncil area, and seems to favour the leaseholder since many loans take years to repay. Unless there is a crop failure, the returns to the leaseholder are potentially great. The return on a $600 investment used to lease (*gadai*) one acre of double-cropped rice land is over 20 per cent per annum. The largest sum recorded during the period of field study for leasing one acre of land is $600; more commonly half this sum would be sufficient. This return to capital is not strictly an 'interest' rate, as there is an element of risk involved. (As Muslims, Malays are forbidden by their religion to earn interest on loans; since in this case there is the risk of crop failure, the money advanced to lease land can be regarded as a potentially profitable investment.) Given average yields and, as is usually the case, assuming the leaseholder will let the holding on a *bagi tiga* basis to the owner, and also hire the latter to harvest his portion of the rice, the following figures indicate the returns possible: one-third of an average yield of 300 *gantang* gives the leaseholder 100 *gantang* which, if harvested and carried by the 'tenant' to his storehouse, leaves a net of 75 *gantang* per season, without his contributing any labour or production costs, or 150 *gantang* per year on an investment of $600; 150 *gantang* is worth approximately $150, or a return of 25 per cent.

As noted above, families which lease out part of or all of their land under *gadai* often take several years to accumulate enough money to regain control of their land. In the absence of other sources of loans for consumption purposes, however, such lease agreements serve a valuable function. Recognizing the difficulty of repaying what is essentially a loan, the farm families of Gong Guncil are reluctant to lease their land out to others, but occasionally are forced by circumstances to do so. The following example illustrates both an important means of economic advancement for a household able to accumulate a small fund of working capital, and the problems faced by a farm family in need of a quick source of money. The example provided is extreme; rarely does a farm family lease out more than one acre of land, and rarely is the outstanding debt more than a few hundred dollars.

One farm family's son was involved in a car accident, which simultaneously reduced this family's labour resource and added major expenses which it could afford only by leasing out an acre of rice land to a neighbouring family for several hundred dollars. Over the next two years the leaseholders gave out loans totalling $1,800 in return for the lease of 4 acres of rice land under *gadai*. Rather than ask the owners to continue cultivating their land, the leaseholders farmed the land themselves; this was to their advantage as they owned only one acre of rice land, and through leasing the additional land they substantially increased their farm size without having to share the production with the owners. It was in this way that the leaseholders, a young and exceptionally hard-working couple, had saved their money. The owners of the land were unable to repay the accumulated loan, and in order to reclaim their rice land they transferred 6 acres of partially cleared rubber land to the leaseholders. The land was worth at least three times the outstanding debt, but as the owners needed their rice land for their basic subsistence, the rubber land was traded away. Neither the parties involved nor other members of the community felt that there was anything unfair in this *gadai* relationship.

The various leasing, renting, and share-cropping relationships formed between farm families in the Gong Guncil area are based on the fluctuating labour and capital resources available to these families, and serve to ensure that virtually all rice land is in continual production. All these relationships are controlled by unwritten but socially approved codes and formulae designed to protect the interests of the parties involved.

THE BASIC RIGHT TO SUBSISTENCE

The rice farmers of Gong Guncil, whether owners or tenants, are concerned first and foremost with producing enough rice to meet their household needs. The assurance of this basic need is not only a major consideration of farm families, it is taken to be a right. This basic right is more powerful than, and has precedence over the distributional formulae of, existing tenancy relationships (see Scott, 1976, for a discussion of this right to subsistence among farmers in South-East Asia). If part of a tenant family's rice crop is lost due to a natural calamity, it may request a modification of the agreed-upon distribution of the remaining harvest or, in the case of a straight cash rental, a reduction in the amount to be paid. In some cases, e.g. a retired farm family owning a small parcel of land, the owners may be less able to weather a crop loss than their tenant, who may be requested to give a larger share of the harvest to them. The agreement between land-owning families and their tenants is conditional and based on the assumption of yields which are expected to provide an adequate supply of rice to the parties involved. Any threat to basic subsistence needs calls for a modification of the agreed-upon distribution of the harvest or rental payment. No modification is called for if the loss is limited to a failure to earn expected cash income from the sale of rice beyond consumption needs, or even failure to meet costs incurred in production beyond consumption needs. Rather, such modifications are expected only when a family's basic subsistence needs are threatened.

During four seasons in the Gong Guncil area there were limited opportunities to observe the consequences of crop loss on tenancy relationships. During one season the field of Pulau Panjang was hard hit by an infestation of the rice bug *Leptocorisa acuta*, resulting in partial or complete loss to several farmers. The most damage was suffered by a family of owners–operators: the husband of this family had left home for several months after transplanting to work in a logging operation some 80 miles away, and no insecticides had been applied to the crop.

Several other families, including owners–operators and tenants, also suffered major losses, but through repeated spraying of insecticides they were able to avert total loss. Two of these tenant families were landless and poor, and even a partial loss of their crop was enough to threaten their subsistence needs. The family owning the land they operated not only agreed to allow them to harvest its share so that they could earn additional grain, even though it usually harvested its own, but also let them harvest an additional 2 acres which it had planted. Though this was not an outright gift, it was considered by the parties involved to be a subsidy in that the owners received less than they normally would while the tenants were able to receive more. The land-owning family in this case could more easily afford to absorb the season's loss than could its tenants, and by doing so demonstrated its willingness to assist its less wealthy neighbours through a difficult time.

The willingness of land-owners to assist their tenants, or vice versa, through a crop loss is a widely accepted social norm for which empirical substantiation is limited. Fortunately for the farm families of Gong Guncil, there was only one significant crop loss during the four seasons of data collection. Widely accepted social norms do, however, have considerable impact on behaviour. A number of practical considerations support the existence of this norm. A wealthy family which fails to consider the subsistence needs of a less fortunate family risks social ostracism; at the very least its tenants can be expected to seek out other land to work. The shortage of available rice land means that an owner will have little difficulty in attracting a new tenant, but this new tenant family will realize that little assistance can be expected from the land-owner in time of need, and its members will be looking for other land to work. It is to the benefit of an owner who has land beyond what his or her family can effectively operate to establish a long-term tenancy relationship with a diligent farm family which will maintain the bunds, fertilize adequately, and in other ways maintain the quality of the land. A tenant family which knows it will work the owner's land for only one season may withhold the use of fertilizer, thus depleting the soil of nutrients, and allow weeds to choke the bunds, providing convenient shelter to rats and insect pests which will plague future crops. There are, therefore, in addition to social pressures, practical reasons for land-owners to encourage the maintenance of long-term relationships with their tenants.

For many families there is another factor to be added to this normative picture of land-owner—tenant relations. It may be recalled that in Gong Guncil 25 out of 49 tenancy relationships recorded during field research were found to be between kinsmen. Kinsmen are expected to assist one another in times of difficulty, and the norm of generosity between owner and tenant easily fits under the rubric of such expectations. Because half of all tenancy relationships are between kinsmen, these relationships influence the nature of all others.

DEVIATION FROM THE NORM

As with any social norm much can be learned from the study of deviation from the norm in question. The basic right to subsistence in rice developed during a period when rice was planted once a year, primarily as a subsistence crop. Since the introduction in the mid-1960s of irrigation facilities, double-cropping with fertilizer-responsive varieties has encouraged the commercialization of rice production. For the first time, many farm families were able to produce a surplus for sale and were, in fact, forced to do so in order to meet the increased production costs of rice cultivation. The extent of the surplus available for sale is limited by the small areas planted by individual families, and the majority of farm families produce little beyond their immediate consumption needs after the costs of production are paid.

For some families, however, rice production is a major source of income. These families are the ones which most easily can afford to be generous to their hired help or tenants. The commercial prospects of rice production in some cases have led to deviation from the traditional norm of generosity to tenant families. Members of the local economic élite residing in Gong Tanah Merah are shifting away from letting their land out to local tenants in favour of managing their own holdings and using hired labour. It is significant that these families are unable to attract local labour for such work. This has less to do with a local shortage of labour than with the fact that local residents who regularly supplement their income by hiring themselves out to work on the fields of others refuse to work the lands of this local élite.

The effective labour boycott maintained against the local élite indicates the kind of social sanctions which can be invoked against deviation from socially accepted norms. This boycott did not seriously hurt production on the fields of the local élite, but it did make their recruitment of labour more difficult and served to further isolate this élite from significant local interaction.

TRADITIONAL AGRICULTURAL PRACTICES

THE PERSISTENCE OF TRADITIONAL VARIETIES AND CULTIVATION PRACTICES

The Besut Agricultural Development Project was established to increase the productivity of Besut District's farmers. Low yields were blamed on the use of traditional seed varieties, the failure to use chemical fertilizers and pesticides, and poor farm management practices. It was thought that the introduction of irrigation facilities would enable farmers to obtain two crops instead of one per year. No longer would farmers be dependent upon the vagaries of rainfall. Water control would be regularized by the timely release of water by the Drainage and Irrigation Department to enable farmers to prepare their fields, plant their seed-beds, and transplant. As the crop neared maturity, the flow of water would be halted, hastening the drying of the grain and facilitating harvest. Careful control of water is a prerequisite for the use of fertilizer-responsive rice varieties. Farmers were encouraged to use these new varieties through seed exchange programmes that gave 2 *gantang* of seed for every *gantang* of seed grain turned in by farmers. Extension agents were to advise farmers on the recommended practices for these new varieties, and credit facilities were provided to assist farmers in the purchase of chemical fertilizers and other inputs necessary for optimum yields.

The receptivity of the farmers to the new set of agricultural practices has been mixed; some adopted them enthusiastically while others continued using the traditional varieties and methods. The majority of farmers, however, have adopted a syncretic mixture of traditional agricultural practices and those recommended by the Project's extension staff. The mixture is a dynamic one, based on the needs and resources of each individual household. If a family is faced with a temporary shortage of funds with which to purchase chemical fertilizers, it may return for a season to the use of a traditional variety and its associated cultivation techniques, and then return again the next season to high-yielding varieties; alternatively, it may continue to plant the new variety but without applying fertilizer.

Sometimes farmers will say that they are planting a traditional variety of rice for reasons of sentiment, as a crop planted by their ancestors ('*bawa padi datuk-nenek*'). They will explain that if the traditional varieties were never planted, the knowledge of those varieties, the practices associated with them, and the very seeds themselves would disappear forever. To some extension agents this would not be an altogether bad thing, but it is clear that farmers feel otherwise. It is significant that fourteen years after double-cropping was introduced to the Gong Guncil area, traditional varieties still retained their popularity.

To understand the continued popularity of traditional varieties and associated production practices it is necessary to comprehend from the farmers' perspective the advantages of these varieties. Any strategy of change must take into account these considerations, and ideally research and extension efforts should start from this basis. To do otherwise would be to assume that farmers are beginning with a 'clean slate' upon which recommended practices may be written at will; as will be shown below, such is not the case.

ADVANTAGES OF TRADITIONAL AGRICULTURAL PRACTICES

Traditional rice varieties are typified by taller plants and larger, heavier grains, qualities that farmers consider positive attributes. They also appear to be quite tolerant not only of flooding during the north-east monsoon but of drought as well. Chemical fertilizers are rarely used with these varieties due to problems of lodging, i.e., the stalk will not support the increased weight of the grain, resulting in the entire plant falling over, especially after a strong wind, thus making harvest more difficult and, if the fields are wet, threatening the grain with rot. Traditional varieties are planted in either wet or dry seed-beds and may be pulled for transplanting at any time from 4 to 8 weeks after seeding. This flexibility is a most important quality of these varieties and contrasts with the relatively more demanding regimen of the newer high-yielding varieties, which lose capacity for tillering when left in the seed-bed for longer than 30 days. Because the seedlings may be left in the seed-bed for extended periods of time, there is less need for a rigid transplanting schedule, which allows the farmer increased flexibility in the timing of his land preparation and his mobilization of labour for transplanting itself.

The taller seedlings of the traditional varieties are more easily handled during transplanting. These seedlings grow quickly into taller plants, and plant height is still a quality to which farmers respond positively. Tall seedlings have a headstart over weeds in the fields, and the traditional varieties compete more effectively against weeds than the shorter fertilizer-responsive varieties, as the greater plant height allows less sunlight to reach the weeds and hence stunts their growth. Even though most of the fields now are planted with fertilizer-responsive varieties, few farmers bother to weed their fields; with traditional varieties this was probably an unnecessary task.

Weed control is a greater problem with the newer varieties, partly due to differences in seedling and plant height, and partly due to changed methods of land preparation. In the past all ploughing was done by water-buffalo or teams of two oxen. First the land would be ploughed and allowed to lie for a week or more so that any weed seeds would germinate; then the farmer would harrow the land, knocking down any weeds that had survived the ploughing and incorporating them into the puddled mud. The land would then be ploughed and harrowed a second time. The first ploughing generally was done in a clockwise direction, starting from a line down the centre of the field, moving to an edge and following the edge of the bund; the ground immediately next to the bund was thus effectively worked and the soil thrown away from the bund. After harrowing and again leaving the land for a week or so (in the meantime moving on to work another piece of land), the farmer would plough a second time in a counter-clockwise direction, throwing the soil back against the bund. The first harrowing was done quickly, the primary purpose being to control weeds, whereas the final harrowing was done more carefully and served to level the land so that the water standing in the field would be even throughout.

Land preparation using draught animals may have stretched over a period of a month or more. The farmer would have worked his animal or animals for only 4–5 hours in the morning and rested them in the afternoon; he also would have alternated working at ploughing and harrowing for their sake. Harrowing is a much more strenuous activity for the animals and the farmer would time his schedule so as not to leave all of the harrowing to be done at one time. The more leisurely pace of transplanting when rice was single-cropped permitted adequate rest for man and beast.

DIVERSITY OF TRADITIONAL RICE VARIETIES

There are a number of traditional rice varieties, each with different rates of maturation. A 9-month variety known as *Padi Sagupa* would be seeded in August, transplanted 6–8 weeks later, and harvested in April. *Padi Pak Saka*, a 6-month variety, would be sown in mid-September or October, transplanted in late October, and harvested in mid-March.

Typically a farm family would plant several different varieties during a single season for at least two good reasons. Different maturation rates allowed the farm family to extend the transplanting season over the months of September and October. Transplant-

FIGURE 3.1

RAINFALL DISTRIBUTION AND RECOMMENDED TIMING OF CULTIVATION STAGES IN BESUT DISTRICT

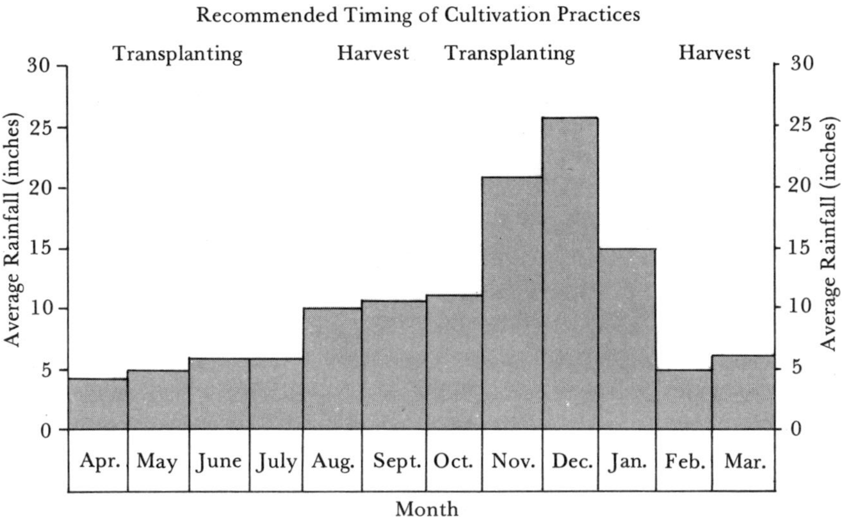

Source: Besut Agricultural Development Project.

ing was (and is) a time-consuming process and the season of peak labour demand in rice cultivation. Secondly, different varieties have different capacities to withstand particular insect pests, diseases, floods, and drought; by planting different varieties, farmers hedged their bets and minimized the possibility of loss. This latter goal also was served by the common practice of planting in different fields. An insect infestation or disease might hit one field, but another field separated by a stand of rubber or a cluster of houses might be unaffected.

The timing of land preparation, transplanting, and harvesting of traditional varieties was tied directly to the annual rainfall pattern. As can be seen from Figure 3.1, the period of greatest rainfall occurs during the north-east monsoon, when more than 25 inches of rain can be expected per month. By April precipitation drops to less than 5 inches per month. With the decreased rainfall came a period of increased solar radiation that coincided with the development of the grain itself; as harvest neared this change in weather assisted in the ripening and drying of the grain in the fields. Drier conditions also made for easier harvesting, as it was much less tiring to walk and work on solid, dry ground than in a field of wet mud that sucked at one's ankles and calves. Furthermore, as the grain was harvested it was possible to lay the bundles of grain on the dry ground; if there was standing water in the field, it would have been necessary to walk through the heavy mud to the bund and leave the bundles there, a time-consuming and tiring task.

Traditional varieties, some with a height of up to 5 feet, were harvested with a small hand knife called a *ketam*. The grains on each tiller were harvested by cutting the base of the panicle. The harvest was gathered into bundles known as *gemai*, which were tied to both ends of a long pole and carried off the field. The rice was stored with the grain still attached to the panicle. Harvesting with the *ketam* involved very little physically hard or stooping labour; one merely moved slowly through the field and plucked the ripe grain, and it was possible to return a week later and harvest grain that previously was immature.

Before double-cropping was introduced, the remainder of the plant was left standing in the field as fodder for livestock, or in some instances may have been cut and burned, especially if there had been an insect or disease problem. In any event, after harvest in April the fields were given over to the grazing of livestock until August when the first seed-beds were prepared and seeded. These would be fenced to keep animals from feeding on the young seedlings. Only from September onwards was livestock restricted from grazing in the rice fields. At that time the heavy rainfall encouraged the growth of vegetation within the orchards, rubber stands, and land around the houses. The advent of double-cropping has greatly reduced the availability of land for grazing livestock and this, together with the displacement of animal traction by tractors for land preparation, has led to a decline in the number of livestock raised in the study area.

DOUBLE-CROPPED RICE PRODUCTION

PROBLEMS OF INTRODUCING A NEW CROPPING SYSTEM

When double-cropping was first introduced to the Gong Guncil area in the mid-1960s there were doubts as to the wisdom of accepting this regimen. In part these worries were based on an understandable reluctance to change production techniques that had provided for the basic subsistence needs of the village for generations. Some farmers were concerned that the land would be exhausted without an annual period of fallow, and all were concerned that the prospects of increased yields and higher standards of living were to be balanced against new risks and uncertainties.

Initial extension efforts were concentrated in the area of Kayu Kelat, a village 2 miles up the road from Gong Guncil. Progress initially was slow and opposition from a number of farmers limited the success of the few farmers who attempted to plant during the off-season, because when a given field is only partially planted the likelihood of crop failure due to insect pests and the depredations of birds is greatly increased. It is also likely that the initial efforts of both farmers and extension agents were hampered by inexperience.

Subsequent extension efforts focused on the village of Pulau Panjang, including one of the fields that came under close observation during the author's own study. This field of some 50 acres lies between the villages of Pulau Panjang and Gong Guncil and a number of farmers from Gong Guncil either own or share-crop land there. Here the efforts of extension agents appear to have been more successful.

One reason for this may have been the influence of one man, a local 'progressive farmer' who encouraged his neighbours and required his share-croppers to follow the planting schedule necessary for double-cropping. This man had inherited 7 acres of rice land, but farmed only 3 acres himself. On the basis of interviews with local farmers it would seem that the influence of this man, a local leader, had much to do with the successful experiment with double-cropping in the area, which in turn contributed to the gradual adoption of double-cropping in neighbouring villages.

Traditional cultivation practices involved little cost other than labour and seed. Most of the labour was provided by the family itself, or supplemented by various cooperative exchanges of labour. The relaxed pace of seed-bed preparation and seeding without the worry of a fixed date for transplanting, the ability to prepare the land bit by bit as the transplanting progressed at a pace determined by labour availability, and harvest unhurried by the advent of a second season—all these were to be changed.

The new varieties require new methods. No longer could the seed-beds be planted on dry ground, so that now the women who pull the seedlings have no choice but to squat in the water and mud. The seedlings have to be pulled 25–30 days after transplanting, an age when by local standards they are considered to be small and hard to handle. Instead of land preparation at leisure by water-buffalo or oxen, the pace must now be quickened and mechanical assistance sought at considerable expense. Cash also is necessary for new production inputs with which the farmers previously had little or no experience. Finally, the pace of the harvest itself was altered, from a gradual and unhurried movement through drying fields to a task that each household raced to complete so it could repeat the whole process.

In sum, farmers adopting double-cropped rice cultivation were faced with not only a major break in their traditional production practices but also a whole series of new uncertainties and dependencies due to a more profound involvement in the cash economy. It should not be surprising that there was doubt on the part of some farmers about whether or not the change would benefit them. A promise of yields of double or more was balanced against unknown risks and major changes in the demands for labour and capital. Given the extent of the change involved in adopting double-cropped rice production, it is indeed remarkable that within a short time—perhaps two or three half-year seasons—the majority of the farmers had adopted many of the new varieties and cultivation practices.

THE CONTINUED USE OF WORKSTOCK FOR LAND PREPARATION

With the introduction of double-cropping the use of draught animals has declined, but not disappeared. Some farmers continue to use only water-buffalo, while others use the water-buffalo exclusively for some seasons but then mix tractor ploughing and water-buffalo at other times; still other farmers depend on tractors for initial ploughing but prefer to use a water-buffalo for the final harrowing. The majority of farmers in Gong Guncil, however, are almost totally dependent upon tractors for ploughing. Most hire privately owned four-wheeled tractors at the rate of $50 per acre, though two-wheeled pedestrian tractors are also used. Only four of these two-wheeled tractors are owned by residents of the study area. None of these locally-owned tractors are hired out to other farmers.

Although the majority of farmers are dependent upon tractors for ploughing, it is unlikely that the water-buffalo will cease to provide valuable and indeed irreplaceable service. When a farm family prepares a seed-bed it probably will be unable to obtain the services of a tractor for such a small plot; moreover, if the seed-bed is in the middle of a field a tractor may be unable to reach it if other farmers in the area are still harvesting their crop. The alternative to a water-buffalo in this case is to prepare the seed-bed by hand, a laborious and time-consuming task that may well conflict with the labour demands of harvest. There are also some fields where tractors cannot be used at all due to the depth of water and mud, and the water-buffalo is the only practical means available for preparing seed-beds or the land on to which the seedlings are to be transplanted.

Water-buffalo have other advantages over tractors: they consume grass and not petrol, and they have calves instead of mechanical breakdowns. But with the advent of double-cropping, the care and feeding of water-buffalo has become a time-consuming chore, and their numbers have decreased markedly over the past 14 years. No data are available to compare accurately the population of water-buffalo before double-cropping with that of today, either from the

Veterinary Department or from local farmers; the Department claims that for Besut District as a whole the population has not decreased, but farmers are unanimous in agreeing that in the Gong Guncil area the numbers have declined.

For the single village of Gong Guncil, in which 54 out of 68 households are actively engaged in rice cultivation, a total of 41 water-buffalo are owned. At least 5 of these animals are less than three years old and cannot be used for ploughing. Only 16 households in Gong Guncil own usable workstock. Based only on an educated guess, it seems likely that twenty years ago at least two-thirds of all farming households might have owned their own workstock, primarily water-buffalo, i.e. it is likely that the number of draught animals in this village would have been double that of the present. (Only one team of oxen was used in the study area during the author's stay. Oxen are said to be superior to water-buffalo for ploughing when the ground is not yet submerged, as was generally the case with rain-fed traditional rice cultivation. Under irrigated conditions, use of oxen has been discontinued in favour of tractors and water-buffalo.)

Farmers report that the cattle population of Gong Guncil also has declined since double-cropping was introduced, although there are no records available to confirm this. In 1978 there were 107 head of cattle owned or being raised by 42 out of 68 households in Gong Guncil. A major factor in the decline of the livestock population has been the lack of grazing land since the introduction of double-cropping. With crops in the fields for so much of the year, it has become necessary to cut fodder for both water-buffalo and cattle. During the ploughing season those farmers using water-buffalo are especially careful to provide adequate feed for their animals, and it would be reasonably accurate to include at least an hour of fodder cutting to the 4–5 hours spent on ploughing for each day of work. Even after the ploughing season, fodder must be cut to supplement the insufficient grazing of the animals, a chore that may add 3–5 hours of work per week.

Because of the size and strength of water-buffalo, and the uncertain disposition of many of them, the men of the household usually are responsible for their care. This will include moving the animals from their corral in the morning and tethering them. A nylon rope is inserted through the nose of each water-buffalo while it is still young, and this rope is tied to another rope which is attached to a wood stake driven into the ground with the heel of the foot. The water-buffalo will need to be moved at least once if not several times during the day due to the lack of adequate feed in any one spot. Raising a water-buffalo is, in short, a great deal of bother, and ties someone in the family—usually the man—close to the village every day of the year. Cattle, on the other hand, are more tractable and much smaller, and a family's children are usually delegated the responsibility for their care.

With the advent of irrigation the amount of time necessary to prepare the land with a water-buffalo has decreased. The soil in the fields never hardens during the dry season and consequently is more easily worked. Instead of working the fields four times as was the case when rice was planted once a year, it is now generally sufficient to plough once and then to harrow and level the field. Farmers still wait 7–10 days between the initial ploughing and harrowing to control the weed population, and sometimes harrow a second time immediately before transplanting, especially if transplanting has been delayed and weeds have again risen. Even working the field only twice, a farmer needs to spend at least 6 days in preparing an acre of land for transplanting. Though a substantial investment in time and energy, preparation of his fields with a water-buffalo saves a farmer the $50 per acre cost of ploughing and harrowing by tractor.

There are few jobs locally that would play a farmer over $8 per day, but this alone does not explain the preference of some farmers for using a water-buffalo for ploughing. Many claim that a water-buffalo does a superior job to either two-wheeled or four-wheeled tractors. Tractors plough and harrow on a single day, resulting in poorer weed control; they also tend to do a poorer job in puddling the soil because the operator is often more interested in completing the job and moving on to the next field, which will increase his income. Having spent a number of hours transplanting both in fields prepared by water-buffalo and by tractor, the author can confirm that fields prepared by the former are better: they contain fewer large lumps of clayey soil and fewer weeds, and are certainly more level than those ploughed by tractor. Levelness of the field is important in ensuring that the whole area is submerged uniformly as high spots in a field allow weeds to compete easily with the rice plants for space and nutrients, while low spots increase the danger of drowned seedlings.

The water-buffalo has other advantages over a tractor: when it is no longer able to plough it may be eaten or sold. A large water-buffalo will weigh over 1,000 pounds on the hoof and may sell for $1,000 or more. Unlike cattle, which are raised for sale, water-buffalo are valued primarily for their use in land preparation and not for the price they will fetch on the butcher's block. But the high price that may be obtained from the sale of water-buffalo, combined with the difficulty in raising these animals and the alternatives for land preparation, has led to a gradual selling off of the local stock. The sale of livestock provides an important source of cash for many families. A healthy 4- or 5-year-old cow may be sold for $500, representing a gain of about $100 per year per animal. Cash from the sale of livestock is often used to meet such major expenses as building or adding to the family's house. Occasionally the animals are slaughtered in conjunction with a wedding feast. During certain religious celebrations, as at the end of the fasting month, as many as 30–40 families will buy shares in an animal to be slaughtered. The majority of the cattle, water-buffalo and goats raised locally, however, find their way to slaughterhouses which serve urban markets.

One major disadvantage of ploughing with a water-buffalo is the time constraint involved when planting two crops per year. The most common high-yielding varieties planted in the Besut area are Mahsuri, Bahagia, and Sri Malaysia II. From seed-bed to maturity these varieties take 135, 145, and 130 days respectively during the main season, and several days less during the off-season due to increased solar radiation. If a farm family plants only these varieties and on an average 280 days per year are required to grow two crops, 84 days remain for land preparation, or 42 days per season. If a farmer needs to prepare 3 acres of land he would need perhaps only 18 workdays to complete this task.

Such simple calculations may be misleading, however. When the harvest of one season is completed a man does not immediately begin to plough his fields for the following season. Several days, and more probably a week or more, are spent on other activities: resting from the strenuous harvest; doing repair work to the house or rice storage shed that had been put off during the harvest; repairing the plough itself; helping friends and neighbours with their harvest; or visiting friends and relatives in other villages and sometimes helping them with their harvest. There are also such factors as the uncertainty of the weather which may delay ploughing. It is also likely that during the 18 days of actual ploughing, several days will be allowed for resting both man and beast. If 7 days pass from the end of harvest until the beginning of ploughing, 18 days are spent in ploughing and 5 days are given to rest, there would still be 10–12 days of leeway per season, assuming that no inclement weather or illness to the water-buffalo or to the man ploughing interferes. The use of animal traction is then possible when double-cropping a farm of 3 acres.

PROBLEMS WITH THE PLANTING SCHEDULE

A major problem which has grown gradually more severe over the past five years or so is the lateness of planting by farmers in the

Stage I area of the Besut Project, of which Gong Guncil is a part. The planting schedule recommended by the Project staff calls for transplanting of the main-season crop on or around 10 November. This would allow the transplanted seedlings to recover and grow tall enough to survive the winds and rains of the north-east monsoon. By 1977 farmers in and around Gong Guncil were so far behind schedule that not only were their seedlings being planted during the monsoon rains, but the harvest of their off-season crop was threatened by the rains. Late harvest presents difficulties in drying grain for sale or for home storage, and late transplanting risks drowning of vulnerable seedlings. The situation had become so severe that halting the flow of water to the Stage I area for one season was considered by the head of the Project to force farmers back on schedule. From the standpoint of the Project, major divergence from the recommended planting and harvest schedules makes it difficult to time the release and withholding of water. Were water to be withheld for one season the effect on farmers, many of whom in the Stage I area live near the margin of subsistence, would be almost disastrous. It is unlikely, in any event, that such action would produce a long-term solution.

Three interrelated factors contribute to the late planting by farmers in the Stage I area of the Besut Project: the continued use of animal traction for land preparation; the continued use of some long-term traditional varieties; and the tendency for farmers cultivating a particular field to time their planting so that all the rice in it will mature at the same time.

While a diligent farmer using a water-buffalo to cultivate 3 acres could manage to keep to the recommended planting schedule, the fact remains that some farmers are less diligent than others. Moreover, some farmers attempt to use animal traction for more than 3 acres. Matters are further complicated by the continued planting of traditional varieties which take 150–180 days to reach maturity. These varieties tend to be planted during the main season and typically are followed by a faster maturing, fertilizer-responsive variety during the off-season; the longer-term varieties are taller and able to withstand the high water conditions of the monsoon period. But combining a variety that takes 180 days with one that takes 140 days allows insufficient time to prepare the land by animal traction, and only barely enough time for ploughing by tractor. Compounding these problems is the tendency for those farmers who plant long-standing varieties to prepare their land by water-buffalo. In some cases the combination of land preparation by water-buffalo and use of traditional varieties is due to a family's inability to pay for tractor ploughing and chemical fertilizers; in others the farmers have no choice due to inadequate drainage which prohibits use of either tractors or short, fertilizer-responsive varieties. In a few cases where neither of these constraints apply, it would appear that personal preference for working with a water-buffalo and eating what is regarded as superior quality rice is the deciding factor. (Grain from traditional varieties is of premium quality and even extension agents, who are trying to convince farmers to plant new varieties, seek to purchase traditional varieties of rice for their own home consumption!)

When some of the farmers cultivating in a particular field are late in completing one cycle and beginning another they influence the timing of operations of their neighbours, and if the number of these farmers and the amount of land they operate is a substantial proportion of a given field they will tend to dictate the schedule to be followed by the others. Farmers attempt to time their activities so that all the rice planted in a given field attains maturity at about the same time; otherwise crop losses due to insects and birds would be much higher. Simultaneous harvesting does not ensure total protection against these predators, but it does minimize the degree of loss suffered by individual farmers.

The most destructive insect pest in Besut, known locally as the *kesin* (*Leptocorisa acuta*), attacks grain at the soft, milky stage and leaves the plant empty of grain. Within a limited area the *kesin* is migratory, whirling through the air from one plot to another as the grain ripens. If only one plot is at the milky stage the entire population of *kesin* is likely to be found there, and the spraying of insecticides on that plot alone will have only a temporary effect as the *kesin* will fly away to an adjoining plot, only to return when the insecticide has diminished in potency, as after a shower of rain. Birds also tend to cause the greatest damage when they concentrate on individual plots which ripen ahead of others in a field.

It became apparent that farmers cultivating a particular field would tend to plant the same varieties, or varieties with similar maturation rates, to ensure uniform ripening, and that the farmers would consult with others operating in the same fields on the timing of their operations. When it is considered that most farmers operate plots in several different fields each season (see Map 2), one can appreciate the amount of consultation that takes place.

Where a number of farmers are late in their planting, the rest may decide to delay their own operations. Departure of only a week or two from the recommended planting schedule per season is enough to place farmers in the unenviable position of harvesting the off-season crop in the rain and transplanting the seedlings of the main-season crop during a period threatened by flood. Farmers recognize this problem and yet, seemingly inexorably, cultivation in some fields digresses further and further from the planting schedule.

LABOUR DEMANDS OF RICE PRODUCTION

Most of the labour invested in rice production is provided by the individual farm family itself, though occasionally supplementary labour may be provided by friends, kinsmen, and neighbours either on the basis of cash payment (*upah*) or reciprocal exchanges of labour. The labour necessary to cultivate one acre of rice per season will vary from family to family and depends upon their diligence and efficiency, such conditions as the depth of standing water in the fields, distance travelled from the home, and distance of the plot or plots from a road or irrigation canal. For the figures given below it is assumed that land preparation (including seed-bed) will be done by tractor and that the amount of time necessary for arranging for tractor services, directing the tractor to the farm family's plot or plots, and supervising the work of the tractor is valued at one man-day.

Table 3.7 illustrates in outline form the approximate labour required to cultivate one acre of rice on the basis of workdays. If the farmer uses a water-buffalo for land preparation, at least 6 workdays per acre must be added to the total.

The amount of time required for repairing bunds and small irrigation and drainage canals will depend on whether a water-buffalo or a tractor is used for land preparation. If a tractor is used, the

TABLE 3.7

LABOUR REQUIRED PER ACRE PER SEASON FOR RICE PRODUCTION

Task	*Workdays*
Repairing bunds and canals	1.5
Seeding seed-bed and seed-bed water control	2.5
Supervision of ploughing	1.0
Pulling and transplanting seedlings	16.0
Fertilizing	1.0
Periodic visits to plot to check water and other conditions	1.0
Pest and weed control	1.0
Harvest and transport	10.0
Winnowing	5.0
Total	39.0

bunds across which it moves will require repair, and this may include bunds on the land of other farmers through which the tractor must pass. The amount of labour invested also varies considerably from family to family; some keep their bunds completely clear of weeds and are careful to fill in any holes which may harbour rats and through which water may escape, while the bunds of others are less well kept.

The amount of time spent in seeding and seed-bed maintenance also will vary. Some farm families plant only one seed-bed and plant all their seeds at one time; this practice minimizes the difficulty of maintaining the proper level of water in the nursery. Other farmers have multiple seed-beds, one for each plot of land operated. Occasionally farmers will use only one seed-bed but stagger their planting. This is relatively rare due to problems of maintaining the proper level of water in the nursery for seedlings at various stages of growth.

The labour involved in the application of fertilizer and pest and weed control also varies, but to a lesser extent. In any event, these inputs of labour generally do not conflict with other labour demands and can be assimilated into the mid-season schedule of a farmer without difficulty, unless he has left the area for short-term wage employment. Almost invariably the tasks of bund and canal maintenance, seed-bed sowing and maintenance, fertilizer application, periodic visits to the plot to check on water level and general crop conditions, and pest and weed control are performed by male members of the household.

TRANSPLANTING

Transplanting accounts for over one-third of the total labour demand in rice production. During both transplanting and harvest seasons, most farming households are busy constantly, and their resources of labour are fully exploited, even though the farm families of Gong Guncil typically stagger their planting and harvest among several plots in different fields. This staggered planting schedule reduces not only the problem of labour supply during transplanting and harvest but also, as discussed earlier, the risk of a total crop failure due to localized infestations of pests or diseases.

As noted, a farm family's seed-bed often is sown at one time, with seed enough for all or most of their land. With traditional varieties this presents no problem, since the seedlings may be pulled anywhere from 40 to 60 days after sowing. With the newer fertilizer-responsive varieties such flexibility is not possible; after 30 days the capacity of these varieties to produce tillers is seriously and adversely affected. Nonetheless, it is common to see farmers transplanting seedlings as old as 40 days; having begun their transplanting 10 days previously, they pull their seedlings as they need them.

Once seedlings are ready to be pulled, the most critical period of labour demand begins. The pulling of seedlings, *cabut semai*, is exclusively a woman's task, though occasionally young boys will help their mothers. There is no particular taboo associated with this division of labour, but it is felt that a woman's fingers are more deft than a man's and women are said to be better suited to this important but rather monotonous task.

Seedlings are pulled from the nursery one or two at a time. The motion is towards the puller at an angle of about 45 degrees to minimize damage to the fragile roots. The women squat or sometimes sit on small benches in the mud and pull the seedlings with each hand, occasionally shaking a handful of seedlings in the water, striking them against their arms, and then running their fingers through the mass of roots to remove the remaining mud. Bunches of seedlings, *unting*, are tied together and attached to the ends of long poles and in this form transported—usually by men—to the plot being planted. The number of seedlings per *unting* will vary according to the size of the seedlings themselves, but typically the diameter of an *unting* at the point where it is tied is 8–10 inches. Farmers calculate that on an average 400 *unting* are required to plant one acre, although this figure would vary depending on the number of seedlings per *unting* and the number of seedlings planted per hill. A woman who is quick at pulling seedlings may produce as many as 60–70 *unting* per day, though 50 is a more realistic goal for most.

Traditional rice varieties do not produce as many tillers as the new high-yielding varieties, and consequently farmers using these traditional varieties typically plant as many as 5–6 seedlings per hill. This practice has carried over to the new varieties, and though the recommended number is 2 per hill, farmers feel that only 2 of these delicate looking seedlings are inadequate and continue to plant 5 or more per hill. The effect of this bunching is to decrease the number of grain-bearing tillers per plant. Traditional varieties also require wider spacing between hills because of the mutual shading effect of these tall plants, whereas the new varieties are characterized by upright leaves which reduce mutual shading, and their shortness allows for closer spacing and a larger number of hills per acre. Many farmers planting high-yielding varieties continue to space their hills as far as 12 inches apart, although the recommended interval is 6 inches; by spacing such plants as they would the taller traditional varieties, farmers are making inefficient use of their land and allowing increased weed growth as well.

The actual planting of seedlings, *cedung*, is a task that men, women, and youngsters of both sexes perform. (In other parts of Malaysia, such as Kedah, men neither *cabut semai* nor *cedung*.) When seedlings have been pulled and bundled, they may be left overnight or even for as long as two days in the wet mud of the rice field. To plant the seedlings, the *unting* is held in the crook of one arm and several seedlings are pulled loose; while standing in a stooped position, the planter pushes the roots into the mud with the thumb while holding the stalks with the first two fingers. A person quick at transplanting may be able to finish 40–50 *unting* in a day. This, however, is not the most accurate way to measure the efficiency of planting, as a person putting 5 or 6 seedlings in a hill will finish an *unting* faster than a person using only 2. If 50 *unting* are transplanted per day, it would take one person at least 8 days to transplant one acre.

INTERDEPENDENCE OF FARM FAMILIES DURING SEASONS OF PEAK LABOUR DEMAND

Most families rely on their own labour to transplant their crop, but occasionally they must turn to others for help. This may be the result of an illness in the family, a woman's advanced pregnancy, or the recent birth of a child, all of which would reduce the family's available labour. Over time virtually all farm families are likely to experience these or other reductions in their productive capacity and find themselves dependent on their neighbours to get the crop into or out of the ground.

There are a number of ways in which this can be done. If the needs are limited, a family may ask a fellow kinsman to contribute one or more days of work to complete a task, with the implicit understanding that in future need this assistance will be reciprocated. In many cases the need for help will be anticipated, and if kin and close friends have completed their work they may volunteer their assistance to another family. It is also common to see members of two or more families working together, timing their activities so that each will help the other in turn. The reason for this may be related to efficient use of labour, but it often seems that the primary goal is simply social: work is more enjoyable and seems to go more quickly when people work together.

Tolong-menolong

Such informal assistance, whether based on pressing need or sociability, is known locally by the term '*tolong-menolong*'. The root word '*tolong*' translates as 'help' or 'assistance' and the verb form '*menolong*' in this context carries the implication of mutuality and reciprocity. Generally the numbers of people mobilized through *tolong-menolong* are small, from one to perhaps three or four people, and the duration of their assistance is limited. It is unlikely that a family will be able to depend on *tolong-menolong* for a major part of its labour needs, but the ability to call upon such assistance is sometimes crucial to timely transplanting or harvest activities.

Pinjam Orang

A second way in which a household can mobilize supplementary labour is called *pinjam orang*, literally 'borrow people', through which a large number of people can be mobilized for a single afternoon of work, primarily for transplanting. As many farmers sow all the seeds in one seed-bed, resulting in a large number of seedlings ready for transplanting at one time, it is often necessary to call upon additional labour beyond the immediate family. This additional labour may be provided by hired help, a few friends and relatives on the basis of *tolong-menolong*, or a call upon a larger number of people through *pinjam orang*.

The number of people to be called out by a family for an afternoon's work will depend upon the amount of labour required, an estimation of how pressed other villagers are in their own planting, and how many other people the family has helped in similar circumstances in the past. It may vary from 10 to over 60 on a particular afternoon. No direct payment is expected by the helpers, but the family which has called the workers is expected to provide tobacco, together with tea, coffee, and local sweets, e.g., a rice and bean gruel cooked in coconut cream and sweetened with coconut sugar.

Ketua Pinjam Orang

The manner in which a labour force is mobilized through *pinjam orang* varies according to how many people are required. If a family requests only 10–15 helpers, its members are likely to visit the other households and invite their participation on the morrow, or perhaps the day after; but if it expects to call out a larger number of workers, it will depend on either one or both of the men in the village who act as labour mobilizers.

The influence of these men appears to be great, and they operate not only in the realm of *pinjam orang* for rice production, but whenever there is a need to mobilize large numbers of people for other sorts of activities, such as a house-moving, the construction or repair of a small bridge, the maintenance of village paths, or the periodic cleaning of the village mosque. These men are referred to as *ketua pinjam orang*: '*ketua*' means 'head' or 'headman'. The position is not so formal as this may imply; it is occupied through self-selection by a man who over a long period of time has involved himself in activities that bring together the labour of a village or even several villages to a single task. Through manifest leadership qualities, such a man comes to be recognized as the person to see when a task requiring the mobilization of large numbers of people is at hand.

Ketua pinjam orang can be found in most of the villages in Besut's rice plain, and it is significant that they form a local network through which large numbers of workers from neighbouring villages can be mobilized. The most common need for such intervillage mobilization is when a house is to be moved. This may occur when the owner of a house buys a new piece of land, when he wishes to use the present house site for another purpose, when the present house site is deemed unsuitable (prone to flooding or dampness during the rainy season), or if there has been a quarrel with an in-law or neighbour. When a house is to be moved, long poles (often from a split betel-nut palm, *pinang*) are first lashed to the stilts and floor supports. The whole house is then lifted by these poles upon the shoulders of as many as 300 men, and with much shouting, groaning, and laughter, carried to the new site. The men are recompensed for this hard work by being fed local cakes and delicacies and by the air of festive sociability that always seems to accompany large congregations of Malays. A certain amount of intervillage rivalry occasionally adds to the interest, but such gatherings mainly provide an opportunity for friends from different villages to meet and exchange news.

Mobilizing the large number of men needed to move a house requires the assistance of several *ketua pinjam orang* from different villages. The owner of the house will contact such a leader in his village, telling him when and to where the house is to be moved, and together they will estimate the number of men required for the task. The local *ketua pinjam orang* will then call upon his counterparts in surrounding villages for the necessary assistance on the appointed day. Only rarely would such an activity occur during transplanting or harvest seasons or during the monsoon rains, but during other seasons house-movings occur quite frequently. The two men who act as *ketua pinjam orang* in Gong Guncil mobilize their fellow villagers at least two or three times a month during such seasons for house-movings, either within Gong Guncil or in other neighbouring villages.

Because of their pivotal role in mobilizing labour, the *ketua pinjam orang* are men whose call for assistance cannot be ignored lightly. If a man repeatedly fails to turn out when called upon to assist others for a house-moving, he will be unable to depend on the help of others if he is subsequently in need of assistance. This threat also applies to a family which fails to assist others in transplanting; when a request is made to help a neighbour it is expected that at least one member of the family will turn out on the appointed day. If the father is unavoidably engaged elsewhere, his wife or one of his older children may take his place. Absence due to a family emergency is of course excused, but repeated absences are remembered and will result in the absentee family being unable to call upon *pinjam orang* for any purpose. No *ketua pinjam orang* would bother to help a family that did not turn out to help others. Even families which prefer not to use *pinjam orang* labour in transplanting often continue to help their neighbours, partly to ensure that in an emergency they will have recourse to this assistance. More is involved than self-interest, however: the shared experience of *pinjam orang* is valued in its own right as a means of fostering a sense of community solidarity. Through *pinjam orang* the mutual interdependence of rice farming families is made manifest, and reciprocal labour obligations are incurred which serve to bind the community together.

During the off-season of 1977 there appears to have been an inordinate amount of reliance upon *pinjam orang* labour for transplanting. Between April and May, the period of transplanting, over 30 families used *pinjam orang* to supplement family labour, reported by farmers to be higher than average. During both the main season of 1977/8 and the main season of 1978/9 fewer than 10 cases per season were noted. (Data for 1978/9 were sent through the mail by a farmer of Gong Guncil; no data are available for the off-season of 1978.) These lower figures are probably more representative of the average use of *pinjam orang* labour. During the main season, many farmers plant traditional varieties for which timely transplanting is less important, whereas during the off-season a higher proportion of farmers plant high-yielding varieties for which timely transplanting is crucial.

One reason for the increased use of *pinjam orang* during the off-season of 1977 was the intensive extension effort in the Pulau Panjang area by MARDI, in which farm families were given free seed and fertilizer for one season on the condition that they followed MARDI's recommendations. Since one of the key features of this production package was the timely planting of seedlings, the farmers operating in this field had need to call upon the help of their neighbours.

Of the more than 30 cases of *pinjam orang* during this season, 8 took place in Pulau Panjang. This created a snowball effect (a curious phenomenon in a tropical setting) whereby other farm families found their own work delayed after helping so many of their neighbours, and they in turn were forced to call upon help through *pinjam orang*.

Pinjam orang is perhaps the single most important factor binding farm families together into a conscious community, one defined by more than mere arbitrary geographical boundaries. Yet not everyone is bound up in these ties of recurrent reciprocal obligations. The nine families of Gong Tanah Merah who comprise the local economic élite are effectively outside the network, neither participating in nor requesting the assistance of their neighbours through *pinjam orang*, depending instead on hired workers to work their lands.

AGRICULTURAL WAGE LABOUR

The élite are not the only families to utilize hired help to meet labour requirements beyond their capacity, however. There are several households in Gong Guncil that claim they have never called upon the labour provided by *pinjam orang* for work in their fields, and they advance reasonable explanations. These households prefer to supplement family labour by hiring people, claiming that the quality of a hired helper's work can be more easily controlled and is superior to that of a worker obtained through *pinjam orang*. If a person has come out to help in the fields under *pinjam orang*, the farm family cannot easily complain if the work is done in a slipshod fashion without appearing ungrateful. With a large number of people transplanting it is almost impossible to produce even rows of seedlings, uniform distance between hills, or a consistent number of seedlings per hill. Each of these factors may reduce the productivity of a given plot of land.

As 'progressive farmers', these households do in fact achieve higher yields per acre than their neighbours. They typically sow their seed-beds at intervals, and thus rarely face the problem of large quantities of seedlings which need immediate attention. These families also point out that with *pinjam orang* people arrive at 3 p.m. and are ready to leave the fields at 5 p.m. Though their labour is free, they must be provided with tobacco, food, and drinks, and when the amount of work accomplished by a crew of *pinjam orang* workers is considered, there is little or no savings over the cost of hired help. There is also the trouble involved in mobilizing the work-force and preparing the food and drink for their refreshment. Although these families willingly assist their friends and kinsmen who call upon their help in *pinjam orang*, they pride themselves in the quality of their crop management, and prefer not to use *pinjam orang* labour on their own land.

There is reason to suppose that the introduction of new high-yielding varieties and the practices associated with them will gradually erode reciprocal exchange of labour. In some ways the demands of double-cropping increase the interdependence of farmers due to the need for timely transplanting, but, over time, the higher yields of the 'progressive farmers' may have some influence, particularly with younger farmers whose level of education and general disposition make them more receptive to the advice of extension agents. By staggering the sowing of seed-beds the demand for labour in transplanting can be spread out over a longer period, reducing the need for mobilizing large numbers of people. Indeed, unless there are many seedlings ready for transplanting at the same time, there is no need for the large-scale mobilization of labour represented by *pinjam orang*. There are clear agronomic reasons for the staggering of sowing operations and the timely transplanting of seedlings in an orderly manner.

Even if most farmers adopt staggered sowing of seed-beds, there will be continued demand for labour beyond the resources of a single household. As at present, this periodic demand may be met in part through *tolong-menolong* between neighbours and kinsmen. It is likely, however, that as rice production becomes increasingly commercialized through increased use of cash inputs (fertilizers and tractor ploughing) and increased marketing due to a larger surplus of grain produced by each household, extra labour demands will be met by recourse to hired labour.

During 1977 and 1978 the costs of hired labour were fixed at $7 for pulling 100 *unting* and $8 for planting 100 *unting*. If 400 *unting* are required per acre of land, the total labour cost per acre is $60. Hired help is enlisted primarily from among local residents. Those people willing to work for a cash wage tend to be landless tenant farmers who supplement their income by working for others; owners—operators or owners—tenants operating small farms may also work for others if such work does not conflict with their own cultivation schedule.

A LABOUR BOYCOTT

Unlike their neighbours, who look to local residents when hiring help, the local economic élite of Gong Tanah Merah rely on agricultural labourers from villages five or more miles away, where rice is either single-cropped or not planted at all. These land-owners claim that there is not sufficient local labour to work their land, but other local residents tell a different story. Until perhaps 1976 several families from Gong Guncil helped to work the lands of these wealthy land-owners. Since then, however, an effective labour boycott forced several of these wealthy families to find other sources of labour. This boycott was instituted after it was claimed that several such owners delayed payment for work done by their less wealthy neighbours, even after repeated attempts to collect the sums due.

One of these land-owners is the *ketua kampung* of the area encompassing Gong Tanah Merah, Baruh Kual, and Gong Guncil. Now most of the labour required to cultivate his lands (and the lands of several of his relatives living in Gong Tanah Merah) is obtained from other villages. Three families from those villages are now full-time residents of Gong Tanah Merah, share-cropping land of local land-owners. Other workers come into the area during periods of transplanting and harvest, either returning to their home villages on bicycles in the evening or staying in some small huts on the land of the land-owners. One family spent their nights in the rice and fertilizer storage shed attached to the house of the headman.

For the more wealthy land-owners, hired workers provide a large proportion of the labour used in their fields. For most farmers of Gong Guncil and the surrounding area, wage labour tends to be supplementary to family labour. The majority of those using hired help to supplement family labour are farmers operating larger than average holdings (e.g. 4 acres) who see themselves as providing needed employment and income for a few of their kinsmen, friends, and neighbours. There is certainly no question of superordinate/subordinate roles involved in such relationships. Negative social sanctions such as the boycott are likely to exert a strong influence towards maintaining friendly and non-exploitative labour relationships among the small farmers of Gong Guncil for the foreseeable future.

LABOUR FOR HARVEST

Pinjam orang is used almost exclusively for transplanting; there was only one case of *pinjam orang* for harvest during the period of the author's residence in Gong Guncil. This is explained by the difference in the nature of transplanting and harvest activities. During transplanting, there may be a large number of seedlings that have to be planted in a short period of time. Timely harvest is also important, but in this case a matter of a few days is not so crucial, and under most circumstances ripened grain may be left in the field a week or more without problems. People work hard during harvest, but the pace is not as frantic as it is during transplanting.

In addition to the more flexible nature of harvest operations, farmers typically plant different varieties with slightly different maturation rates. Consequently, there is no need to mobilize a large number of workers on any one day. The labour resources of farm families is more likely to be adequate for harvest operations; when it is not, families may turn to their friends and neighbours for *tolong-menolong* assistance, or they may hire a fellow villager.

If anything, *tolong-menolong* is more prevalent during harvest than during transplanting: the work of harvesting is more enjoyable and people are more likely to volunteer their help. Moreover, during harvest the range of volunteers is expanded to include kinsmen from other villages, especially non-rice producing villages. In such cases the effect of *tolong-menolong* is to decrease the amount of grain the cultivating household obtains from its farm as such help is expected to be rewarded by a gift of grain. Even if relatives from such villages do not come and help with the harvest, they may still be given rice when they come to visit or when a family from Gong Guncil goes to visit them after the harvest. Such giving is not strictly one-sided, however, and the rice is likely to be greeted with a reciprocal gift from the other family's efforts, e.g. fish, fruits, or coconuts. Unless one or the other family is materially better off, it seems, from the author's experience, that the value of gifts is roughly comparable, although the exchange may not occur simultaneously. Gifts of rice also are made to children of local farmers who have found wage employment in the urban sector or in the military. In such cases reciprocal gifts are likely to be made in the form of cash, and in value are likely to represent a net gain in income to rice farming families.

Labour for harvest beyond that provided by members of a household may also be obtained by hired help, and for many tenant farmers this is an important source of rice. Unlike payment for transplanting, men and women hired to help with the harvest are paid in grain, at the rate of 20 *gantang* for every 100 *gantang* harvested. If the rice is transported to the storehouse of the owner, the rate is 25 *gantang* per hundred. The same proportion is used whether or not the grain is winnowed, though generally those hired prefer to winnow as it increases their share of grain. In those few cases where there is no female labour available in a farm family, due to illness, etc., a woman from another family may be hired to winnow the rice before it is stored or sold. There does not seem to be any clear formula, but it appears that this labour is generally paid in cash rather than in kind.

ADOPTION OF THRESHING

When rice was planted once a year, there was less pressure to complete the harvest in a short period of time. There was no second crop which followed immediately, and the grain could more safely be left in the fields since there was no danger of flood during the dry months following the north-east monsoon. Today timeliness has become a major factor.

Harvesting with the *ketam* is a slow process. At present it is rarely used even where traditional varieties are planted. Instead the stalk is cut near the ground and sheaves of grain are threshed into an oblong or square wooden tub which measures 3 feet per side, within which is the threshing board, a ladder-like frame of wood slats.

Most threshing tubs are built by the men of the farming household, though they may be purchased in some shops in Jerteh, or built to order by a fellow villager. The tub is surrounded on three sides by a fabric curtain or woven mat held up by thin wooden poles about 4 feet high, which serves to trap the grains as they are shaken loose. Threshing was introduced in the last fifteen years by local farmers who learned the practice as migrant workers in Kedah during the harvest there. When asked why they prefer to thresh rather than use the *ketam*, the immediate response of farmers is that threshing is much quicker than harvesting with the small hand knife. Because the *ketam* was so infrequently used during the author's stay in the village he was not able to collect comparable time-budget data on harvest with this tool. While threshing is more efficient in terms of time, it is less efficient in terms of yield. Despite the use of the curtain around the threshing tub, some grain is scattered and lost on the ground. Moreover, both mature and immature grain is harvested simultaneously as it is not practical while reaping to leave an individual plant, much less an individual tiller, standing. When harvesting with the *ketam* this is possible, and two or three passes through the field can be made to ensure harvest of only mature grains.

The adoption of threshing coincided with the introduction of double-cropping and the use of shorter-stalked high-yielding varieties. The panicles of these new varieties are prone to breakage and it is impossible to tie such grain into the small bundles known as *gemai*. Farmers in Gong Guncil report that when rice was harvested with the *ketam*, grain from plants least affected by disease and insects, and which had the greatest number of filled grains, were kept aside as seed for the next crop. With the introduction of threshing, however, this is no longer done, and seed is simply chosen at random from the rice storehouse.

Threshing is a quicker method of harvest than cutting with a *ketam*, but it is also more strenuous. Reaping of the grain is done with a hand scythe and is almost purely stoop labour and very hard on the back. Ideally, if the weather and fields are dry, the rice is reaped and allowed to lie in the field or along the bund for several hours or even overnight, as this speeds the drying of the grain and facilitates threshing by making the rice shake free more easily. Men, women, and even younger children can easily manage reaping, but threshing of the grain requires some strength. Though women also thresh, one usually finds the men doing most of the threshing and the women and children doing the reaping. Each sheaf, measuring about 18 inches in diameter at the base of the stalk, will require a variable number of blows on the threshing board, depending on the rice variety and on the dryness of the stalk and grain. More easily threshed varieties may release all their grains after 3–4 strong blows, while others may require 10–12. Obviously, farmers take this matter into consideration when deciding which variety to plant. Harvesting one variety may take as little as 8 workdays per acre, while another may take half again as long.

It is evident that the labour demands of the two methods of harvest vary in important ways. Harvesting with the *ketam* is time-consuming, but the number of people within a household and a community who are able to do this work is larger than that available for threshing, for which the physical demands are greater. Only physically vigorous men and women can contribute their labour in threshing, whereas the limited exertion of harvesting with the *ketam* allows older men and women to participate.

No matter which method of harvest is used, the rice must be transported back to the house of the farming family for storage in the storehouse, *rumah padi*, usually a separate structure near the home. Wherever possible, sacks of grain are transported from the fields on the back of a bicycle. The sacks used for this purpose are readily available, having originally contained fertilizer. With very few exceptions the men of the household do the transporting of rice from the fields to the home. Many of the bunds along which people move in the field are too narrow for riding or pushing a bicycle, and the grain must be carried several hundred yards to a point where a bicycle may be used. Almost all households own bicycles, and those that do not are able to borrow one from a neighbour. Occasionally, however, the grain must be carried home from a distant field on the shoulders.

CLEANING AND STORING RICE

What happens to the grain after harvest depends on a number of different factors. It may need further drying before storage, in which case it is spread out on woven mats in the sun. If it needs no further drying, as is generally the case with the main-season crop harvested in April, it may be placed directly into the storehouse. Those families which sell the rice immediately after harvest need to clean the grain of chaff before the sale.

Cleaning of the unmilled rice is a job for the women, and a number of different methods are employed. If there is a good breeze winnowing is done by simply pouring grain into a pile on a woven mat while the wind carries off the lighter chaff; under this condition, a woman could clean 100 *gantang* in a day. If there is no breeze, however, winnowing is slower, and perhaps only 40 *gantang* can be cleaned in one day. In this latter case, the grain is placed in a shallow round basket and a vigorous swirling motion sends the heavier grain to the edge. After scooping out the bulk of the chaff, the grain is cleaned again by flipping the furthest edge of the basket in a rapid up-and-down motion combined with a slight pulling back of the basket on the down stroke, which has the effect of spilling the remaining chaff (and a few grains for the ever-present chickens) off the end.

Most of the grain consumed by the family is stored chaff and all and is cleaned just before it is milled. Before rice was double-cropped, milling was done by hand in a large mortar using a heavy wooden pestle. This also was the work of women, and only done in quantities sufficient to last a family several days. Since the mid-1960s, however, women have been relieved of this task. A rice mill powered by a small diesel engine was built in Gong Tanah Merah by a group of local residents who formed a Cooperative Society. More recently another privately owned mill was established in Gong Guncil.

The polished rice produced by these mills is deemed superior in quality to pounded rice due to its fine white colour, even though it is nutritionally inferior because all the bran is removed. Almost all the rice consumed locally now is polished, and a sack of cleaned grain is taken to the mill every week or two. Rice is pounded by hand only when the local mills are temporarily out of operation due to mechanical breakdowns. The existence of these small mills has taken a burden off the women of the household, but it has also added a recurrent expense to the family budget. The cost of milling 10 *gantang* of grain is $0.50, and this will produce 4 *gantang* of polished rice. If a family's average consumption is one *gantang* of polished rice (*beras*) per day, the annual cost to the family would be over $45. Even the poorest families are willing to pay this price; it is just one of a number of small incidental costs that have gradually crept into the local economy and which make earning money an unquestioned necessity. Traditional agricultural practices required virtually no cash investment from planting to consumption. As will be seen in the section which follows, such is not the case today.

COSTS OF PRODUCTION

Accurate data upon which to base a discussion of the relative merits of single- and double-cropping rice regimens are hard to come by. Villagers who wish to justify planting only a single crop may overestimate the yields of traditional varieties, while those who argue the advantages of double-cropping may overestimate the potential yields obtainable by farmers under existing field conditions. Farmers who in the past planted traditional varieties and continue to do so today claim that in a good year as much as 450 *gantang* per acre is possible. Figures published by various government agencies (e.g. Yap and Dixon, 1972) show that average yields in Besut were only 270 *gantang* per acre with traditional varieties and practices. When the Besut Project was first envisioned, it was claimed that yields of 800 *gantang* per acre per season were possible with double-cropping of new varieties. This, however, was based on the results of double-cropping in Kedah rather than on field trials in Besut. More recent data indicate that yield potentials are in the range of 500—550 *gantang* per acre per season due to the poorer soils of Besut. Even this is considerably higher than actual average yields reported by villagers, which range from 300 to 350 *gantang* per acre per season.

In the Gong Guncil area, yields of 550 *gantang* per acre per season would represent a substantial increase in productivity. Attempting to get such yields, however, would mean accepting certain economic risks and devoting greater effort to crop management and practices associated with new varieties of fertilizer-responsive rice. This in turn must be balanced against certain opportunity costs, since farmers would be tied more closely to their fields and less able to seek alternative employment, especially far from the home village.

Traditional agricultural practices cost the farm family only seed and labour. No chemical fertilizers were used, and land preparation was done by water-buffalo or teams of oxen. A family with its own workstock which planted a traditional variety with its own labour would incur no cash costs to obtain 300—400 *gantang* of rice per acre per year. Based on an effective farm size of 2 acres and a yield of 300 *gantang* per acre, the family obtains 600 *gantang* or about $600 per year from rice cultivation.

If the family were to follow the Project's recommendations and obtained 550 *gantang* per acre per season for a 2-acre farm, they would have a gross yield of 2,200 *gantang* or $2,200 for the year, from which must be subtracted costs of production of just over $100 per acre per season (tractor ploughing $50, compounded fertilizer $35, urea $11, plus weedicides, pesticides, and seed-bed fertilizers). At least double the amount of labour is also required. The net income per year for a family farming 2 acres at optimum yield is therefore nearly $1,800, three times the income level from traditional agricultural practices. In both cases there is a certain amount of risk involved: if the crop is lost in the former case, the family has lost seed and labour and may have trouble meeting subsistence requirements; in the latter it risks losing not only rice for home consumption but working capital as well.

There are also opportunity costs for both land and labour associated with double-cropping which cannot be given an exact monetary value. The land could be used for such cash crops as tobacco, or at the very least to provide grazing grounds for the family's livestock. Though the local opportunities for off-season employment are limited, men not tied to the land by double-cropping could find work elsewhere (see below) or engage in carpentry or other local trades and services. The difference in income of $1,200 between using traditional and recommended varieties and practices for a farm of 2 acres is indeed substantial but has to be seen in light of the above.

Estimated yields using traditional rice varieties and cultivation practices can be compared to both the average yields and costs obtained by farmers during the period of field research and with the government agronomic field trial data. Average yields reported by farmers were 350 *gantang* per acre per season; thus for a 2-acre farm over one year, gross yields would be 1,400 *gantang*. Production costs vary among farm families. Some families use mixed or compounded fertilizers together with urea, while others use only urea. An educated guess would be that an average of $25 per acre per season currently is expended on fertilizers, with a range from zero to almost $50. With another $50 for contract ploughing, average production costs are in the region of $75 per acre per season, or $300 per year for a 2-acre farm; net income would be $1,100.

Actual costs of land preparation vary depending on whether private contract tractors are hired, the Besut Project's tractor service is utilized (at $34 per acre), or animal traction is employed. Although the Project's tractor service is less expensive, most farmers in the Gong Guncil area use private contractors, as scheduling a tractor from the Project must be done and paid for weeks in advance of the actual ploughing, and often the tractor does not arrive on the appointed day. This presents major difficulties to farmers with seedlings ready to transplant. Private tractors remain in the area while there is work to be done and ploughing usually can be arranged on short notice.

If a farm family uses animal traction for land preparation, production costs are substantially reduced, although there is the factor of labour to be considered. A family not owning a water-buffalo may need to hire workstock, paying at the end of the season either in cash or in grain. Though the amount of rent varies, the average cost is $50 per season. If the crop were to fail, local farmers say that this rent would be reduced or waived; such would not be the case with contract work by either private tractor operators or the Project tractor service. If a family owns a water-buffalo and prepares its land with this animal, it would save as much as $200 in the course of a year for a 2-acre farm.

From net yields must be subtracted approximately 900 *gantang* ($900) of unmilled rice, the amount necessary to meet annual consumption needs of a family of six. A family consisting of two adults, two adolescent and two pre-adolescent children will likely consume one *gantang* of milled rice (equivalent in volume to 2.5 *gantang* of unmilled rice) per day. In a given year this family will consume at least 900 *gantang* of unmilled rice, though the actual amount required for a family's needs probably is closer to 1,000 *gantang* when social obligations, such as contributions to local feasts, are taken into consideration. Some households will have lower consumption needs due to having fewer household members or younger children, while other households may find one *gantang* of unmilled rice insufficient.

The following analysis considers 900 *gantang* of unmilled rice as the consumption needs of a family. A 2-acre farm cultivated with traditional varieties and methods would not provide such a family with its basic consumption requirements. Optimum yields using recommended varieties and practices would give it an annual cash income of $900, or $75 per month. In practice few farm families obtain such yields. Using the figures suggested above for production costs and yields of current production practices (assuming tractor ploughing), after subtracting 900 *gantang* for consumption requirements, the family is likely to have at most a surplus valued at $200 available for sale. This income works out to less than $17 per month. Table 3.8 summarizes these data.

TABLE 3.8

COMPARISON OF THREE RICE PRODUCTION REGIMENS FOR A TWO-ACRE OWNER-OPERATED FARM PER YEAR

(in $)

	Traditional Practices (1 crop)	*Optimal Practices (2 crops)*	*Current Practices (2 crops)*
Gross yield	600	2,200	1,400
Production costs	0	400	300
Net yield	600	1,800	1,100
Consumption	900	900	900
Surplus (deficit)	(300)	900	200

These figures are rough approximations of production costs and yields for rice farmers in the Gong Guncil area. They assume ownership of 2 acres of rice land; obviously some families have more land and some families have less. Yet other families are share-croppers who share both the costs and the yields of the land they work. The assumption of a 2-acre farm used in these figures is for illustrative purposes and may be compared with Tables 3.2, 3.5, and 3.6 which provide data on land-ownership and farm size.

No detailed family budgets were collected, but absolutely minimal consumption needs of a family (a little fish, cooking oil, kerosene for light, tea, sugar, and the like) cost at least $1.50 per day, $45 per month. This figure may be doubled without extravagance, and it does not take into consideration regular and recurring expenses: children in school who need books and uniforms and pocket-money for a snack, tools, utensils, clothing, etc. At present, rice farming alone does not provide an adequate income for most families, and even at optimum yields a cash income of $75 per month is only one-third of the income obtained by the lowest paid government labourer. Additional sources of income are an absolute necessity for almost all rice farming families in the study area.

PRODUCTION CONSTRAINTS

According to the staff of the Besut Agricultural Development Project, farmers in Besut obtain below optimum yields due to three factors: the use of rice varieties other than those recommended; inadequate use of chemical fertilizers, weedicides and pesticides; and poor management practices in general. This section will focus on the different selection criteria used by farmers and government agronomists in choosing rice varieties and on constraints on the use of recommended levels of chemical inputs.

Rice farmers are inveterate experimenters, constantly willing to try a new variety, whether it be one recommended by extension agents or one that they have seen grown in another area. Farmers visiting relatives in the neighbouring state of Kelantan may bring home with them seed of a variety planted there for trial on their own land. Even Kedah and Perlis have been sources of new varieties, especially in the past when men from Besut and Kelantan travelled to those states to take part in the harvest.

Virtually no farm family in the Gong Guncil area plants only one variety of rice, a practice that may be justified by the spreading of risks associated with disease and insect susceptibility. It is not altogether clear that reducing the number of varieties to the three or four recommended by the Project authorities would be in the best interests of the farmers themselves. Varietal diversification and experimentation by farmers are likely to persist, and future agronomic research and extension efforts should recognize this reality rather than try to develop a more simplified, and hence more vulnerable, varietal pattern.

Farmers select or reject rice varieties on the basis not only of yield potential or resistance to damage by insects and diseases, but also for cooking quality, ease of harvest, and suitability to their individual plots. Agronomic research conducted by government experiment stations also takes these considerations into account in so far as possible, although there is a tendency to concentrate effort on those varieties which are responsive to high levels of chemical fertilizer. But unless farmers can afford to apply adequate amounts of fertilizer, these varieties may produce no better than those selected by farmers on the basis of a wider range of criteria.

PRODUCTION CREDIT

Use of fertilizer below optimum levels can be attributed chiefly to insufficient working capital and reluctance to go into debt. Even though credit facilities are available, many farmers, especially those close to the margin of subsistence, are reluctant to borrow money for production inputs. If they lose a single crop, such a debt (and the mounting interest payments on this debt) would be nearly impossible to repay.

Production credit is available to farmers from Farmers' Cooperatives (previously known as Farmers' Associations) at 4 per cent interest per season. The funds for this loan programme in Besut come primarily from Bank Pertanian. Not all farmers are members of the Farmers' Cooperatives, however, and Bank Pertanian has established other Local Credit Centres to increase the availability of production credit.

Beginning in 1977, a number of local notables, e.g., village headmen and religious leaders, were asked to administer loan applications and the distribution of fertilizer to farm families which, as non-members of the Farmers' Cooperatives, previously were ineligible to receive production credit. This programme was hastily conceived and applied in Besut as a result of pressures from the Ministry of Agriculture and certain politicians to increase production. It became apparent that these Local Credit Centres were improperly used to obtain credit for farm families which not only were members of the local Farmers' Cooperative, but had failed to repay previous loans and hence were ineligible to receive further production credit. The records of the Farmers' Cooperative in the Gong Guncil area show that the most wealthy farm families had the worst repayment records from previous loans. These same families, however, were the first to take advantage of this new source of credit. The local head of the Local Credit Centre knew that many applicants were members of the Farmers' Cooperatives and therefore ineligible. This problem was circumvented by the simple expedient of registering the loan in the name of whichever spouse was not recorded on the membership rolls of the Farmers' Cooperatives. As Bank Pertanian could not ensure that only non-members obtained loans through the Local Credit Centres, however, even this subterfuge was unnecessary.

Since production credit was first offered to Besut's farmers in the off-season of 1971, there have been serious repayment problems. Including the off-season of 1976 (the last season for which figures were available) total production credit given to farmers totalled $183,752, of which $53,553 (29.1 per cent) remained unpaid. The bulk of these loans ($140,913.48) were advanced to members of the Farmers' Cooperative serving the Stage I area. Of this, 25.8 per cent remains unpaid.

The apparent inability or unwillingness on the part of the Farmers' Cooperative and Bank Pertanian to press for repayment when loans begin to fall in arrears has had much to do with the appalling repayment record. Loan repayment rates for the first two seasons were quite acceptable, but after that the situation deteriorated dramatically, as demonstrated by Table 3.9.

TABLE 3.9
REPAYMENT OF PRODUCTION CREDIT
(in $)

Season	*Total Loan ($)*	*Outstanding ($)*	*Per Cent of Loans Outstanding in 1977*
II 1971	29,013	nil	nil
I 1972	18,669	288	1.5
II 1972	14,988	2,297	15.3
I 1973	11,414	1,651	14.5
II 1973	7,529	1,404	18.6
I 1974	28,643	11,804	41.2
II 1974	4,421	1,985	44.9
I 1975	13,435	6,376	47.5
II 1975	12,798	10,560	82.5
I 1976	6,214	1,006	16.2

I = Off-season
II = Main season

During the main season of 1975 there were widespread crop losses due to insect damage by *kesin*. Some portion of the outstanding debts from other seasons may also be due to crop losses, but it is more likely that simple disregard has been a significant factor. Bank Pertanian is willing to waive interest penalties on outstanding loans when the crop has been lost due to natural causes, but many farmers appear to be unaware of this policy and, in any event, the principal must be repaid. If there is a major crop loss, in the absence of any crop insurance scheme, farmers near the level of subsistence would find themselves with a debt which would take many seasons to repay. The logic of the Ministry of Agriculture, the Project staff, and Bank Pertanian is that farmers should accept this risk and increase their usage of fertilizer to optimum levels since the increase in production would allow farmers to repay their loans and leave a healthy surplus for their own use or sale. Many farmers, particularly the more vulnerable small farmers, adopt a more conservative approach which minimizes risk. Minimizing risk, from the standpoint of the government agencies involved, is virtually synonymous with a subsistence orientation to farming, a traditional value they feel a duty to counter.

SECONDARY ECONOMIC ACTIVITIES

The application of increased amounts of chemical fertilizers can be shown to increase productivity in the Besut area, but only with appropriate attention to crop management. It is at this point that the approach of the government agencies and the farmers diverge. The agencies involved in agricultural development in the Besut Project area begin with the assumption that the farmers are full-time rice farmers, and ignore important sources of off-farm employment on which farmers depend for their cash income. This may include rubber tapping, animal husbandry, petty trading activities, or wage employment in distant urban centres. Men who leave the area to find employment after transplanting and before the harvest are unable to check on their fields, see to the application of fertilizer at the proper times, weed, or adjust the water level in the fields. They may ask a friend to keep an eye on their crop, but if an insect infestation occurs, this friend cannot be expected to do anything about it. Farmers engaged in other economic activities in the immediate area at least are available for crop maintenance, but the amount of time devoted to the rice crop may not be worth the added yield if such labour were to detract from their other employment. For both the government and the farmers the question ultimately seems to come down to economics. The various government agencies see farmers as planters of rice who need to improve management practices. Farmers, however, see themselves as engaged in a multitude of other time- and energy-consuming activities which diversify their sources of income and decrease their dependency on any single source. As was clearly shown in Table 3.8, the majority of households in the Gong Guncil area cannot earn adequate incomes from rice farming alone, even under optimal conditions.

Almost all families in the Gong Guncil area have some source of income other than that provided by rice cultivation. The relative importance of these other sources of income varies from household to household, but with very few exceptions the cycle of rice production dictates the timing and extent of such secondary activities, and not the other way around.

A number of villagers are involved in full-time or part-time trading. Two families are engaged in full-time trading, regularly travelling to local weekly markets in their small pick-up trucks to sell rice, fruits and vegetables. Once a week these two families are joined by three women from Gong Guncil who together go to the weekly market in the village of Penarek, 2 miles from the fishing community of Mangkok. In addition to these traders, several women in Gong Guncil buy seasonal fruits, especially *durian*, acting as primary bulking agents for fruit dealers who transport the fruits to urban markets hundreds of miles away. Also resident in the Gong Guncil area are part-time barbers, carpenters, and the owners of three sundry goods shops. Four men own and pedal trishaws when not busy with transplanting or harvest. Another four men have found employment with the Drainage and Irrigation Department as labourers, and one man is a labourer with the Project itself. Yet another man rides a motor cycle to Kuala Besut (11 miles away) to buy fish which he peddles in Gong Guncil and surrounding villages. One family processes and bottles *budu*, a sauce made of *ikan bilis* (anchovies), salt, and spices which is eaten with rice.

Besides this wide range of local enterprises, a large number of both married and unmarried men between 17 and 40 years of age regularly work in Singapore in the construction industry. When the author first arrived in Gong Guncil, nearly 20 men from the study area were working there, earning $10–12 per day. This is a much higher wage than could be earned locally, even if regular wage labour were available. Once transplanting has been completed, these men travel in small groups of three or four by bus to Singapore, returning when the crop is ready for harvest. When harvest is completed and the next crop planted, they are ready to repeat the cycle. While in Singapore the men live rent-free in barracks provided at the construction site, and cook their own meals. Estimates of their daily expenses range from $3.00 to $5.00, enabling them to save at least $30 to $40 per week over a period of perhaps ten weeks. Transportation costs amount to less than $40 for a round-trip ticket. Some men send home postal or money orders to their families; others keep the money and take home what is left after buying clothing, radios, and cassette tape recorders in Singapore (where prices of these goods are much lower due to its free port status). A few of the younger unmarried men manage to take home next to nothing, having succumbed to the various charms of life in the big city.

RUBBER TAPPING

Alternative sources of income provide the cash necessary for contemporary existence. The single most important source of cash for rice farming households of Gong Guncil is rubber tapping; 40 out of 134 households are directly involved in rubber production, and another 20 households earn income from rubber land they own but do not tap themselves.

Table 3.10 provides data on the ownership of rubber land in the study area. It is readily apparent that, as with ownership of rice land, the largest acreages are controlled by residents of Gong Tanah Merah. Verifying the extent of rubber holdings is even more problematic than for rice land, since in many cases rubber land

TABLE 3.10

OWNERSHIP OF RUBBER LAND BY HOUSEHOLD IN STUDY AREA

(Acres)	*Gong Guncil*	*Baruh Kual*	*Pulau Panjang*	*Gong Tanah Merah*	*Total*
< 1	4	1	nil	nil	5
1–1.99	4	3	2	5	14
2–2.99	5	1	2	2	10
3–3.99	1	nil	nil	1	2
4–4.99	nil	nil	1	nil	1
5–5.99	nil	nil	2	nil	2
6–6.99	1	1	nil	nil	2
7–7.99	nil	nil	nil	nil	nil
8–8.99	1	nil	nil	nil	1
9–9.99	nil	nil	nil	1	1
> 10	nil	nil	nil	4	4
Total	16	6	7	13	42

owned by local residents may be located further away and may have escaped the author's attention altogether. Of the four households owning more than 10 acres, it appears that two own 20 acres, one owns 15 acres, and another owns 16 acres. In each of these cases, the land is worked by others on a *bagi dua* basis whereby the production is divided equally between the owner and the tapper.

Of the 42 households owning rubber land, 6 own land that recently has been replanted with new higher-yielding rubber varieties. Sixteen households own rubber land but hire share-croppers, including owners of small as well as large holdings. Twenty-four households which own no rubber land earn a cash income by tapping the trees of others, and in all of these cases *bagi dua* is used.

The income to be earned tapping rubber tends to be irregular and varies depending upon the prevailing market price. During peak labour periods in rice cultivation tapping ceases altogether. There is also the monsoon season to contend with; when it rains heavily in the late afternoon or evening, tappers are unable to work the following morning because the water dripping off the leaves and down the trunk causes the latex to spill out of the grooves tapped into the bark of the tree. (Tapping in wet conditions also increases the trees' susceptibility to fungus diseases.) During the 2 months of almost constant rains little tapping takes place. When the 3 months of transplanting and harvest over the course of a year are added, only 6–7 months are left for tapping. Income from tapping is also limited by the quality of trees found in the area. Many rubber stands are composed of old trees, some planted before World War II, which provide a poor yield.

The Rubber Industry Smallholders Development Authority (RISDA), the government agency responsible for the production and marketing needs of the smallholder sector in the rubber industry, provides materials for the building of processing sheds and the heavy mangles used for pressing the latex into suitably thin sheets. RISDA also assists the tappers in selling their product by accepting tenders from private buyers and acts as buyer of last resort if the proferred price is deemed too low. In 1975 such a Smallholders Processing Centre was established at Pulau Panjang.

As of 1978 there were 23 members of the Smallholders Processing Centre in Pulau Panjang who, in return for being able to use the Centre, pay $1.00 for every *pikul* (133.3 lb.) of rubber sold. Part of this money is to be used for maintenance and cleaning of the facility, and the remainder may be used for any other purpose that the members choose.

Some of the 23 members are residents of villages outside the study area itself, and only approximately one-third of the 40 tap-

TABLE 3.11
QUANTITY OF RUBBER SOLD PER HOUSEHOLD AT RISDA PROCESSING CENTRE, 1975–1977

Quantity (pikul)	*No. of Families*
1–5	5
5–10	3
10–20	4
20–30	4
30–40	1
40–50	1
50–60	1
60–70	2
70–80	2

ping families enumerated in this study process their rubber at the Centre. Nonetheless, in terms of acreages tapped and yields obtained, the data from the Centre may be taken as representative of the area as a whole. The local RISDA office in Besut was kind enough to provide figures for total sales at the Centre in Pulau Panjang for the years 1975, 1976, and 1977. The total amount of rubber marketed by this Centre in the three-year period 1975–7 was just over 600 *pikul*. Table 3.11 indicates the distribution in terms of quantity sold per household.

The sellers who produced less than 5 *pikul* include 3 members who joined in September 1977; the other 2 are members who have stopped tapping rubber, or tap infrequently. Those members selling the most rubber are owners–tappers who also sell the rubber produced by share-croppers who tap part of their holdings.

Share-croppers are not eligible to become members of such Smallholders Processing Centres. As the price paid for rubber sold through these Centres is slightly higher than that obtainable through local rubber dealers, these share-croppers prefer to allow the owners to sell their share of the production. Hence, the households selling the most rubber actually share part of the proceeds with their tenants.

Taking these adjustments into consideration, it can be estimated that most households engaged in rubber tapping obtained less than 30 *pikul* of rubber over the 3-year period. Among the eight cases from Table 3.11 in the 10–30 *pikul* range there was a total production of 163.33 *pikul*, just over 20 *pikul* per household for the period, or almost 7 *pikul* a year. This may be a close approximation of average production for many households that tap rubber on a regular basis. The income from this rubber can only be approximated due to the extreme variations in price. (A more detailed discussion of rubber production, marketing, and price variations will be given in Chapter 5.) Taking $70 per *pikul* as an average price, each of these families would have earned $490 annually. This figure would represent the income of a family which owned their own trees, not that of a share-cropper, whose income would be half that amount. There are of course wide variations among households: some families tap a small number of relatively unproductive trees and may only produce 2 *pikul* annually, while others will produce or earn ten times as much or more from their investment in land. Whatever the yields and incomes from rubber tapping, this and other alternative economic activities provide the main sources of regular cash income to the majority of households in Gong Guncil.

MARKETING OF RICE

The combination of small farm size and low yields per acre means that most of the rice harvested by farm families in and around Gong Guncil is consumed by these families. What surplus is available for sale beyond household needs often is sold immediately after harvest. Rice prices are usually lower at this time, but farm families need the cash to purchase fertilizer for the following season, or to repay production loans. If possible, families sell only enough rice to cover these production costs and store whatever additional grain is not needed for their own consumption until just before the following harvest. This marketing strategy is preferred not only because the price is higher at that time, but because grain in storage provides a hedge against crop failure. Once the success of the next harvest is assured, the store of grain may be safely sold.

Rice may be sold either in large or small quantities. To meet production costs or repay production loans, relatively large quantities of rice are marketed in gunny sacks which hold more than 20 *gantang* of unmilled rice. Most rice marketed is sold in this fashion. Rice is also sold in quantities as small as 10 *gantang* at a time. Often this will be done when a household is short of cash and makes a small withdrawal from what is essentially the family's savings.

In many villages there are two or three regular buyers of rice who operate out of their homes or sundry goods shops. A number of other people in the village also occasionally buy small quantities of rice to be sold along with the fruits and vegetables they offer at various weekly markets. The regular buyers also purchase rice in small quantities throughout the year, but the bulk of their purchasing comes immediately after harvest. Some of this grain is sold by the buyers directly to the Lembaga Padi dan Beras Negara (LPN, the National Rice Board), the government agency which regulates the marketing and distribution of rice in Malaysia. Alternatively, the rice is sold at one of the numerous weekly markets held throughout the state of Trengganu.

Rice may be sold at a good price outside rice farming areas, where it will receive a premium of between $0.20 and $0.40 per *gantang* of milled rice over the price obtainable in Gong Guncil. Many of the regular rice buyers in Besut also own and operate small vans and use these vehicles to travel between different parts of the district and state, supplying rice to areas where it is not grown. In Besut, the supply of rice to such areas is accomplished primarily through these small-scale entrepreneurs. The buyers follow a regular circuit of weekly markets from the inland hills, to the rice plain, and down to the coastal villages. Each area specializes in different kinds of produce which are needed by the others. The flexibility of the small vans allows these traders to move quickly when a shortage of a particular commodity occurs, and provides an important marketing outlet for the surplus production of each of the three zones. The staple item of this trade is rice, but by itself rice probably would not be sufficiently profitable. Seasonal and non-seasonal fruits from the interior, and coconuts and *nipah* roofing material from the coast, are important supplementary trade items. Local petty traders effectively integrate the three zones of Besut's economy. The two families in Gong Guncil who engage in full-time trading typically work long hours and by local standards are deemed prosperous. Their life-styles are not noticeably different from their fellow villagers, however, and they continue to cultivate rice together with their neighbours and to participate in *tolong-menolong* and *pinjam orang* exchanges of labour. They are able to do so because rice cultivation is essentially a seasonal endeavour which allows ample opportunity for alternative employment.

The price of rice in Gong Guncil and the surrounding area is relatively stable and in essence is controlled by the National Rice Board. Occasionally there are differences of opinion between buyers and sellers as to the deductions taken from the gross weight of the rice for chaff, moisture content, and percentage of immature grains. Though these deductions are based on the judgement of the buyers, the sellers are sufficiently knowledgeable to understand the reasons for and the reasonable limits of these deductions. The ability of the buyers to treat the sellers in an unfair manner is limited by this, and by the effective competition maintained among the buyers.

1A Ploughing with water-buffalo

1B The traditional plough used in rice fields and pulled by water-buffalo or a team of oxen

2A Gathering bundles of rice seedlings (*unting*) in preparation for transplanting

2B Transplanting rice

3A A small *pinjam orang* work party helping to transplant rice

3B Carrying a sheaf of *padi* to be threshed during harvest

4 Winnowing rice in the breeze

5 House moving

6 Pounding the sedge known as *kercut* which is later woven into mats for fish drying

7 Cleaning a drifting gill net (*pukat hanyut*) off the stern of a fishing boat in Mangkok

8A Throwing a cast net in the surf off the beach at Mangkok. The fleet of boats on the horizon are seineing for *ikan bilis*

8B Boat captain at tiller with a non-motorized boat in tow. The two boats work together in using a small purse-seine

9A Operating a small purse-seine (*pukat jerut udang baring*).
The boat on the right is motorized; the one on the left is not and
is towed to the fishing grounds

9B Gathering in the purse-seine (*pukat jerut udang baring*)
off the beach near Mangkok

10A Gathering in the purse-seine (*pukat jerut udang baring*)
off the beach near Mangkok

10B Gathering in the purse-seine (*pukat jerut udang baring*)
off the beach near Mangkok

11A Early morning activity at fish landing in Mangkok with buyers crowded on the deck of the boat in the foreground

11B Small pick-up trucks used to carry fish to market from Mangkok, and for carrying all manner of goods in and out of other rural communities

12A Drying small shrimp (*udang baring*) on the beach at Mangkok

12B Drying small shrimp (*udang baring*) in the sun

13A Carrying boxes of *ikan bilis* up the beach to the processing shed

13B Cooking *ikan bilis* prior to sun drying

14 Market scene in Penarek, near Mangkok, frequented by sellers from Gong Guncil

15A Tapping rubber

15B Collecting latex from rubber trees

16A Latex collecting in coconut shells at base of rubber tree

16B Processing ribbed sheet rubber. Note shallow tin pans for coagulating latex

As will be seen in the following chapter, marketing relationships in the fishing village of Mangkok tend to be fraught with conflict. Tensions between boat owners, captains, and crewmen also characterize production relations in Mangkok, in contrast to the much more harmonious relationships between rice farmers. These differences are directly related to relationships formed in production activities. While rice farmers have a clear need to cooperate in the scheduling of planting and in the exchange of labour, fishermen operate more independently and form smaller and more short-lived cooperative associations—the fishing crews. Gong Guncil and Mangkok represent distinctly different economic and environmental adaptations, and these differences shape and condition a wide range of economic and non-economic social relationships.

4 Mangkok: A Fishing Village in Trengganu

THE SETTING

KAMPUNG MANGKOK is a village of 121 households situated on a spit of sand between the South China Sea and the Sungai Setiu, 50 miles north of the state capital of Kuala Trengganu. The houses of Mangkok are spread over approximately one mile of what is essentially a stabilized sand-bar which is nowhere wider than one-half mile. Mangkok is reached by a dirt road through the neighbouring village of Penarek, which is served by a paved road and regular bus service. This bus makes seven round trips daily along the 9 miles connecting Penarek and Kampung Buluh, a village straddling the main East Coast Highway.

From Penarek the traveller may walk the 2 miles to Mangkok, or for a small fee he may have someone with a small motor cycle carry him to Mangkok as a pillion passenger. The traveller may also time his arrival to coincide with the school bus schedule. Adult passengers regularly ride the school bus in and out of Mangkok, leaving in the early morning and returning in the late afternoon. Another means of transportation is the legally licensed taxi which is supposed to be based in Mangkok. Such licences are valuable and in rural areas usually are granted with the stipulation that the taxi be available to provide emergency transportation to the villagers. In fact the taxi that bears the name of Mangkok rarely is seen in the village, though a taxi registered elsewhere began to come to Mangkok on a regular basis during the period of field-work. This taxi is available during the night for emergencies, and for transporting people out of the community early in the morning and bringing them home at dusk, but during the day the driver generally plies the major roads and is not available for local transport.

A somewhat more flexible means of transportation available to the people of Mangkok is provided by a resident 'pirate taxi', an unlicensed vehicle hired out on a charter basis by its owner. Such unlicensed vehicles are common in rural areas and provide valuable

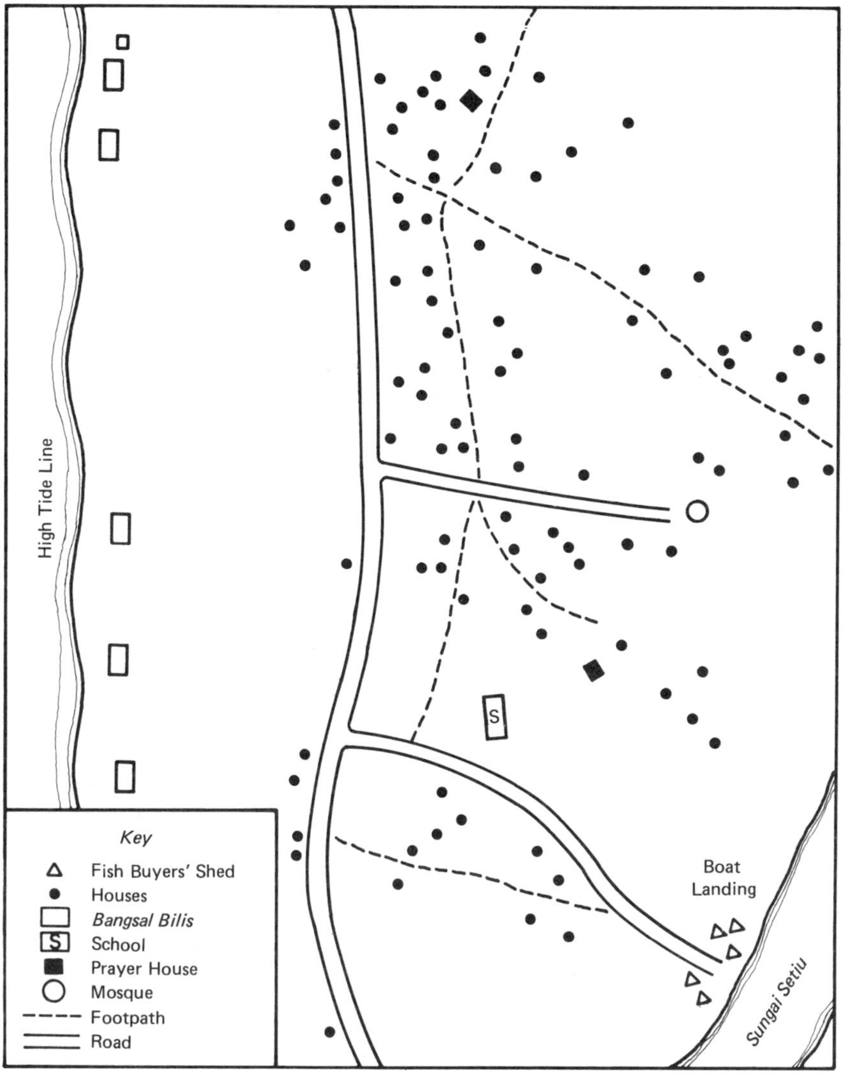

Map 3: Mangkok

services to the community, allowing families to travel to areas not served by regular taxis or buses, or a fisherman in need of a spare part for his boat to make the trip to Kuala Trengganu and back quickly. If the fisherman has to wait for other means of transport he might miss a day at sea.

In addition to the 'pirate taxi' there also are a number of small Japanese-built pick-up trucks, known locally as 'vans', which transport fish and other local products to the markets in Kuala Trengganu and Kota Bharu. These vans also are available for charter, though they are more suited to carrying goods than passengers.

Until recently Mangkok was physically isolated. The road that connects Penarek with the East Coast Highway has been paved only since the mid-1960s, and the bridge which crosses the Sungai Setiu (a single-lane Bailey bridge) was built several years later. The dirt road into Mangkok itself is of even more recent origin, and four-wheeled vehicles have been able to enter the village only since 1973. Before that only small motor cycles and bicycles could enter the village along sandy paths across which coconut fronds were strewn to provide some traction.

Despite the building of this dirt road Mangkok in many respects remains quite isolated. The nearest secondary school and the nearest newsagent are in Kampung Buluh, 11 miles away. Though the road opened the possibility that more children from Mangkok could attend secondary school, the cost is either prohibitive or a major expense for most families. The daily fare, plus pocket-money for the student's snack, will cost a family at least $1.00, or $5.00 per week. Attending to business with a government agency or visiting a sick friend in the hospital involves a major investment in time and money. A visit to the state capital of Kuala Trengganu is likely to require several hours each way. Such trips are not only time-consuming but expensive: a trip to Kuala Trengganu by taxi costs $4.50 each way. By the time a villager returned home he would have spent perhaps another $5.00 beyond transportation in having lunch in a small shop and buying a few 'treats' for the family, such as vegetables or fruits unavailable in the Mangkok area.

In addition to travel by road, people and goods may be moved by fishing boats along the Sungai Setiu and its tributaries. A boat may travel on these inland waterways over 10 miles either up or down the coast and, were it not for the recent construction of small bridges, as far inland as Kampung Buluh. Boats are used for visiting relatives in other villages and obtaining lumber from sawmills, and firewood for cooking. In some cases the river provides the only suitable thoroughfare between villages. The large neighbouring village of Fikri is about 25 miles by road but can be reached in only half an hour by even the slowest boats.

The importance of river travel can be seen on Fridays when there is a weekly market in Penarek. Such weekly markets bring traders from the towns of Kuala Trengganu and Kota Bharu as well as from certain villages in the interior, including the rice farming community of Gong Guncil. Travelling by boat, most families within a 5-mile radius of Penarek regularly visit this weekly market and purchase fruits and vegetables which cannot be grown locally. Cloth, clothing, kitchen utensils and tools also are available in greater variety than in the small local shops. Many families purchase their rice at the weekly market because it is of better quality and cheaper than that retailed in the local shops, being sold by traders like those from Gong Guncil who sell rice they have grown themselves or have purchased from their neighbours.

THE SEA

Fishermen know the sea in a manner analagous to the knowledge that inland villagers have of their fields. The predominantly sandy sea bottom off the Trengganu coast is shallow and is marked by a number of natural and man-made points of interest to fishermen. Submerged rock formations and even a small freighter, victim of an American submarine during World War II, act as natural reefs harbouring certain species of fish. These points are located while at sea by a simple geometry, using various landmarks (mountains, estuaries, and islands) as bearings. Fishermen also are keen observers of the behaviour of marine life, their habitats and breeding grounds. They know when the fish will be found near the surface, or at the bottom, and when it is best to fish during the day or at night. Fishermen use a wide variety of gear to exploit the fishing grounds under the various conditions which prevail during different seasons.

Fishing on the East Coast of Peninsular Malaysia is a seasonal activity. The north-east monsoon, which begins in November and continues until January, is accompanied by heavy seas and high winds which make the operation of the local fishermen's typically small and shallow-draughted boats quite hazardous. Unable to put to sea, the fishermen of Mangkok (and of course the fish buyers, shopkeepers, and others dependent upon fishermen as primary producers) must cope with a period of minimal income. It is a time for net-mending, boat and engine repairs, visiting friends and relatives, repairing or extending the house, working as casual labourers or, for some families, working in the rice fields. The monsoon period is one of privation, when accumulated savings are consumed, debts and obligations assumed, and fishermen and non-fishermen alike are reduced to eating dried salted fish with their rice.

Yet it is the north-east monsoon which brings the most productive fishing. During the monsoon, stormy seas combine with the increased run-off from rivers to produce a nutrient-rich environment in which plankton thrive, and this in turn supports a wide variety of marine life. Most importantly for the fishermen, carnivorous fish species such as Spanish mackerel, wolf herring and tuna are attracted to the coast. These fish are among the most highly

FIGURE 4.1
SEASONALITY OF CATCH, 1978
(YAHYA)

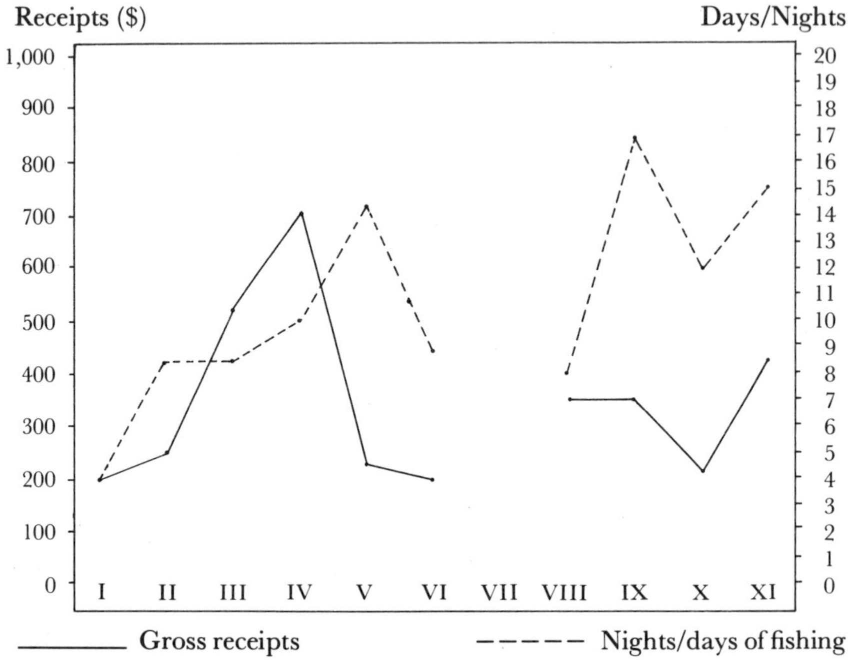

Note: Roman numerals refer to the following fishing periods:

I	14–19 January	VII	30 May–16 June
II	24 January–2 February	VIII	28 June–7 July
III	7–15 February	IX	21 July–8 August
IV	3–15 March	X	21 August–2 September
V	29 March–18 April	XI	20 September–5 October
VI	20 April–12 May		

prized and priced fish in the country. As soon as the boats can put to sea, including short lulls during the monsoon itself, very good catches are landed by the fishermen of Mangkok. The period from January to March is one of great activity as a number of different types of fishing gear are employed to exploit this opportunity. This seasonal variation is illustrated by Figures 4.1 and 4.2.[1]

By April the catch is already declining, and during May and June the catch is so poor that fishermen often do not even bother

[1] The author left Mangkok in late April, and an assistant hired to continue data collection left in mid-May. No data are available for the period of late May to mid-June, at which point Yahya began to provide him with data through the mail.

FIGURE 4.2
SEASONALITY OF CATCH, 1978
(DAHAT)

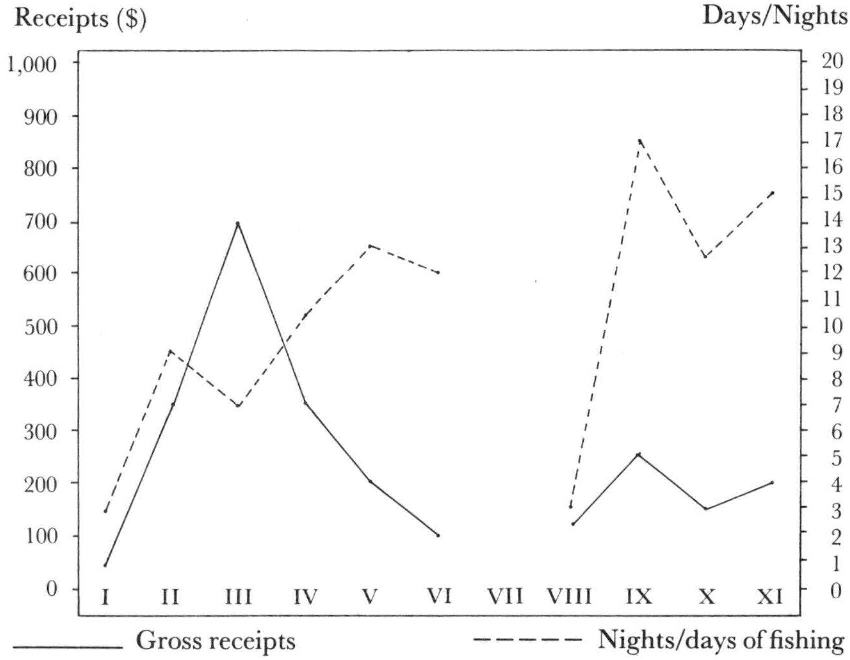

Note: Roman numerals refer to the following fishing periods:

I	14–19 January	VII	30 May–16 June
II	24 January–2 February	VIII	28 June–7 July
III	7–15 February	IX	21 July–8 August
IV	3–15 March	X	21 August–2 September
V	29 March–18 April	XI	20 September–5 October
VI	20 April–12 May		

putting to sea. The slack season actually does not end until August or September. This is the season of *air jernih*, or clear water. The fishermen know that when the turbidity of the water (*air keroh*) is reduced, so is their catch; they do not realize that the murky conditions signify greater organic content in the water and hence more marine life. Rather, on the basis of numerous informal discussions, the most common understanding seems to be that with *air keroh* the fish are unable to see the net of the fishermen and therefore are more easily caught. They claim that during the calm period (which coincides with the south-west monsoon) the fish are present, but because they are able to see they escape the nets. During the period from May to August, some fishermen turn to the rice fields in villages 5 miles or so inland, or set off for fishing grounds to the south near Kuala Dungun or Kuantan, as far as 20 hours away by boat. Others go overland to these ports to work temporarily with boats which operate fish traps off their coast. Fishing in these areas appears to be less variable than in northern Trengganu. It may be that the ocean currents set up by the south-west monsoon carry with them nutrients which enrich the fishing grounds to the south of Mangkok, while the northern Trengganu and Kelantan coasts are sheltered by the bulge of the coastline near Kuala Dungun. The surface currents of the north-east monsoon, on the other hand, move in a south-westerly direction, striking the entire East Coast of Peninsular Malaysia (Marr, 1976: 8–9).

The species of fish exploited commercially by the fishermen of Mangkok are not really migratory, but they are sensitive to major seasonal variations. During and immediately following the north-east monsoon these species are concentrated close to the shoreline and are normally found within 5 miles of the coast, but when the seas enter the prolonged calm which coincides with decreased river discharge, the nutrient level drops and the fish tend to disperse over a wider area in search of food. This annual cycle determines the pattern of fishing activities and community life in general and has important implications for the potential development of the fishing industry on the East Coast.

RESOURCES ON LAND

IN THE VILLAGE

The primary economic resource of Mangkok has always been the sea, but there are important resources on land as well. Within the confines of the village itself the soil is almost exclusively sand, with little organic content; yet coconuts grow and in some places even thrive. Most families grow enough coconut for household consumption; 14 households (out of 121) reported regular sales of coconuts, either dried (copra) or as fresh nuts, while about the same number of households claimed their coconut production was insufficient even for their household needs. Coconut is used in the cooking of many local dishes, and a vegetable oil is also extracted from it.

Coconut palms located near a house tend to grow much better than those further away. Villagers frequently explained that coconut palms 'like' people and the sounds of human habitation, but whether or not one gives credence to such beliefs, it is true that palms planted near a home are more productive than others. There are practical reasons for this difference. Palms nearer a house have the benefit of refuse and sweepings from the house and grounds, perhaps some ash from the cooking fire, wash water and bathing water from the well, animal dung and the more or less random droppings of small children; those in the vicinity of fish processing and drying sheds also tend to do better than others, probably because the water used to cook the fish, rich in nutrients, is dumped at the base of the trees.

Most coconut stands in Mangkok are old and poorly maintained, and consequently are not highly productive. The sandy soil precludes profitable application of chemical fertilizers, and irregular rainfall—periods of heavy rain followed by drought—also reduces productivity. During the high winds and heavy rains of the north-east monsoon, many of the buds are blown off. The time from budding to harvest is one year, so there is an annual shortage of coconuts during the monsoon season. Only in the months of May and June is there sufficient quantity for copra production, otherwise it is almost always more profitable to sell coconuts fresh.

Cashew nut trees (*jambu golok*) grow wild in the village, but they are not very productive and are economically unimportant, even though a good price is paid for the nut. Other fruits and vegetables rarely are found due to soil constraints: very heavy manuring and constant watering would be required. Manure itself is in short supply due to the small numbers of livestock that the available ground cover, a tough, wiry grass, will support. From July or August to January there is adequate rainfall to encourage this grass to grow (see Figure 3.1), but during the dry season even this minimal vegetation withers.

Virtually all households in Mangkok raise chickens,[1] yet less than half engage in any other forms of animal husbandry. Not a single water-buffalo is raised locally, and there are only a few hungry-looking cows to be found in the village. Goats, however, appear to thrive on the tough grass; they are allowed to roam freely during the day, but at night are returned to their small corrals and shelters. Voracious scavengers, the goat population has forced those who wish to plant new coconut palms or any small patch of vegetables to protect their efforts with elaborate and (because the materials are not locally available) expensive fencing. At one time, informants report, it was decided at a community-wide meeting called for this purpose, that all goats had to be tethered so as not to interfere with such planting, but this scheme quickly collapsed: due to the sparseness of vegetation the goats would have starved unless moved every half

[1] In 1978 Mangkok's chicken population twice was decimated by a fowl disease.

hour. The goats in this area need to be allowed freedom of movement. As long as goats are not tethered, they are easy to raise and in three years' time may be sold for as much as $70 each. Some of these goats are consumed locally during feasts associated with weddings; others are sold to people from neighbouring villages for similar purposes. Only rarely do urban people enter Mangkok in search of goats, and there is no marketing relationship with urban abattoirs.

ACROSS THE RIVER

Across the river the land is low-lying and swampy, the primary vegetation being *gelam* trees, *nipah* palms, and various grasses and sedges. The most important of the latter is a sedge called *kercut* which is used for weaving baskets and mats for fish drying.

In order to gather *kercut*, both men and women cross the river in a fishing boat and walk through the low-lying, often swampy land. The *kercut* is cut with a small scythe and bundled into sheaves perhaps 8 feet long with a diameter of about 2 feet. It is then soaked overnight in a watery mud to soften the fibres and make pounding of the *kercut*, the next step, easier. The women use a large wooden pestle about 4 feet long to pound each sheaf for approximately one hour on a hard platform. Finally the *kercut* is ready to be woven, by the women. Weaving these baskets and mats is an important activity during the monsoon period when there is no other gainful employment to be found. It may be done at a woman's convenience while caring for children, cooking, etc. In a day a woman will probably manage to weave the equivalent of four small mats, measuring about 2 × 3 feet, the most common item produced. These are used for drying fish and shrimp, and local fish processors assure a steady market. Each mat fetches $0.50; calculating the amount of time taken in each step, from gathering to final weaving, about $0.15–0.20 is earned per hour of effort. Though minimal, this income is crucial during the monsoon when the seas are too rough for the boats to go out.

The *nipah* palm is exploited in a number of ways. The mature leaves are collected and used for roofing materials, either for personal use or for sale. The long, slender leaves are folded over a 3-foot strip of bamboo and stitched into place, and the sections are then placed on the roof and stitched down. *Nipah* thatch may last 7 years or more if closely spaced; if they are not overlapped, they may last less than 3 years as the ends give way. The tender young shoots of the palm also are collected and dried, becoming the wrapper for hand-rolled cigarettes, again for use or for sale. The *nipah* palm also produces a small fruit which children enjoy.

The *gelam* tree, found across the river in swampy or semi-swampy areas, is an important source of firewood for cooking, as is the pine-like *ru* tree, which prefers the sandy conditions found in the village itself. The wood of the *gelam* tree is most valuable for making charcoal and there are several kilns within a 5-mile radius of Mangkok. Its soft bark is used in boat building as gasket material between planks to give a water-tight joint; it is impervious to marine worms and lasts as long as the wood itself.

CULTIVATION OF RICE

Also across the river and 2 or 3 miles by foot is land that the government alienated to residents of Mangkok and neighbouring villages for rice production. The suitability of this land for the cultivation of rice is questionable. After two good years production dropped and wild boar, insect pests, and rats took a heavy toll of the remaining crop. Because of the swampy soil, tractors could not operate in the area, and land preparation was accomplished by hand with a *tajak*, a scythe-like instrument; this work may take upwards of a month for a 2-acre holding. When yields were high it was considered a worthwhile activity, especially in the light of the fact that the month of land preparation—May—coincided with a sharp drop in fishing activity. But when increasingly heavy losses by predators and pests coincided with declining soil fertility (no chemical fertilizers appear to have been used), most people of Mangkok gave up working those fields.

As of 1978 about one-quarter of the households in Mangkok continued to grow some rice, but this is generally on a share-cropped basis on more established rice growing land along the road to Kampung Buluh. Less than half of these families produced enough rice for a whole year's consumption, and only one family produced a modest surplus for sale. As in Gong Guncil, rice grown by the family is often stored for consumption during the monsoon or other slack period. When a steady income is earned from fishing, milled rice is purchased and consumed, leaving the family-grown rice as a hedge against difficult times in the future.

RIVER AND BEACH

The river itself provides important, though to most families supplementary, sources of food and income. Many years ago the river was infested by crocodiles, but there have been no attacks in at least fifteen years. Crabs, shrimp and fish are plentiful, and they are exploited particularly when ocean fishing is poor. The river also is the home of two kinds of edible shellfish and a large river turtle (*tuntong*) whose eggs are greatly enjoyed and may be preserved for many months in salt. Six households within Mangkok derive a substantial portion of their income from netting and trapping on the river, an activity particularly suited to the efforts of older men who prefer to work at their own pace in the solitude of their own small boats.

The shallow water right off the beach of Mangkok is a valuable natural resource for the villagers. During the monsoon and other lulls in fishing activity, it is common to see people catching small fish with either a small throw net, *jala*, or with a scoop-net, *sauk*. Edible bivalve shellfish, *remis*, also are plentiful. These all are important sources of protein in the local diet when other sources of fish are unavailable.

FAMILY STRUCTURE

Mangkok's 121 households contain a total population of 541 people, or an average of 4.5 per household. The range of household size is from one to fifteen, but the most commonly found are households containing a nuclear family of five (26 cases). There are only 3 cases of extended families, where a son- or daughter-in-law has been brought to live in the parents' home. In one of these households separate kitchens are maintained, and expenditures on such items as food and clothing are kept separately.

The local pattern of endogamous marriages is an indication of the relative isolation of Mangkok. In general for rural Malay society there is no clearly stated preference for endogamous or exogamous marriage, and the evidence from the other two communities studied shows a significantly higher proportion of exogamous marriages than in Mangkok, where 48 out of 100 married couples consist of people born in Mangkok. If villages in the immediate surrounding area (within 5 miles) are included, the proportion is even higher (74 out of 100). It also is interesting to note that only in 6 cases was neither spouse locally born, and even then in 4 cases one or both partners had been resident in Mangkok for a decade or more.

Another demographic feature of Mangkok that seems to stand out, certainly in comparison to the other two communities studied, is the large number of single individual households (11) comprising either widowed or divorced older women, who are typically semi-independent economically, earning small incomes from a variety of occupations such as making mats, sewing, or cleaning and drying fish on a piece-rate wage. They are dependent to some extent on their children for regular supplies of fresh fish and sometimes rice, cash or other essentials to supplement their own earnings.

Several factors account for the large number of households of single women in Mangkok. Availability of land is no problem as the land itself has such a low productive value that there is no question of economic cost for such use. The expense of constructing a modest house also is small, and if the materials are procured across the river or further up river, the house may cost virtually nothing but the time it takes to build (and obligatory refreshments given to the work crew). These latter factors, however, would also apply to the other two communities studied, and yet there the proportion of single individual households is nowhere near 10 per cent as in Mangkok.

The most plausible explanation may be that the village economy of Mangkok allows an elderly individual to remain materially independent or semi-independent longer than the economies of rice farming or rubber tapping. Though it is true that in any village an elderly person may weave mats and baskets, it is in a fishing community such as Mangkok that there is a ready market and fixed prices for such endeavours. Collecting and processing the raw materials is physically demanding, but it is common to see a woman's children involved in the more arduous tasks of collecting, soaking, and pounding the *kercut*. The mother will then weave and sell the mats, the effort of her offspring being essentially a subsidy which costs them time and effort but no money. Though the earnings are small in mat-making, such employment gives the option of substantial self-sufficiency if one's son or son-in-law is a fisherman and gives one free fresh fish whenever he has been to sea, and if other wants are modest.

The obvious question, at least in the context of rural Malay society, is why an aging woman would want to live alone. The answer given by each of the women is that they do not want to be bothered by the noise and fuss of their grandchildren. At first glance this answer is surprising, as everyone in the village apparently likes babies and toddlers and showers them with affection. These grandmothers are, in fact, no different, but prefer to have their own abode and retreat, and their sleep undisturbed.

It is interesting that while there are 11 cases of women living alone there is only one case of a widower living alone. His situation is quite different. Since the death of his wife he has been listless, lethargic and unable to care for himself, and is so irrascible that even his siblings, who presently care for him, finally had to build a small separate dwelling for him. There is only one other household in Mangkok where an adult male has no sister, daughter or other woman to cook and wash for him; he has instead a 14-year-old son to help him with such chores.

Generally, elderly men separated by death or divorce from their wives do not form separate households but reside in the same house with one of their children. The reason for this seems to be simply that men in rural Malay society are unaccustomed to the necessary domestic duties which would enable them to function independently. Most fishermen do possess rudimentary culinary skills, and many have cooked for themselves when fishing beyond the home village; but no rural Malay man ever met by the author has claimed to enjoy cooking. The division of labour within a family is such that the man is discouraged from involvement in the skills and inclinations necessary for an independent existence.

FISHING BOATS, GEARS, AND METHODS

Of the 121 households in Mangkok, 41 are not directly engaged in fishing activities. These include the 12 single-occupancy households, shopkeepers, fish buyers, and households comprising the aged and infirm. Within the remaining 80 households there are 103 active fishermen, of whom 7 concentrate their efforts on river fishing and 9 work on the large purse-seiners which operate from Kuala Trengganu.

BOAT DESIGNS

Most fishermen in Mangkok use boats 25–35 feet in length with a beam of 6–7 feet. These boats displace 3–6 tons and are powered by 6–8 horsepower diesel engines. The boats are moored along the river bank within the village and there are protected from storms. They are far too heavy to drag up on to the beach as was done with the small boats, *perahu*, that were used before the introduction of diesel engines in the early 1960s. The boats are of shallow draught, typically 3 feet, which enables them to pass over the sand-bars that lie before the river mouth; even so, at low tides the boats must be skilfully guided so as not to run aground. This shallow draught, however, makes these boats bob like corks even with moderate swells, and in heavy seas they are most uncomfortable, even dangerous.

The traditional boat designs and gear types used in the Mangkok area resemble closely those described and illustrated by Raymond Firth (1966) in Bachok, Kelantan (about 40 miles north of Mangkok). In Mangkok the *pukat tangkol* was the dominant gear, and the graceful *kueh* and *kolek* were used, but they are no longer common.

When diesel engines were first introduced, the powered boats were used to tow the smaller boats used for the *pukat tangkol* to the fishing grounds and to transport the catch back to the beach. But in Mangkok the adoption of diesel power led to the increased popularity of the drift net, and this has led to the introduction of a new boat design.

The new 'square butted' boats, *pantat potong*, are not picturesque or attractive, but they are functional. The bow is shaped and raised so as to cut through waves at the river mouth and at sea. There is an engine compartment amidships which also affords some protection for the crew from the elements or the cold when fishing at night, but it has only headroom enough for sitting. There is ample room for two men to lie down or for three men if well placed around the engine. It is an unpleasant place to be in if one is not used to inhaling diesel fumes, but the deck in a cold rain at night is not pleasant either. The space behind the engine compartment (maybe 8 feet long by 6–7 feet wide) is used for carrying and storing the drift net. There also is deck space in front of the engine compartment, and it is there that the catch is displayed when the boat returns from the sea. Often meals are eaten and prayers offered on the roof of the engine compartment or on the foredeck, but not in the work area of the aft-deck. Shoes never are worn on board a boat, just as they never are in a Malay home.

The 'square butted' design allows the drift net to be played out over the stern as the boat chugs slowly forward until the full length of the net (often over 1,000 yards) is in the water. The square stern is even more important when the net is pulled in. When fishermen pull in the drift net they essentially are pulling the boat back along the course of the net, the net acting as a kind of sea anchor. This task is physically taxing with a square sterned boat, but if the net had to be hauled over the side, as it would be with the traditional boat designs, the boat would be hauled sideways, a much more strenuous task which also would present the danger of swamping the gun-wales.

THE DRIFT NET

There are various kinds of drift nets in use, with mesh sizes ranging from $2\frac{1}{4}$ inches to 4 inches. The most common mesh sizes are between $2\frac{1}{4}$ inches and 3 inches. This net, called a *pukat hanyut*, is made of nylon, typically light brown in colour. Quite often local fishermen will mix mesh sizes. During the peak season from January to April the 3-inch net is more productive, while at other times the finer mesh will catch the smaller fish that are available.

The larger mesh of 4 inches is restricted in season to the north-east monsoon (roughly November to January), and is known locally as a *pukat hijau* after its characteristic green colour (*hijau* = green). Because the *pukat hijau* is expensive and only can be used for two or three months of the year, and because the seas are too rough for the small boats when these nets are at their most productive, no fishermen in Mangkok own the *pukat hijau*. But they are familiar with it as fishermen from the village of Batu Rakit, almost 30 miles down the coast, use the *pukat hijau* and sell their catch in Mangkok. Not only is the mesh size larger, but the net itself is heavier and more suitable for the relatively heavy seas during and immediately after the monsoon period. The six boats using these nets and selling their catch in Mangkok also are larger (about 40 feet with 22 horsepower diesel engines) than those used by the fishermen of Mangkok, enabling the Batu Rakit fishermen to operate in heavier seas and further from shore than Mangkok fishermen. The *pukat hijau* is particularly effective in capturing large Spanish mackerel (*ikan tenggiri*; this net also is known as the *pukat tenggiri*). Since it is used in conditions when most other boats are unable to put to sea, the prices obtained by fishermen using the *pukat hijau* are likely to be at annual high levels.

Both the *pukat hanyut* and the *pukat hijau* are used at night, the net being let off the stern as the boat moves slowly away from the coast. The fishermen of Mangkok typically operate $\frac{1}{2}$–3 miles off the coast. The prevailing currents move up and down the coast, depending on the tides, and so the fish—which generally swim against the current—find themselves trapped in the nets which run perpendicularly. A small kerosene hurricane lamp fixed on a wooden floating platform is attached to one end of the net. Another lantern is placed on the boat itself, and these two lights mark the location of the net so that other boats passing in the night will not cross it. The net itself is attached by nylon rope to a string of plastic floats which allows the net to hang about 3 feet below the surface; the netting runs 30 feet deep and is of variable length.

The fishing boats of Mangkok typically leave the village around 4 p.m. and reach the river mouth by 4.30 p.m. Sometimes the boats cast their nets near the river mouth, but generally they will move either up or down the coast, depending on the judgement of the captain (*jeragang*) and crew. This decision is crucial and is in part determined by the success of the previous night's fishing for that boat and the other boats from Mangkok. There is a free exchange of such 'intelligence' among fishermen. On arrival at the selected spot the net will be played out, this task being completed by sunset. The religious will say their evening prayers, the hungry will eat their evening rice, and all will settle in to wait; talking, smoking, and napping in the engine compartment until around midnight. At this time the net will be pulled in, a process that takes 45 minutes to an hour or more, depending on how many fish need to be cleared from the net. This must be done carefully so as not to damage the fish, which would lower their value. When species such as wolf herring, sting rays, and sharks are brought on-board still alive, clearing the nets can be a dangerous job. After the net has been pulled in and cleared, it will probably be cast again, unless the moon has risen, in which case the boats will begin to return, arriving in Mangkok at two or three o'clock in the morning.

Fishing with the drift net is done only during the darker phases of the moon as it is said that when the moon is out the fish can see the shadow of the net, and will avoid it. It also is said that during the bright phase of the moon fish will not rise to the surface where the *pukat hanyut* hangs. This is understandable as any fish swimming near the surface when the moon is bright would cast a shadow and be an easy target for predators such as the shark and dolphin. This is another reason why fishermen do not go out during the bright phase of the moon; fish trapped in the nets will be taken by sharks and dolphins, leaving only gaping holes where the fish had been. Consequently, fishing activity usually stops from the eighth, ninth, or tenth day of the lunar calendar and is only resumed again on the seventeenth to twentieth day; the exact day will depend on weather conditions and the catch of the few boats that may still venture out when their colleagues either have ceased or not yet begun fishing. Each fishing period is called a *kelam*, from the Malay word meaning 'dark or obscure', and *sekelam* (one *kelam*) usually refers to a period of 18–22 nights of fishing.

In many ways, night fishing is a pleasant experience. The men put to sea after the heat of the day has been relieved, watch the sun set after casting the net, and enter the river again at sunrise. At the landing area in Mangkok there is a small shop operated by the Fishermen's Cooperative where a hungry fisherman can buy a cup of hot tea with milk and perhaps a dish of local cakes or glutinous rice. But fishing at night has its drawbacks as well. If boats venture out in the afternoon, a storm may build up later in the darkness of the night and catch them unawares. At the least they will spend an uneasy evening at sea, and they will find their passage back into the river mouth treacherous. In 1976 two boats capsized while attempting to enter the river at dawn in such circumstances. The boats and nets were recovered, and the fishermen reached shore safely by hanging onto plastic floats, but what catch they had and such incidental equipment as lamps, poles, fuel cans, and personal effects were lost. Fear of such an eventuality keeps many fishermen from venturing out even if there has been a calm spell during the monsoon period, but the attraction of putting to sea is great, as it is during the monsoon season that fishing is often most profitable.

OTHER NETS USED IN MANGKOK

In December 1977 a new type of net came into use, a bottom-set gill net known as *pukat tansi*, which is made of clear mono-filament nylon and used during the day. The lower edge of the net is weighted with lead sinkers which carry the net to the bottom which is where the fish are found during the turbulence of the monsoon season, and the upper edge is attached to small plastic floats which hold up the body of the net. The *pukat tansi* used in Mangkok has a mesh size of $2\frac{1}{2}$ inches. Because the nylon is clear it is not readily detected by the fish in the murky conditions during the monsoon. When the monsoon has passed and the water again clears, this net is no longer used as the fish are said to be able to see even the clear netting; the *pukat hanyut* is used instead. In the years preceeding 1977 there had been only two such nets in Mangkok, and they had attained indifferent success, but in 1977 the catch obtained by the *pukat tansi* suddenly increased dramatically and, sensing opportunity, many people in Mangkok began to invest in the new net. By mid-January there were 17 *pukat tansi* operating from Mangkok.

Because the *pukat tansi* is used during the day the fishermen are less likely to be caught unawares by a storm. Not only does this contribute to the peace of mind of the fisherman and his family, but it increases his productivity during the monsoon season, which in the past was a period of inactivity. Unlike the *pukat hanyut*, which is cast only once or twice during a night, the *pukat tansi* is cast and hauled in as many as eight times during a single day. Fishermen explain that this is necessary so that shark and dolphin, which see more clearly during the day than at night, will not destroy their nets. Being weighted with lead sinkers, this net makes fishing a very laborious task. While a *pukat hanyut* can be operated easily by 2 men, a minimum crew for the *pukat tansi* would be 3 men. In fact, crews often number 4 or 5 men, a 'feather-bedding' situation caused by the large number of available fishermen, many of whom are able to call upon ties of kinship or friendship to secure a place with the limited number of boats using this type of net.

In addition to the *pukat hanyut* and *pukat tansi* there are other nets owned and operated by fishermen in Mangkok, as shown in Table 4.1.

The *pukat dalam* in use in Mangkok is essentially a seine net using the materials from a drift net, and is a much smaller version of that used further down the coast. This net is used from May to August when the drift net is locally unproductive; tuna and other schooling fish are the main catch. The *pukat dalam* is used either by day or by night and, once sighted, the school of fish is encircled. Chumming is not used.

The *pukat kokoh* is a trawl net. The size of the net is dependent upon the size of the boat which pulls it, and in local terminology the *pukat kokoh* refers to the trawl net pulled by the small boats found in

TABLE 4.1
NETS USED IN MANGKOK

Type of Net	*Number*	*When Used*
Pukat hanyut	28	Year long, weather permitting
Pukat tansi	17	November to March, weather permitting
Pukat hijau	1	Year long, weather permitting
Pukat jerut udang baring	3	January to March
Pukat dalam	2	May to August
Pukat kokoh	2	May to August
Pukat tiga lapis	2	January to March
Pukat jerut bilis	1	March to October

Mangkok. It is used primarily to catch non-commercial fish species, or 'trash fish', which are sold at a low price and used for poultry feed. The *pukat kokoh* in Mangkok is used only during the slack period from May to August as a means of earning a small income. Use of a trawl net within 12 miles of the shoreline is prohibited during these months, but in the absence of any effective patrolling this is ignored both by a few local fishermen and by the larger trawlers from the major fishing ports of Kuala Trengganu and Kuala Besut.

The *pukat tiga lapis* is a small trammel net used by a single individual from a *perahu* to catch large prawns which are in season immediately after the monsoon period. This net is not common in Mangkok, but is common in Penarek and several other villages further down the coast.[1] The prawns fetch a very high price (over $5.00 per lb.), and a lucky fisherman may be able to recoup the cost of his net (about $450) in a single day of fishing. More usually it will take an entire season to recover the initial cost, and the net itself, due to the fineness of the nylon used, will need to be replaced after two or at most three seasons, even with diligent repair work.

In Mangkok the most important net other than the *pukat hanyut* is a type of purse-seine used for catching a small translucent shrimp called *udang baring* (*Acetes sp.*). This is a fine mesh nylon net approximately 200 yards long and 30 yards deep, and a crew of 10–15 men is required to handle it. Typically two boats are used. The first is a standard local diesel in-board boat which tows a second boat. The latter usually is an older boat without an engine and it carries the

[1]Letters received by the author from fishermen in Mangkok indicate that the *pukat tiga lapis* is now in widespread use.

net. The *udang baring* season also comes after the north-east monsoon, in Mangkok peaking in March. Only when the sea is glassy smooth will this fishing be successful, for otherwise the *udang baring* will not school. The fishing takes place during the day close to shore, and the schools are spotted when the *udang baring* hop along the surface when disturbed by a passing boat. The boats encircle the shrimp in a clockwise direction, the trailing boat laying out the net over the right side. The two ends of the net are then joined, completing the circle. At the bottom of the net are lead weights and large brass rings through which a nylon rope is threaded and manually hauled in, causing a pursing of the net from which the name 'purse-seine' is taken. Once this arduous work has been completed, the net is hauled in from both boats simultaneously, the shrimp being shaken back into the portion of the net still in the water until at last the catch is trapped in a small pocket of netting. This is then lifted on to the rear deck of the lead boat. The work is hard, but there is often a good deal of good-natured joking and laughter as one person or another loses his footing on the shrimp-covered and slippery deck.

PUKAT KILAT VERSUS *PUKAT HANYUT*

Many fishermen of the neighbouring villages of Penarek and Kuala Baru work on boats which use a gear type which requires a crew of up to 20 men. There are at least eight such boats crewed exclusively by fishermen of one or the other village. Known locally as the *pukat kilat*, this gear is a large purse-seine in which the net is hauled in by a power winch. In Malay '*kilat*' means 'lightning', and the name of the gear refers to the speed at which the power winch tightens the bottom rope of the net. It is, the author believes, significant that only 9 men out of over 100 active fishermen in Mangkok work with these boats, even though it would appear that the annual personal income from such employment is higher. Good reasons for preferring to work with the drift net are given by the fishermen of Mangkok. Their opinions concerning the pros and cons of this or that style of fishing are illuminating as to what are considered to be the important aspects of employment. In simplified form the debate centres around a possible trade-off between increased personal income and other, less tangible, but no less important, social and personal costs.

The boats using the *pukat kilat*, including those operated by fishermen of Penarek or Kuala Baru, are based in Kuala Trengganu, putting to sea in the afternoon and only returning to market the catch in the early morning. Only during the bright phase of the moon do the boats return to the villages, which means that for three weeks out of the month many of the men are absent from the village. Kuala Baru is especially affected as over 80 per cent of the fishermen, which includes most of the able-bodied men over the age of 15, are gone during this period. The crew members themselves have no say in the marketing arrangements and often have no idea of the value of their catch. Their income is based on a complex share arrangement and there is no way for them to check the accuracy of the calculations, as they know neither the proceeds from the catch nor the expenses (fuel, food, etc.) incurred during the fishing period. Moreover, the owners of the boats and nets (which together may cost $70,000) are not from the village, but rather are wealthy merchants, some of whom are engaged in fish marketing. The crew captain is a fellow villager but he, too, is quite at the mercy of the person who keeps the accounts. Although there are no indications at present that the owners of the boats operating out of Penarek and Kuala Baru have been cheating their crews, it is said by local fishermen that incidents of this nature are common occurrences. It is easy to see how this could happen, or could be perceived to happen. When the boat arrives the catch often is removed directly to the van of the boat owner without it being weighed or a price being set; and if, as is often the case, the owner is Chinese, the accounts of income and expenditure will be kept in Chinese characters.

There are other tensions involved in working with the *pukat kilat* which are significant and, in fact, often mentioned by the fishermen. With the *pukat kilat* a large number of men are confined for long periods of time on a single boat. Though these boats are sometimes over 60 feet in length, the amount of available space is quite limited by the netting, the power winch, the light lures, and other equipment. This crowding, it is said, often leads to strife and even violence. Added to this, there are certain functional specializations involved in this style of fishing which in most cases require no particular skill but are rewarded by extra shares. These may produce jealousies and hard feelings among the fishermen, especially if one man is passed over for a particularly choice assignment. It is not that there are no tensions on the small boats of Mangkok, or even that there are no accusations of unfairness. But in Mangkok the problems are on a smaller scale and occur when one is at home and hence less vulnerable. It is much easier to quit fishing with one boat and take up with another in Mangkok; with the large purse-seiners operating from Kuala Trengganu, a person who is dissatisfied may not be able to switch boats in the middle of a fishing period unless a timely opening occurs, and even then the dissatisfied fisherman may be refused by a captain who does not want a 'troublemaker' on his crew. In Mangkok the uncertain position of a crewman and the possibility of wholesale cheating on the part of the owners is quite impossible. This is one important factor that fishermen mention in explaining their preference for working on the smaller boats using the drift net. They fear being cheated by non-villagers, who are not amenable to traditional social controls.

The majority of fishermen from Mangkok prefer to operate from their home village, to work with boats and equipment that are locally owned, and to sell to buyers who are local residents and with whom they have regular social or even kinship relationships. There is ample opportunity for them to be boat captains, and at one time or another most of them have been *jeragang*. Even as ordinary crewmen many fishermen of Mangkok take part in such important decisions as to where and how often to cast the nets, but with the large purse-seiners there is no room for individual initiative; all that is required is simple regimented labour.

Involvement with the large purse-seiners is said also to result in feelings of resentment towards those who are perceived to be gaining an unfairly large share of the income. The owner of the boat and net, in this case, has a much higher capital investment than those with smaller boats and less expensive equipment. Consequently, he will demand a larger proportion of the total catch. To fishermen accustomed to operating on a much smaller scale, the share accruing to the owner may appear excessive. It is not that the fishermen do not recognize capital as a factor of production, but rather that the sums earned by the owner of a large purse-seiner are so much greater than those earned by the average crewman that their sense of fairness is outraged. The formula used in Mangkok for distribution of the proceeds of the drift net catch is simple and provides the observer with an understanding of the relative values placed on labour and capital.

DISTRIBUTION OF THE CATCH

Fish is marketed daily in Mangkok, but the buyers do not hand over cash on the day of the sale. Instead, at the end of a given fishing period, or when there is a break in fishing caused by a storm, the captains of the individual boats will inform their buyer or buyers that they are ready to distribute the proceeds to their crews. Generally on the following day the boat captain will visit again the house of the buyer or buyers and collect the money. That afternoon or evening the crew will assemble at the house of the captain who, with a pile of money before him, will proceed to distribute the earnings according to an established formula. The formula itself is simple enough, but the calculations become complex if for one reason or another a crew member had not joined the boat for a given evening, or if perhaps another fisherman had joined for part of the fishing period. As such is often the case, instead of going through the calculations once for a twenty-day fishing period, there may be five or more separate calculations to be made.

As the men sit on the floor in the front room, the wife of the captain and quite possibly the wives of the other crewmen will be in the kitchen, preparing tea or coffee and snacks. Quite often rather than actually working out the distribution with pencil and paper, money will be physically taken from the middle of the floor and set aside into different piles. The women are quite attentive to the proceedings in the front room, and the author observed that they are not at all averse to correcting their husbands' calculations or voicing an opinion on the interpretation of a particular distribution formula. It should be kept in mind that many of the fishermen are either illiterate or nearly so. In some cases younger fishermen with primary education, even from other crews, are asked to help with the calculations. The author watched several distributions and offered no comment when an error in calculation was made. Errors invariably were caught, and more often than not it was one of the women in the kitchen who supplied the correct answers.

After calculations are completed, drinks and snacks are served. At this point, or possibly later in their own homes, the fishermen will hand over their income to their wives, keeping back only a few dollars for personal expenses. Young unmarried men living at home will turn over most of their money to their mothers, keeping some cash aside for the more flashy clothes of a young man.

CALCULATION OF THE DISTRIBUTION

The first call on the gross total of each boat's earnings are the operating expenses. These include fuel and cylinder oil, which may total $5.00 per outing, and the tea, snacks, and cigarettes the crew consumed upon their return. Once these have been set aside from the pile of cash on the floor the basic formula calls for 20 per cent to be paid to the owner of the boat as the boat share. The remainder is divided into three equal parts, with one share going to the owner of the net (often also the owner of the boat). The remaining two shares are then divided equally among the crew, including the captain, who may also be the owner of the boat and net. Regardless of ownership, a further calculation is made: charged against the shares given to both the boat and the net is the *bahagian bawa*, or 'operating share', amounting to 20 per cent, to recompense the captain for his added responsibility in looking after and maintaining the equipment.

It is expected that the captain will distribute some of the *bahagian bawa* among his crew, especially if they have assisted in maintaining the net (a continual, almost daily task) and boat in operating order. The engine should receive routine maintenance, and the hull requires at least annual painting in addition to periodic scraping of barnacles and general cleaning. There is neither a formula to guide the captain, nor a formal requirement that he give away any of the *bahagian bawa*. There is, however, a general standard of generosity and fairness by which captains are judged. The existence of this standard is evident from the number of complaints made by fishermen. Failure to distribute a satisfactory share of the *bahagian bawa* is claimed to be the cause of many crew members leaving one captain and joining another. It would seem that the captain who owns no part of either boat or net may keep a larger than equal share of the *bahagian bawa* for himself. Not only is he ultimately responsible for the boat and net, he is responsible for dealing with the fish buyers at the time of sale and when collecting money, and during the actual distribution of earnings to the crew he also is expected to provide tea and snacks. But if any of his crew helped to clean the boat, mend the net, or work on the engine they would still expect adequate recompense from the *bahagian bawa*. On the other hand, if the captain also owned the boat and net, he would be expected to share the greater part of the *bahagian bawa* with his crew; it is considered that he needs little or no recompense for looking after his own equipment. In addition to his crew share he also will be receiving the boat and net shares, which are almost half of the total earnings.

If a crew of three men using a *pukat hanyut* earned $100 after expenses had been met, the owner(s) and crewmen would receive the following income (assuming equal division of the *bahagian bawa* among the three crewmen):

Owner of boat	$16.00
Owner of net	$21.33
Crewman's share	$20.89

The total share earned by the owner(s) is $37.33, while the share earned by the fishermen is $62.67. (In contrast, the owners of the *pukat kilat* take an even $50.00 of each $100.00 earned, after expenses.) If the captain of the boat is also the owner of the boat and net, he would take home approximately $58.21 from every $100.00.

INCOME FROM FISHING

The incomes earned by fishermen vary considerably from season to season. Figure 4.3 graphically depicts the seasonality of fishing in the Mangkok area. Data for this Figure (and the other Figures and Tables in this chapter as well) were collected by a locally born field assistant under the author's supervision. After the author left Mangkok on 20 April, he continued to collect data until 12 May, at which time he left to take a job elsewhere. 12 May was the sixth day of the lunar month, meaning that there were still probably at least four if not six nights of possible fishing. However it is clear from the data that, due to the poor catch of the nights immediately preceding 12 May, a major change in the figures was unlikely.

Data on the value of fish landed and approximate distributions are provided in Table 4.2 for five cases from Mangkok. This Table includes data from 14 January to 15 March 1978, the peak fishing season of the year. An estimate is taken for operating costs using the figure of $5.00 per day or night of fishing, which includes fuel, engine oil, and refreshments for the crew after a day or night at sea. Not included are major expenses, e.g., engine repairs, which are paid for by the owner of the boat. The *bahagian bawa* has been subtracted from both the 'Boat Share' and the 'Net Share', and added to the 'Crew Share'.

Table 4.2 indicates that there is considerable variation in the

FIGURE 4.3

FRESH FISH LANDINGS IN THE MANGKOK AREA, 14 JANUARY–12 MAY 1978

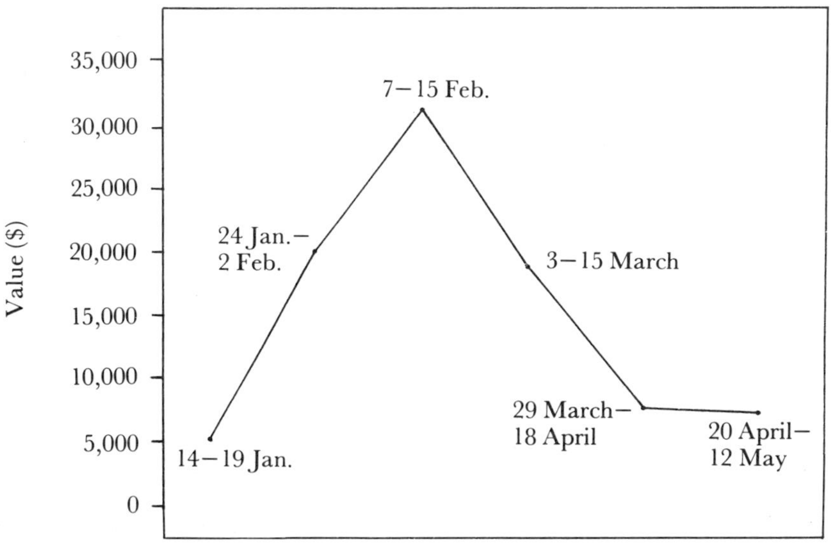

TABLE 4.2
CATCH, DISTRIBUTION, AND INCOME FOR FIVE CASES, 14 JANUARY–15 MARCH 1978

Case	*Total Catch ($)*	*Costs ($)*	*Boat Share ($)*	*Net Share ($)*	*Crew Share ($)*	*Number of Crew*	*Approximate Crewman's Income ($)*
I	964	105	137	183	538	3	179
II	2,236	140	335	447	1,314	3–4	375
III	1,356	145	194	258	759	3	253
IV	2,268	140	340	454	1,333	3–4	381
V	1,810	125	270	359	1,056	3	352

success of the fishermen of Mangkok. The captain of Case I, the least successful of the five cases presented in Table 4.2 and one of the least successful captains in Mangkok, suffered not only below average income but had great difficulty attracting an adequate crew. Early in the season his average crew consisted of three men. By April, however, they had left him to work on other boats, and on nine separate occasions in April he had to go to sea alone. It is possible to operate the *pukat hanyut* alone, but the work is lonely and arduous, and not particularly efficient as the net is likely to be cast only once per night, instead of twice, which increases the likelihood of captured fish being taken by sharks and dolphins. If this occurs the catch is diminished and the net damaged. With no other crewmen to help, the increased work of mending the net is left to only one man.

Success in fishing is partly a matter of the skill and luck of the captain and crew, but the condition of the nets is perhaps a more important element. The *pukat hanyut* is rarely if ever purchased new, but it is constantly being repaired and renewed section by section as funds are available: netting in a poor state of repair may have gaping holes and thread so weakened by age that even a small fish may be able to break free. Fishermen operating nets in poor repair will find it most difficult to meet depreciation and maintenance costs associated with the net precisely when the need is greatest.

In Case I the captain (Dahat, see Figure 4.2) is part-owner of the boat and both the *pukat hanyut* and *pukat tansi*. The boat and nets are in poor condition. The *pukat tansi* was purchased second-hand and is too short to be effective; moreover, the mesh size of $2\frac{1}{4}$ inches seems to be too small for the larger Spanish mackerel and wolf herring which predominate during and immediately after the monsoon.

In Case II the captain operates the boat of the only Chinese family in Mangkok but is partner with this family in both the *pukat hanyut* and *pukat tansi*. The boat is in good condition as is the *pukat hanyut*, but the *pukat tansi* has begun to yellow with age. This captain was the first to use the *pukat tansi* in Mangkok, and while he was successful with it in early 1978, others with newer nets had markedly greater success.

The captain of Case III (Yahya, see Figure 4.1) also operates the boat of another, but unlike Case II, he does not own shares in the nets, which are in only fair condition. In Case IV the captain owns his own boat and nets; the boat is new and the nets are in fair condition. This boat brought in the year's single largest catch, valued at over $636 or 28 per cent of his total catch for the 2-month period.

Finally, in Case V the captain is owner of his new boat and nets which are in good repair. Having a new boat does not directly contribute to the catch—nets, not boats, capture fish. But a boat is appreciated for its seaworthiness, especially when the seas are rough. This captain will take his boat out with confidence when others will worry about older planks and joints and may not go to sea. A fast boat also is an asset, and a newer boat tends to be faster, and also to require less general maintenance; and for these reasons, fishermen prefer to work on such a boat.

It is the author's impression that the cases chosen are representative of boats and nets in differing conditions. The most significant variable in terms of increased catch appears to be the relative condition of the nets used. Chance and luck are other factors in the success of fishing, as are skill and perseverance. But without a decent net of suitable size, even the best fisherman of Mangkok will have difficulty earning an adequate living.

We see from Table 4.2 that over a 2-month period (mid-January to mid-March, the best fishing of the year) a crewman on the boat of Case II may earn almost $375, or $187.50 per month. In addition he will bring home enough fish to feed his family, at least $1 worth per day of fishing (perhaps $2—3 at retail price levels). But if the case of Yahya, Case III, is taken to be closer to the average, as the author believes is true, the average cash income for this period is approximately $125 per month. Comparing Figures 4.1 and 4.3 it is obvious that the average income is not maintained throughout the year. In the absence of adequate data it is only possible to offer an educated guess that average monthly incomes from fishing based on a 12-month year are almost half the average from mid-January to mid-March. It should be noted here that fishing with the drift nets in 1978 was reported to be as good or better than average compared to recent years. Price levels also have been maintained although there was some turbulence in the field of marketing.

MARKETING

THE FISH MARKET

Marketing of fresh fish in Mangkok takes place along a sandy beach on the bank of the Sungai Setiu. Gently grounded on the sand, the boats often do not require further anchoring. By coming in bow first rather than completely parallel, as many as 25 boats can be accommodated at one time. Though as many as 45 boats may come in during a single morning, they tend to be staggered over a period of two hours or more. When a boat comes in the crew will disembark for a short time to sell the catch and to patronize the small coffee shop owned by the local Fishermen's Cooperative, where they spend some time discussing the night's fishing, where they cast their nets, where the fish seem to be most plentiful, and where they will operate that evening.

The landing area itself is dotted with the open pole sheds of the various buyers which contain insulated boxes (approximately 4 feet by 3 feet by 4 feet high) in which ice is stored; also in or near these sheds are the packing boxes in which the fish are packed in crushed ice and sent to Kuala Trengganu. A fuel tank owned by the Fishermen's Cooperative, which sells diesel fuel and cylinder oil, also is located at the landing. Plans are being made to operate a store to provide supplies and spare parts for nets and boats which during the period of research could only be obtained in Kuala Trengganu or Kota Bharu.

In June 1978, the government built a small dock at the landing beach presumably to facilitate loading and unloading the boats; however, at best only three boats can use the dock at the same time, so its utility is limited. Moreover, as the dock seems to have been built high enough to prevent its being submerged in a flood, during normal conditions it is quite difficult to climb up to it from the small local boats. It is much easier to wade a few feet in knee-deep water to reach the boats. At the landing area also may be found two structures known as *wakaf*, open raised platforms with tiled roofs which are commonly used by people on the East Coast as places to rest or wait. Finally, there is a fresh water well at the landing area used for bathing and to supply potable water to the coffee shop.

MARKETING ARRANGEMENTS OF THE PAST

Until the dirt road was extended from Penarek to Mangkok five years ago there was no marketing of fresh fish in Mangkok, the bulk of the fish being dried before sale. Greater profits tended to be earned in the processing than in the catching of fish. To be a successful processor of dried fish, however, required a constant source of materials without which a steady supply of labour and a good return to the investment in drying mats and other equipment would have been impossible. In Mangkok, fish drying tended to be concentrated in the hands of a few men, and in an effort to achieve a certain supply of fish they also invested in fishing boats. At one time at least half of the boats operating from Mangkok were owned by three or four fish processors. The catch was automatically sold to the owner of the boat, who set the price. Those fishermen who owned their own boats could sell their catch to these processors, process the fish themselves, or sell to small-scale fish vendors who would enter the village on bicycles or small motor cycles. For independent fishermen drying their own fish was not a viable alternative partly due to certain fixed costs, partly to the uncertainty of an individual boat's catch, and partly to the lack of regular marketing outlets. The small-scale vendors provided important outlets only during periods of relatively poor fishing. When the catch was substantial they could not handle the quantity landed, and the bulk of the fish had to be sold to the local fish processors.

It is not necessarily true that the fish processors took unfair advantage of their position, cheated their fellow villagers, or made unreasonable profits on their investments of energy and capital. But it is clear from their present economic condition that they prospered.

NEW MARKETING ARRANGEMENTS

When the road into Mangkok was completed, small vans were able to enter and fresh fish could be sent to the market in Kuala Trengganu, only 50 miles away. The opening of Mangkok to fresh fish marketing produced a major structural change in the local fishing economy. Its most immediate effect was to raise the price of the fish. In 1972 the price obtained for spotted Spanish mackerel (*tenggiri papan*) was $0.53 per lb. When this popular fish could be sold fresh the price jumped to $0.80 per lb. and gradually increased to present levels. The price for other varieties commonly caught by the fishermen also increased. As of early 1978 fishermen of Mangkok were receiving the prices indicated in Table 4.3.

The building of the road and the consequent changes in the price structure and marketing relationships had a beneficial effect on the incomes of local fishermen. Instead of selling their catch to processors of dried fish at prices over which they had no control, fishermen, including those operating the boats of the fish processors,

TABLE 4.3
1978 PRICES FOR COMMERCIALLY IMPORTANT SPECIES OF FISH

Species	*Price per lb. ($)*
Spotted Spanish mackerel	1.20–1.35
Spanish mackerel	0.90–1.05
Large wolf herring	0.95–1.09
Small wolf herring	0.53–0.60
Bonito	0.19
Bluefin tuna	0.26–0.30
Scabbard fish	0.23–0.26

began to sell to the highest bidder. As owners of boats and nets, these processors received a larger income from the boat and net shares, but their profitable trade in dried fish itself dwindled. The rationale for maintaining a small fleet of boats to supply fish for processing no longer existed. With their increased incomes, fishermen were in a position to buy used boats and nets, which the erstwhile processors no longer found as profitable.

The owner of several boats and nets can earn a reasonably good income from the boat and net shares alone, but only if he can find captains and crews to operate the fleet. As the fishermen themselves increasingly have sought to purchase their own equipment it has become more and more difficult for the owners of boats to man them. In most cases the processors sold their boats, but in some cases they have entered into a partnership with their captains. Known locally as a *kongsi*, such partnerships are formed by the original owner giving a half share of the boat and sometimes of the net as well to the captain. This may be done outright, but typically the owner proposed to his captain that the boat is worth, for example, $2,000. If the captain continued to operate the boat until $2,000 was earned for the boat share, then he was given half ownership in the boat itself, and one half of the boat share thereafter. This effectively tied the captain to the particular boat, reducing the risk to the owner of having a boat for which he could find no captain and which consequently produced no income. The owner also appeared generous though at the same time he was sharing not only the profits from the boat but the expenses as well. An inactive boat also incurs expenses and, in fact, depreciates in value more rapidly than an active boat. During the period of field research there were always at least two boats inactive due to lack of a captain.

THE NEW FISH BUYERS

The processors of dried fish seem to have been unable to adapt to the new marketing situation. The marketing of fresh fish today requires the establishment of trade relationships with other middlemen in either the state capital or the major urban centres in Singapore or on the West Coast of Peninsular Malaysia. The work tends to be hard and involves long hours and, significantly, requires a level of literacy which few rural people born before World War II possess. Marketing of fresh fish requires record keeping at multiple stages: there are the daily records of purchases from fishermen and records of the sales to the buyers of their fish consignments, as well as costs for ice, packing materials, and transportation which need to be accounted for and controlled; in some cases these may involve credit relationships.

As a consequence, fish buyers now tend to be men in their twenties and thirties; older men are less prepared by education, experience, or desire to adapt to these changed circumstances. Previously the only expenses that a processor of dried fish incurred were for locally produced materials and labour from their neighbours; the only other relationship that was necessary was with the Chinese buyer of the dried fish, who paid for his purchases with cash.

It was difficult for these older fish processors to adapt themselves to the new marketing pattern, though one of them tried. Instead of being able to conclude sales from the comfort and security of his own village, he had to travel daily to a large town and deal with buyers on their home turf, accept payment by cheque, and deal with banks, ice factories and even car dealers and mechanics. To move the fresh fish quickly he purchased a small van and hired a driver. He said he found the experience both physically and financially exhausting. An older man who is functionally illiterate, he found the long days were too much of a strain on his constitution. Possibly because he was inexperienced in fresh fish marketing, and possibly because he also was involved in a number of other merchandising activities which distracted his attention and energy, he lost money and finally sold the van and stopped buying fresh fish.

During the peak fishing seasons, a fish buyer in Mangkok may work 18 hours per day. He will need to be at the marketing place by 6 a.m. at the latest. Sometimes the boats will come in as early as 2 a.m., continuing until 7 a.m. or later. As the fish is purchased it is packed into crates with crushed ice and loaded onto the vans. Between 9 a.m. and 10 a.m. the vans are ready and are driven to Kuala Trengganu, about $1-1\frac{1}{2}$ hours away by road. The sale of the fish to the dealers in Kuala Trengganu typically takes little time; the buyers of Mangkok have established relationships, sometimes involving credit, with certain dealers there. The various dealers generally offer the same prices, and there is no need for a daily checking of prices among each of the dealers. The buyers each sell to different dealers anyway, and they know what their fellows received for their consignments. More often the buyers will switch dealers for reasons of real or imagined personal slights, disagreements on the grading of the fish delivered, or if one dealer is willing to provide needed credit when another is not.

The dealers pay the buyers on the basis of price per unit of weight for the given species of fish. Generally the fish are not unpacked from their crates but are sent off directly to the urban centres of the West Coast. If there is any problem in the quality of the fish, the dealer will hear of it when the fish reaches its destination. Lorries leave Kuala Trengganu with the fish between noon and 3 p.m., arriving in Kuala Lumpur, Singapore, or Johor Bahru by 3 a.m. There the major urban buyers accept the consignments and distribute them among retail sellers.

When the fish buyers of Mangkok have delivered their fish they will need to buy ice for the next day's catch; it is at this point that the buyers often extend their working day and their costs. At the fish marketing centre in Kuala Trengganu there is an ice factory, but during the peak fishing seasons there is a serious shortage of ice, which is sometimes sent up from Kuantan, over 200 miles away. To the initial cost of this ice is added the transportation costs and the 'depreciation' caused by melting in the unrefrigerated lorries. The buyers often wait for hours to obtain their ice, and sometimes in desperation drive 80 miles north to Kuala Besut in the hope of obtaining it there, but as there also is a shortage at this port, and because they cannot place a telephone order for the ice they require, they usually face a long wait there as well and may even have to return to Kuala Trengganu once again. Many nights while up late typing field notes the author saw fish buyers returning to Mangkok after midnight with their precious cargo of ice. Without ice fish cannot be purchased on the morrow, and if there is not ice immediately available then wait they must. When the shortness of the peak seasons is taken into consideration, such exertions are placed in proper perspective. A buyer of fish in Mangkok will earn a substantial proportion of his annual income during a 2- or 3-month period, and while it is exhausting, he knows that a season of relative idleness or alternative employment will follow. But in calculating costs and margins, the extra expenditures for fuel and meals for both buyer and driver in this seasonal search for ice must be considered substantial.

It often has been claimed in government and academic circles that 'middlemen', the buyers of fish, are largely responsible for the impoverishment of Malaysia's coastal fishermen. As with most sweeping statements there are important exceptions to be made, and the author's data indicate that an exception could be made in the case of the buyers in Mangkok. It is beyond the scope of the present study to attempt an analysis of marketing relationships from producer to consumer. There may be good cause for claims that other middlemen are cheating the fishermen while robbing the consumer. It is true that some varieties of fish, such as the Spanish mackerel, double in price from Mangkok to Kuala Lumpur, and that even considering costs and risk there is a lot of profit being made. But if unfair market practices are taking place they would appear to be at a different level from what the author is prepared to discuss on the basis of field data from Mangkok.

Neither is the author willing to argue that the buyers of fish in Mangkok are unconcerned with their profit margins or are unwilling to take advantage of superior market information in their dealings with fellow villagers. There is, in fact, considerable room for conflict among fishermen and fish buyers, and it would appear to be a regular feature of life in the village. This was graphically illustrated soon after the author arrived in the village when the fish buyers attempted to impose a new method of fish marketing on the fishermen of Mangkok.

THE MANNER OF SELLING FISH

When fresh fish marketing came to the Mangkok area the system adopted was that of the Dutch auction, known locally as *borong* (wholesale), whereby the captain of the fishing boat would quote a value for the whole of the catch displayed neatly on the foredeck of the boat. While various onlookers crowd around, the fish buyers climb up on the boat and wait for the captain to start lowering his quoted price, in the meantime quickly calculating the approximate weight of the different species of fish displayed and the price they are likely to fetch in Kuala Trengganu. The captain, having originally asked a price he knows no buyer would pay, will begin to lower it in increments of $5 or $10. The buyers meanwhile likely will be making disparaging comments on the quality of the fish presented for sale, noting how this one was damaged while being removed from the net, or that one had been nibbled at by another fish while in the net. Several minutes later when the price has reached a level that a buyer feels he can afford and still turn a profit, he will say (or often shout) '*Beli!*' (Buy!).

Sometimes if a price asked by the captain, e.g. $140, is close to a buyer's estimation of the catch's value but no other buyer has committed himself, he will anticipate the next price level and shout an offer to buy at $130. This is a reflection of the competition under *borong*, the buyer feeling that one or more of his fellows would want the catch at that price. No buyer could use such anticipatory bids regularly without endangering necessary working relationships with his fellow buyers, but it is considered fair to use this strategy on occasions, especially when the buyer has been unsuccessful in purchasing a catch on that day, or when purchase of another catch will give the buyer enough fish to make a trip to Kuala Trengganu worthwhile. The process is quite public, with six or more buyers competing for the catch and with sundry other villagers observing.

THE BUYERS FORCE A CHANGE

In December 1977, the various fish buyers of Mangkok met and decided they would begin to buy fish on the basis of weight instead of buying by *borong*. They argued that they sold their purchases on the basis of weight and that if they misjudged the catch they would lose money; they also pointed out that miscalculations went the other way as well and that to sell by weight would be fairer to all concerned. They promised to offer a fair market price to the fishermen. No large public meeting was held, but rather the individual buyers talked with a few fishermen and the word spread quickly from there.

The fishermen were not happy with this suggestion, fearing that the buyers would establish a price cartel and that their interests would not be served by the new system. In public the fish buyers adopted the position that the fishermen owned the fish they caught and it was up to them how they chose to dispose of their catch. Giving way to the desire of the fishermen, the buyers continued to buy the fish on the basis of *borong*, but with a difference. Deals which previously would have been concluded in 2 or 3 minutes now took 20 minutes or half an hour as the buyers would not accept the prices asked by the fishermen. It happened that this confrontation coincided with the *pukat tansi* season, and these protracted negotiations were carried out under a sun still hot at 4 p.m. after the fishermen had been out on the boats in the sun all day. The un-iced fish on the foredeck were not improving with age. Tempers began to flare as buyers suggested that the fish be weighed as a solution to the deadlock, and moved on to another boat if the captain refused. Previous locally accepted procedure held that the buyers would conclude a deal with the boat which came in first and only would move on to succeeding boats after the earlier boat's catch had been sold. By their delaying tactics the buyers effectively tied up most of the boats as they came in, and then went from boat to boat without concluding any sales. Some fishermen gave in to the pressure and had their fish weighed, but others held out this first day and finally sold by *borong*. The second and third days the confrontation was repeated, but with increasing numbers of fishermen shifting to selling by weight. This was encouraged by the fish buyers who would tell the arriving fishermen that everyone before them had sold by weight (though this was untrue). By the end of five days all fish landed at Mangkok was sold by weight; the buyers had been successful in imposing their goal.

THE BUYERS' UNITED FRONT BREAKS DOWN

The confrontation seemed to solidify into two opposing groups with different interests. It had been obvious from the start that the buyers and sellers of fish had opposing interests, but as time passed it became clear that among the buyers themselves there were competing interests, and that buying fish on the basis of weight favoured some buyers more than others. Under the new marketing arrangement the element of competition was reduced. Initially the prices offered by the different buyers were the same, and some fishermen decided which buyer to deal with on the basis of convenience. The shed of Tenaga Baru, a partnership of three men, was advantageously located on the landing beach, and with three men there were extra hands to help carry and weigh the fish and to write out the receipts. At first fishermen appeared to take their catch to this group out of convenience, but soon it became obvious that the crews were being treated to refreshments and cigarettes at the local coffee shop, a practice quickly picked up by the other buyers.

While convenience may have directed some fishermen to certain buyers, most sold their catch on the basis of more important considerations and relationships. During this period as many as 43 boats were selling in Mangkok; 29 boats sold their fish exclusively to one or another of the local buyers. Table 4.4 illustrates the type and extent of the ties which came to bind particular boats to certain buyers; all the buyers operated in Mangkok, with the exception of Osman, who bought fish in Kuala Baru.

Under the heading of 'Economic' would be included loans for the purchase of nets and other gear, personal loans for consumption at some time in the past (which may or may not have been repaid), or even outright ownership of or partnership in the boats and nets being used by the fishermen. The category of 'Kinship' needs little explanation; while a fisherman may be able to trace ties of kinship to several buyers, in some cases the tie is so close, e.g. brother, that a fisherman under the new system felt obliged to sell to this par-

TABLE 4.4
REASONS FOR PREFERENTIAL RELATIONSHIPS BETWEEN FISH BUYERS AND FISHERMEN

Buyer	*No. of Boats*	*Reason for the Relationship*		
		Economic	*Kinship*	*Friend/ Neighbour*
Tenaga Baru	6	5	0	1
Aziz	5	0	2	3
Tok Su	4	3	1	0
Osman	5	5	0	0
Rashid	3	2	1	0
Rokid	3	2	1	0
Jaafar	2	1	0	1
Pak Weng	1	1	0	0
Total	29	19	5	5

ticular buyer. Under the category 'Friend/Neighbour' are included fishermen whose immediate neighbour was a buyer and who felt obliged to sell to him if there were no stronger reason to be linked to any other buyer. Similarly, a fisherman would sell to a close personal friend in the absence of a more compelling bond.

One of the buyers, Tok Su, had not previously engaged in fresh fish marketing. He is an old shopkeeper who owns two boats and a half interest in a third, the remnants of a small fleet which he had owned when the local production of fish was dried. When fish was sold by *borong* he did not buy—wading out to the boats and then climbing up onto them was too strenuous for him—but when it was sold by weight he could stay on the beach and let the fish be brought to him. In essence Tok Su was acting as a *dagangan*, an intermediate fish buyer who guaranteed a market to the fishermen (though this service met no pressing need) and who in turn sold the fish to another buyer. Tok Su entered into a working relationship with a regular buyer who owned a van; through him Tok Su sent his fish to market and they jointly shared the profit that came with the added volume. The packing, transporting and selling were done by the regular buyer, and what Tok Su did was to interpose himself between the buyer and the fishermen, taking part of the buyer's added profit for himself. The price paid to the fishermen was unaffected, but Tok Su was able to make a small profit in addition to his regular income from boat and net shares.

Although each of the buyers was able to form at least one firm relationship to a boat, it was clear that these marketing links introduced some disequilibrium into a situation that had been totally open. Some buyers began to complain publicly that their business had slackened so much that they could not even put together a viable consignment of fish, and that the new marketing system was threatening their livelihood. This latter point is a particularly strong one in rural Malay society, where the right to earn a living is held to be pre-eminent, a basic right. Their complaints grew louder as the partnership of Tenaga Baru began to offer higher prices than their competitors, attracting the boats which were not firmly linked to other buyers. At this point the complaining buyers claimed that the original agreement among the buyers was to offer a uniform price, vindicating the fears of the fishermen that the new method of marketing would lead to a price cartel (though the fairness of the prices offered is a separate question). The partnership of Tenaga Baru (literally 'new strength'), however, claimed that they were able to offer higher prices because they marketed their fish directly to the urban centres on the West Coast. In fact, it seemed that the real reason they raised their prices was to meet the competition offered by Osman, the sole buyer of fish in the neighbouring village of Kuala Baru.

Osman also sells his fish directly to buyers on the West Coast and in Singapore, the only other buyer to do so. Osman is an interesting character, a hard-nosed trader who publicly proclaims his disdain for public opinion. He has managed to alienate virtually the entire population of his own village by being proud and aloof and for allegedly reneging on a promised gift to the local mosque. During *ikan bilis* season he must recruit labour from Mangkok to dry the catch because not one individual from his own village will work for him. His personality is abrasive, and he views his fellow villagers with ill-disguised scorn, which they return in equal measure. His relationships with fellow buyers of fish are as bad as or worse than with his neighbours. His willingness to engage in cut-throat business practices once elicited fisticuffs from a buyer in Mangkok, and Osman, who had briefly moved his buying operations to Mangkok, moved back to Kuala Baru. There he bought the fish from the five boats owned by his wife and from any other boats that cared to sell to him. He purchased fish on the basis of weight long before the buyers in Mangkok.

When the buyers at Mangkok began to buy fish by weight they found that Osman was outbidding them by about 7.5 cents per lb. on some of the more important varieties and even more on others. Several fishermen from Mangkok compared the prices and began selling their catch to him, and his business flourished. It was this competition that forced the partnership of Tenaga Baru to raise their own prices. At the same time pressure was put on those fishermen who were selling to Osman to sell to one of the Mangkok dealers. On this latter point all the buyers were agreed, and a considerable number of the fishermen also spoke to the 'mavericks' on this issue. Besides the personal antipathy towards Osman, both the buyers and fishermen also were interested in maintaining Mangkok's control over fresh fish marketing.

When the road was built connecting Mangkok and Penarek, it was extended to Kuala Baru, and initially the fresh fish marketing was carried out in that village. Most of the fishermen selling fish were from Mangkok, however, and they wanted to land in their own village. Informants recall that those seeking to move the landing site to Mangkok were mindful of the government aid to the fisheries sector which would tend to be attracted to marketing centres. The fishermen of Mangkok wanted to maintain Mangkok's place as the local fresh fish marketing centre, the only one between Kuala Besut and Batu Rakit. Although the new jetty built at Mangkok was recognized by the fishermen to be a waste of money, it also was seen as a symbol of the government's recognition of Mangkok's place as a fishing centre. Indeed, it was the local Fishermen's Cooperative which requested this project, a request that won out over the simultaneous request for a jetty by fishermen in Kuala Baru.[1]

This competition between the villages, combined with the removal of the price differential between Osman and first one and then several buyers in Mangkok, convinced the fishermen who had strayed to return to the fold. Some buyers attempted to raise their prices, if not across the board then for selected species, in an effort to attract more of the total catch. But most of the buyers were clearly unhappy buying fish by weight, and whereas previously the author had been told in public (and loudly for all to hear—a case of field-worker as sounding board) that buying fish by weight was fairer to all concerned, now buyers told him privately that buying on *borong* was more advantageous to them. A clever buyer, it was said, could make a better profit with *borong* than was possible with the fixed margins of buying by weight.

It seemed to be true that buying the fish by weight limited the profit margins of the buyers. The present writer has seen, and more to the point, the fishermen have seen the buyers' receipts with the prices they obtained in Kuala Trengganu. He also verified these

[1]At the end of 1979 the author revisited the Mangkok area and discovered that the village of Kuala Baru had been abandoned by everyone except Osman due to simultaneous erosion by the ocean and the Sungai Setiu. The inhabitants have relocated several miles down the coast.

receipts by travelling to Kuala Trengganu with the buyers. Compared to the prices actually paid to the fishermen, the buyers were receiving a margin of between \$10 and \$15 per *pikul*. Fish are transported in crates which when full hold 1.4 *pikul* (about 190 lb.) of fish; it costs at least \$11.50 per crate to market the fish in Kuala Trengganu, including \$5 for transportation, \$4 for ice, and \$2.50 for the crate itself. In addition a few dollars may be paid to a casual helper who assists in packing the fish and ice. At a margin of \$15 per *pikul* there would be about \$20 of margin per crate, or a profit of about \$8.50. If the margin drops to \$10 per *pikul*, the profit per crate of fish is only about \$3. It should be noted that the \$5 transportation charge is the cost which van owners themselves have calculated as sufficient to cover maintenance and depreciation costs and fuel. If a single buyer is unable to purchase enough fish to justify sending his own van to Kuala Trengganu, he may join with another to send his consignment at this rate.

During the peak fishing period between January and March a fish buyer may manage to purchase 6 crates or more in a day, in which case his daily profit is substantial; but when fishing is poor it is often difficult to accumulate even one crate, and sometimes the volume of fish marketed in Mangkok will amount to only 3 crates. When the catch is this poor it may not be worthwhile to send the fish to Kuala Trengganu; instead it may be stored in the large wooden insulated ice chests of the buyers. Buyers say that fish stored in ice instead of immediately marketed loses between 10 and 15 per cent of its value, which wipes out the profit margin for the buyers. It is in fact disadvantageous for the buyers to participate in buying during periods of poor fishing, but they are held, and hold themselves, responsible for buying the fishermen's catch. Table 4.5 indicates the value of fish landed at Mangkok between 14 January and 12 May 1978. This Table, which may be compared with Figures 4.1, 4.2, and 4.3, and Table 4.2, clearly shows the seasonality of fishing in Mangkok and the effect of this seasonality on local buyers.

Even during periods of good fishing the buyers may suffer losses. The peak post-monsoon season is prone to stormy periods when fishermen may not be able to go to sea for a week or more at a time. If a buyer has filled his chest with ice in anticipation of the next day's buying, he will stand to lose his store of ice (worth \$36) if a storm halts fishing for even 4 or 5 days. This happens regularly and means that the buyer must make a special trip to purchase ice. Normally ice is purchased on the return from delivering fish to Kuala Trengganu and the transportation costs are not a major factor, but they must be included when the trip is made only for this

TABLE 4.5
VALUE OF FISH PURCHASED AT MANGKOK,
14 JANUARY–12 MAY 1978
(figures rounded to nearest whole $)

Buyer	*I*	*II*	*III*	*IV*	*V*	*VI*	*Total*
Tenaga Baru	915	3,191	4,021	2,297	335	137	10,896
Osman	1,629	4,582	4,412	4,476	516	nil	15,615
Rashid	432	2,518	5,996	2,061	316	8	11,331
Aziz	1,003	3,012	3,937	2,447	750	505	11,654
Rokid	115	2,332	3,592	1,507	1,342	1,651	10,539
Jaafar	332	1,547	1,751	1,154	319	nil	5,103
Pak Weng	nil	1,034	3,674	2,160	1,408	65	8,341
Tok Su	nil	760	1,667	1,882	22	nil	4,331
Praih Moto	78	705	1,920	1,118	1,662	3,985	9,468
Total	4,504	19,681	30,970	19,102	6,670	6,351	87,278

Note: Roman numerals refer to the following fishing periods:

I	14–19 January	IV	3–15 March
II	24 January–2 February	V	29 March–18 April
III	7–15 February	VI	20 April–12 May

purpose. The commonly agreed cost of a round trip to Kuala Trengganu is $40, including the $5 paid to the driver.

Added to these risks are uncertainties within the market itself. The price of fish is effectively set in the urban markets, which transmit the prices back to the major dealers in Kuala Trengganu by telephone. The fish buyers from Mangkok arrive in Kuala Trengganu in the mid-morning, and only then learn what price they will receive. Their dealers in fact do cushion any major fluctuations in price so that the small buyers rarely have to absorb an outright loss, but they also take any windfall profits that result from suddenly higher prices paid in the urban markets. They will advise local buyers on what the following day's prices are likely to be, but they cannot be sure.

The profits and earnings of Mangkok's fish buyers are closely tied to the success of the local fishermen. The buyers are all locally born men resident in the immediate area and, with the exception of Osman noted above, they are subject to a certain amount of social control. Their standard of living is not noticeably higher than that of a successful fisherman. When fishing is good their income can be quite substantial, as of course is that of the fishermen themselves, but this period is quite limited; when the catch is poor the price margins no longer match the risks or the effort involved in buying and selling. For several months of the year they must seek alternative employment, such as hiring out their small vans to haul locally produced coconuts, copra, or dried fish. In sum, it does not appear that the local fish buyers are making unreasonable incomes at the expense of the fishermen. Even the effort to influence fishermen to sell their catch by weight was not so much to increase profits as to remove a source of risk.

When the peak fishing season ends in late March the importance of local fish buyers who operate vans gradually decreases, while the importance of the more numerous small-scale buyers using motor cycles increases. This latter group are known as *praih moto* (motor cycle traders), while the fish buyers who operate vans are known as *praih van*. As many as 22 *praih moto* buy fish directly from the boats as they come in, before the bidding under *borong* is completed. (When fish was sold on the basis of weight the *praih moto* also had access to the fish, but they had to act quickly before the *praih van* took their purchase off the boat.) Until a deal is concluded between a boat captain and a particular *praih van* the fish displayed on the deck of the boat is literally 'up for grabs'; individual consumers from the village or from other villages may walk up to the boat and remove whatever fish they want from the foredeck, paying the captain after the bulk of the fish is purchased. When a *praih van* has concluded his deal with the captain the *praih moto* will approach him asking the price for the fish that he has removed from the boat and placed on the beach. Generally the captain will set a price that will be accepted, but occasionally there is some haggling and the price may drop.

The fish removed by the various *praih moto* and other individuals generally are of lower value (scads and sardines) than the Spanish mackerel or occasional pomfret landed in Mangkok. The *praih moto* sell their purchases in the surrounding villages, as far as 20 miles inland, but their customers are almost exclusively villagers. Spanish mackerel and other high quality species of fish caught in the drift nets generally are sold to the wealthier urban markets, and local fishermen themselves rarely eat these fish. Other lower priced fish from the nets are kept for the home consumption of the fishermen themselves and generally are to be found on the rear deck when the boat lands. If fishing has been good, there will be enough fish there for the consumption not only of the immediate families of the fishermen, but also probably one or more related households (aged parents or non-fishing families). Sometimes some of this fish will be sold or more often shared with friends who have come down to watch the boats land, hoping perhaps to take a few small fish home. A fisherman who was unable to go to sea (e.g. mechanical breakdown), or the wife of a fisherman who has gone fishing elsewhere for a period of time, or the non-fishing owner of a boat captained by another man will be able to obtain free fish for home consumption. In times of plenty the fishermen are generous, but when less successful they may not have left enough for their own immediate families.

When the peak fishing period ends in late March or April the *praih moto* begin to dominate fish marketing in Mangkok. During the peak season most boats will land over $100 of fish per outing, and occasionally $200 or more. But in April some boats are able to land only $10 of fish in an outing and many arrive with nothing at all for sale. The *praih van* gradually withdraw, leaving the market to the *praih moto*. The larger, higher priced fish become conspicuous by their absence after March, leaving a few of the smaller, less expensive fish to be trapped in the nets. These are the fish that the *praih moto* find most easy to sell in the villages.

Each *praih moto* follows a regular circuit of villages, and his customers come to depend on him for their daily fish. These customers may require occasional credit for a day's purchase. The *praih moto* will probably grant this request; if he does not he might lose a customer besides the particular sale. But his capacity to give credit generally is limited by his small working capital and by the fact that he must pay cash for the fish he buys from the boat captains. The occupation is one that a man may move in and out of easily and quickly, and it would be unwise for a captain to sell his fish to the *praih moto* without immediate cash payment. This is especially so as the majority of the *praih moto* are not residents of Mangkok itself. Most are younger men who own small motor cycles and pick up this occupation as a sideline to other occupations such as rice farming or rubber tapping simply by adding a basket made by local tinsmiths to their motor cycles. A *praih moto* may be able to carry $20 of fish on his rounds, from which he may be able to realize a profit of $5–15. The profit margins of the *praih moto* are necessarily high due to his limited carrying capacity and his need to make enough money to maintain both his family and his motor cycle.

THE BEACH ECONOMY

As one enters the village of Mangkok, a number of shelters and sheds may be seen nestled among the coconut palms just above the high tide line. These structures, made with *nipah* thatch and either milled lumber or split bamboo siding, are rough and weathered looking and usually deserted. But when the *ikan bilis* and *udang baring* are in season, these shelters and sheds are hives of activity. It is here that many of the women of Mangkok work, and it is here that some of the most profitable business within the community occurs.

Mangkok and the surrounding villages of Penarek and Kuala Baru are advantageously situated to engage in the processing of *ikan bilis* and shrimp. To the north, there are no other villages along the shore for over 10 miles; to the south, there are only a few small and scattered villages until one reaches Merang, 12 miles away. Because the *ikan bilis* and small shrimp spoil very rapidly, they must be landed and processed as quickly as possible to receive a good price. Consequently, boats cannot return to their home villages or ports with their catch and must sell to processing sheds along the beach wherever they are fishing. On the West Coast, especially around Pangkor and Langkawi Islands, *ikan bilis* are processed on boats specially designed for this which follow the actual fishing boats. There are no such processing boats in the area of Mangkok, or for that matter on the East Coast, as far as the author is aware.

The small shrimp have a short local season of only one month. Some fishermen of Mangkok and other villages extend this season by following their migration down the coast as far as Kuala Trengganu. The *ikan bilis* season is longer, running from around March to September or October, when the seas begin to run heavy, but is variable within the year and from year to year. Local fishermen claim that the catch of both *ikan bilis* and *udang baring* is declining rapidly. Men catching the *udang baring* claim that previously they could fill a boat after only a few hours' work, and that a crew of 15 men working hard could land over 80 baskets (*raga*) in one day. In early 1978 the best catch recorded was 40 *raga*, but more often the catch would be only 10 or less. Villagers living along the coast also report that they used to be able to wade out into shallow water reddened by shrimp and using a scoop net gather enough of them to make their own *belacan*, a rather pungent but tasty and nutritious paste of shrimp mixed with salt. People still catch the *udang baring* with scoop nets, but the activity is more rewarding in entertainment than in food value. It would appear that the *udang baring* are being over-exploited both by local fishermen and by those operating larger, more powerful boats from Kuala Besut and other major fishing ports, who use trawl nets to pull relentlessly through the schools. The fishermen of Mangkok use a purse-seine instead.

Unlike the *udang baring*, *ikan bilis* is caught in deep water 5–10 miles from shore. To encircle a school of *ikan bilis* requires a larger net than that used for the *udang baring* and therefore larger boats—up to 50 feet or more and powered by 60 horsepower diesel engines. Though the net and other equipment used for catching the *udang baring* are expensive by local standards, the total cost of used equipment is in the region of $3,000. In contrast, to equip oneself to catch *ikan bilis* requires an investment perhaps fifteen times as great. The principle is the same in both cases: the purse-seine net is cast around the school of fish or shrimp and the bottom is closed by pulling in a rope that runs through brass rings at the bottom of the net while the top of the net is held up with plastic floats. In both cases a second boat is used to help haul in the net. In the case of fishing for *ikan bilis* there is often a third boat used for transporting the catch to shore for immediate processing. The one Chinese family in Mangkok owns such an '*ikan bilis* fleet' of three boats, but the boats are operated by fishermen from Fikri, a nearby village. This family owns and operates a processing facility, known as *bangsal bilis*, for the *ikan bilis* brought in by their own boats. The other processors (there are a total of seven in Mangkok) must either rely on other boats to bring their *ikan bilis* to them or, as is often the case, hire the boat of a local fisherman to go out to where the fleets are. A processor purchasing *ikan bilis* will pay a commission of $2 per box to the captain of such a boat for his services. This is an important source of income to local fishermen especially during periods of poor fishing.

In addition to *udang baring* and *ikan bilis*, various other species of fish and 'trash fish' are processed along the beach at Mangkok. The processing sheds are located along the beach above the high tide line for ease of access to the boats fishing up and down the coast. There is no need to use the river entrance to the village as the fishing season for this mix of marine life coincides with relatively calm seas and the boats can be brought right to the beach.

The processing itself varies, not only according to what needs to be processed but also the condition it is in. The simplest way of treating the *udang baring* is to spread the tiny shrimp on the mats of *kercut* in the hot sun to dry; if they are landed fresh they need no cooking or salt. A large area of beach is covered with overlapping mats on which the *udang baring* are spread and, depending on the heat of the sun, after perhaps 2 hours the shrimp are turned by giving a quick shake to each mat; in 3 or 4 hours on a hot day they will be ready to be bagged. Care must be taken to dry the shrimp adequately so that they do not rot in the jute bags, yet if they are too dry they will be brittle and turn to powder, lowering the quality and price. There is also the danger of a sudden squall or wind which could blow the tiny shrimp all over the beach; and a watch must be kept so that goats and chickens do not eat the drying shrimp.

Compared to *udang baring*, processing *ikan bilis* requires more equipment, labour, material inputs, and risk, and not incidentally may produce more profit. When the *ikan bilis* is landed, men carry them up the beach in boxes, dumping the fish into a basin of water for rinsing. A woman will then use a shallow basket of woven split bamboo to scoop the fish out, carrying it into the cooking shed where there are a number of large cast iron pots known as *kawah* which are shaped like a *wok*. There may be 2–8 *kawah* in a row, set roughly waist high in a foundation constructed of stone, clay and cement. Under each *kawah* is a large cavity for the wood fire which heats the mixture of fresh water and coarse salt in which the fish is cooked. The shallow bamboo basket containing the fish is submerged in the *kawah* using a bamboo lid weighted with a brick or rock; when the fish is cooked, the entire basket will rise despite the weighted lid. Each person in charge of cooking, who may be either male or female, will be operating 2–4 *kawah*, setting a basket in one and then removing the basket from another by sliding two poles underneath to lift and swing the steaming hot basket to the side. Another person, a woman, will carry the basket to the drying mats outside. Often when cooking is in full swing she will not have time to carry the baskets outside immediately, in which case they will be stacked temporarily to the side, and as time allows the fish will be carried out to the drying mats.

The amount of time needed to dry the *ikan bilis* is a function of time of day and the heat of the sun. Often, if the fish is landed in the middle of the morning there will be adequate time to dry and box it on the same day, otherwise it may need to be brought inside a shed for the night, and then spread to dry once again the next day. This increases the labour cost of processing and also the risk of breaking off the heads and tails of the small and delicate fish, lowering its quality and price. Increased handling also may be required if there is rain in the late afternoon, a common occurrence, or overcast skies. As with the *udang baring*, a sudden squall may send the fish flying all over the beach. The fish processor's helpers will assist in picking up as many as possible, but a major loss is always possible from a sudden turn of weather.

Unlike the *udang baring*, the price for *ikan bilis* is highly volatile. During the early part of 1978, whereas the price for *udang baring* was within a range of $10 of the median price of $115 per *pikul*, that for *ikan bilis* was more erratic, starting out at $295 per *pikul* in March and within one month dropping to below $200. A daily fluctuation of $20 per *pikul* was common.

Lacking adequate marketing information, the processors in

Mangkok were to a large extent at the mercy of the dealers from Kuala Trengganu, who came to Mangkok daily to buy dried *ikan bilis* and *udang baring*. There are four such dealers who visit Mangkok daily in their small vans. One of them works for himself, and the other three work for wages plus commissions from wholesale merchants in Kuala Trengganu. All the buyers are ethnic Chinese. They claim that there is no pricing agreement between them, and it would be difficult to prove otherwise. The processors in Mangkok, however, are certain that two and possibly three of them actively collaborate on pricing. Whether this is so or not, these dealers are in fact the primary source of regular market information available to the processors. They will advise the processor on the price at which he should purchase fresh fish or shrimp, but they do not guarantee to purchase his product at a set price for even the next day. Occasionally hard feelings arise as a result of this, and a processor will refuse to have further dealings with a particular dealer.

Irregular but less biased market information also is obtained when villagers themselves visit the urban centres of Kuala Trengganu or Kota Bharu. The fish buyers are particularly useful in this regard, and as the peak season for fresh fish tapers off some of these men use their vans for transporting dried fish and shrimp to wherever the price is highest. There is a risk involved in that prices change from day to day, and lacking telephone communications there is no means by which a fish processor may know what price he will receive until he arrives at the selling point. Moreover, unless he has a large amount of dried produce to sell, the price differential may not offset his transport costs. To hire a local van to Kuala Trengganu costs $40; to Kota Bharu the charge is $50. The risk to a processor marketing his own production is alleviated somewhat by the normal movement of people on personal visits and on other business, through whom a certain amount of information filters to the village, but it is an uncertain source both in terms of timing and accuracy. If a processor personally takes his product to sell and finds that the price in that locality has dropped, he can drive through as many small towns and villages as necessary, selling his output in small lots to shops and private individuals. Because it is time-consuming this is done infrequently, but the flexibility of the small vans is important in opening the option of marketing the dried products directly rather than solely through the merchants who come to Mangkok.

In 1978 the price for *udang baring* was higher than it had ever been and the demand was constant. As a consequence, marketing presented no difficulty, which in turn meant that the processor knew at what price he could buy and still make a profit. Drying *udang baring* is a simple matter, requiring only mats and baskets for drying and moving the shrimp, while the jute bags into which the dried shrimp are poured are provided by the wholesale purchaser. All the investment needed to enter this business are enough mats (perhaps $200 worth at $0.50 each) and a storage shed, which may cost well under $100 even if bamboo, which must be purchased in a village upriver, is used. More important, however, is an assured supply of *udang baring*, and this usually comes either through ownership of a pair of boats and the net or through kinship or other close relationship between the owner of the boats and net and the processor. In Mangkok there were two sets of nets for *udang baring* operating in early 1978; in one case the owner did the processing himself at his own *bangsal bilis*, while in the other, the owner had an agreement to sell his *udang baring* to his brother-in-law. The other processors also made some purchases, but on a more irregular basis.

As with *udang baring*, personal contacts are important when purchasing *ikan bilis*, but to a lesser extent. The *ikan bilis* fishermen are not necessarily local men, and there is a greater scope for purely economic relationships, though these relationships often become regularized. The buyer encourages repeated sales by offering tea and snacks to the fishermen, and some buyers give a small cash gratuity to the captains in the form of a commission per box of *ikan bilis* or per basket of *udang baring*. These quasi-economic and quasi-personal relationships are not as permanent as those based on ownership or kinship, but they are nonetheless significant and mutually beneficial. A processor who knows a certain captain's boat is operating offshore can hire a local fishing boat to take him out there, knowing that his trip will be rewarded with a purchase if any fish have been caught. A regular outlet for his catch is also important to the captain, especially when the catch is made in the middle of the day or in the late afternoon, or if the catch of *ikan bilis* is mixed heavily with other small fish of lower value, or if for any other reason the catch is of questionable quality. The captain knows that his buyer will take this catch at a reasonable price despite the added inconvenience or risk involved, because the buyer wants to maintain the relationship. The buyer, for his part, knows that he can approach the captain later if he has suffered a loss and ask for a discount on his next purchase.

One processor of *udang baring* bought two purchases worth $780 over a six-day period. His labour expenses were $84, and included carrying the shrimp from the beach to the drying area, spreading them on the mats, and finally packing them into the bags. He sold the shrimp in a series of daily transactions during this period for a total of $1,006.50, giving him a profit of less than $150.

While $150 over six days certainly is not a low income, especially when compared with the total income earned by the people who did the work, the profit is paltry compared to what he was able to earn from processing *ikan bilis* during the same six-day period.

In mid-March 1978 this man bought three catches of *ikan bilis* valued at a total of $2,105 at prices ranging from $55 to $60 per box, each yielding approximately 30 *kati* (almost 40 lb.) of dry *ikan bilis* depending on the proportion of less valuable fish caught at the same time. The labour costs for processing *ikan bilis* include:

1. Going out to sea in a small local fishing boat to buy the *ikan bilis*;
2. Carrying the fish from the beach to the cooking shed;
3. Fetching water for rinsing and water for cooking the fish;
4. Rinsing;
5. Cooking;
6. Spreading and drying;
7. Packing the *ikan bilis* into cardboard boxes.

Additional costs associated with processing *ikan bilis* include the purchase of firewood for cooking, salt, cardboard boxes for packing the fish, and the wear and tear on the equipment used in cooking; excluding this last cost, and depreciation for the drying mats, sheds and other paraphernalia, the costs for processing work out to approximately $25 per *pikul* of dried *ikan bilis*.

The three purchases noted above ($2,105) produced 12.34 *pikul* (about 1,645 lb.), giving a figure of $308.50 for total processing expenses. Total costs were, then, $2,413.50. The *ikan bilis* was sold over a period of six days in five separate transactions, beginning at $270 and then falling to $160 per *pikul*, for a total income of $3,247.15. The processor earned a net profit of over $830 on a total investment of just over $2,400 in a period of six days.

During this period the fish processor and his wife earned a profit of nearly $1,000 while the people who worked for them earned a total of $392.50. An average of six women worked daily during this period. Daily wages of better than $10 are quite high for such casual labour, but then so is the profit earned by the family owning the *bangsal bilis*. When it was obliquely suggested to the couple who owned the *bangsal bilis* (with whom the author has been on good terms) that their income was disproportionately high in relation to that of their workers, they declined to agree, citing the capital cost of establishing the *bangsal bilis*, the depreciation of this asset, the risk involved in their enterprise, and the managerial and technical expertise involved.

If a family can earn a profit of $1,000 for six days' work, why have not more families gone into this business? One explanation would be the cost of setting up a *bangsal bilis* in the first place. Few families have the requisite $3,000 in liquid capital. But this can be in part remedied by joining the resources (and labour) of two or more families in a partnership arrangement. In fact, this was done during the period of field-work when two families joined to operate a small *bangsal bilis*, buying the sheds and equipment owned by another man who, after a divorce, had left the village. It has been seen that when the profitability of the *pukat tansi* was established a great deal of money was quickly mobilized and invested in this gear, often in the form of partnerships. Capital needs certainly are a factor, but alone they cannot be taken as limiting the participation of larger numbers of families in fish drying and processing.

The most important factor would seem to be the irregular nature of this enterprise. A profit of $1,000 for six days of work is highly unusual. In other transactions this couple suffered one small loss and some small profits. The large profit came early in the season while the price of dried *ikan bilis* was still high, and though they bought at a price higher than had prevailed during the previous year the margin of profit was even higher. Moreover, the weather was fine during that period, and there was no need for excessive handling.

Processing of *ikan bilis* and shrimp is a highly seasonal activity. Due to the short length of time spent in this community, the author was unable to collect data for an entire year. Based on information gathered from residents of Mangkok, both processors and non-processors, one has the impression that there are both seasonal and annual fluctuations in activity and in profits and losses. The *udang baring* season is extremely short, running from mid-February until the end of March. The *ikan bilis* season also begins in mid- or late February, with apparently a slow season beginning in mid-April or May parallel to and no doubt caused by the same factors that affect the other fishing operations off the coast at Mangkok; only in August or September will the *ikan bilis* fishing pick up once again, and sometimes the season will be meagre throughout the year.

Another factor that may serve to discourage wider participation in processing operations is that they entail considerable and regular dealings with hard and occasionally sharp dealers; those based in Kuala Trengganu are Chinese, while those in Kota Bharu are mostly Malays. On the basis of the experience of processors from Mangkok there is at least as much sharp trading and probably more outright dishonesty (in the form of non-payment for delivered goods) from these Malay merchants than from their Chinese counterparts. It is beyond the scope of this study to give an in-depth analysis of the dynamics between racial and economic antagonisms.

But it certainly can be noted that no one ethnic group has a monopoly on questionable business practices. In fact, many of the local processors of Mangkok prefer to deal with the Chinese, who they know will pay them something, rather than with Malay dealers who will promise a higher price but delay payment, perhaps indefinitely.

The significant point for the villagers of Mangkok who may be interested in earning some of the profits from processing dried fish and shrimp is that yet another factor of uncertainty is added to the uncertainties of weather and seasonal and annual fluctuations in catch. Uncertainty and risk are associated with profit and may make the investment in processing facilities unattractive. The same investment will provide a fisherman with a used boat and net with which, it may be reasonably expected, fish could be caught and a living earned. This boat and net are mobile and can follow the seasonal migrations of fish; the boat itself also can be hired out for a number of uses not directly related to fishing, and also serves as a utility vehicle for some family needs. Processing facilities, on the other hand, are more functionally specific, immobile, and depreciate rapidly.

There are, then, serious disincentives for investment in processing facilities for *ikan bilis* and shrimp, and this has limited the number of *bangsal bilis*. It is clear that the families which own and operate *bangsal bilis* make a good living by local standards largely on the basis of these operations. Their homes are larger than average, with more glass windows; but other than this, their consumption patterns are not significantly different from that of their neighbours.

ECONOMIC ROLES OF WOMEN IN MANGKOK

Most families in Mangkok face budgeting difficulties due to the seasonality of fishing and other employment. During the monsoon there may be some limited cash income from the weaving of *kercut* mats, or rice may be harvested. Life does not come to a halt with the rains and stormy seas or with the poor fishing in the middle of the year, and provision must be made for the proverbial rainy day. Accumulating a surplus of rice and cash to tide a family through the monsoon, postponing all expenses not related to immediate and necessary consumption, establishing a credit source from a local man of relative wealth, or borrowing from the captain of a boat or the buyer of the boat's fish—all are logical strategies for seeing a family through periods of limited income.

The competence of rural Malay women in controlling their

families' incomes is amply shown by the financial solvency of the vast majority in an economy which alternates plenty with want. The significance of female roles in East Coast rural Malay society lies in large part in this stabilizing influence. Their influence in a fishing community such as Mangkok is indirect. Unlike conditions reported by Raymond Firth (1966) 40 years previously, and unlike the situation in Malay fishing villages of Southern Thailand 20 years ago (Fraser, 1960), women in Mangkok are not actively involved in the marketing of fish. Neither are they directly involved in fishing or the maintenance of boats and nets. Their productive roles fairly may be seen as of secondary importance to the local fishing industry, and to most households as well. There were 61 households which reported that the women did not seek active employment such as at the various *bangsal bilis*, while 59 women from 57 households were so employed. These figures no doubt vary somewhat from year to year, but they do show the relative lack of opportunity available to women in Mangkok. Of course, it would be a gross misrepresentation to say that women of 61 households are unemployed. They contribute in numerous ways, from planting rice to weaving mats and baskets, but what they do not do is earn regular cash incomes, and what cash they do earn is likely to be in small amounts. The same is true of those women who work at the *bangsal bilis*; during all but the busiest times they may earn only $2 or $3 per day, and that in itself is irregular.

Though women are productively peripheral, their economic dominance is almost complete. As noted above, wives and mothers gain control over the proceeds of the catch. A fisherman may keep a few dollars for his personal expenditure, but once that has been spent he must then ask his wife or mother to replenish his pocket. Men are deemed to be spendthrifts who would squander their earnings on coffee and cigarettes. When a family is considering buying a boat or a net the decision often is strongly influenced by the wife. Women control the finances of an overwhelming majority of households in Mangkok; less than ten exceptions were known to local informants. The exceptions to this rule were well known and frequently they were the object of public discussion, often disapproving. It was usually the wife who would make known the peculiarities of a husband who attempted to control the family purse-strings, or who held back from his wife more than normal pocket-money; she would bring the matter to public attention in order to secure moral support for her position. Not only did this tend to embarrass the husband, but if the disagreement resulted in divorce this man probably would find it difficult to remarry a local woman because of his 'reputation'.

In both the East Coast communities studied, Gong Guncil and

Mangkok, women control the family budgets and share with their husbands the responsibility of making decisions. In Gong Guncil the women not only play an active role in deciding which varieties to plant and how much fertilizers they can afford to use, they provide at least half of the labour required for rice cultivation. The women in Mangkok are not directly involved in the labour of fishing, but they control family finances and often have a decisive influence on whether or not to make investments in boats and nets. It follows that government officers working with rice farmers and fishermen need to take into consideration the influence of women when attempting to encourage the adoption of new production technologies.

Unlike their sisters on the East Coast of Peninsular Malaysia, the women of the West Coast community of Kampung Dusun do not control family finances. The reasons for this difference will be discussed in the following chapter.

5 Kampung Dusun: A Smallholder Rubber Tapping Community in Kedah

THE SETTING

THE forty-five households of Kampung Dusun reside in the hilly interior of Kedah, in the district of Sik, on the West Coast of Peninsular Malaysia. The total population studied is 237, or an average of 5.3 per household. Included in the study area are six households within a village known as Kampung Mandul. This section of Kampung Mandul is contiguous with Kampung Dusun, and its residents are closely related by ties of kinship to the people of Kampung Dusun. Though the number of households surveyed is only one-third the number surveyed in the other two communities studied, the author's long experience in the district of Sik allows for broader understanding than would otherwise be possible from such a small sample (Bailey, 1976).

The primary economic activity of Sik, and of Kampung Dusun, is the production of rubber, a crop well suited to the district's hilly terrain. Almost three-quarters of the district's land area of 636 square miles is in Forest Reserve, accessible only by logging roads and foot paths. Within this Reserve are mountains approaching elevations of 3,000 feet, but for the most part rubber is planted on privately owned land at elevations of well below 1,000 feet. Interspersed between the hills that dominate the terrain are narrow river valleys suitable for wet rice cultivation. Near the town of Sik, several hundred acres of rice land are served by a small irrigation system which supports double-cropping, and in some areas year-round springs which feed narrow stream valleys allow double-cropping. In Kampung Dusun itself an earth dam structurally supported by hardwood posts provides water for double-cropping a small field of 20 acres; another field of comparable size lacks adequate water and supports only a single rain-fed rice crop each year. Most of the rice land in Sik District is dependent on rainfall and is planted once a year.

Kedah lies in a rain shadow caused by a line of mountains which runs down the centre of Peninsular Malaysia. The north-east monsoon brings heavy rains to the rice farmers and fishermen of Trengganu but little to Kedah, which experiences an annual drought lasting as long as three months during which many village wells dry up and rubber trees lose most of their leaves. This 'wintering effect' results in markedly lower production of latex during the months of January, February, and March.

Many of Sik District's inhabitants, including those of Kampung Dusun, are descended from refugees from Pattani during the 1830s, a period of warfare between Pattani and the Kingdom of Siam. The flow of immigrants from Pattani has continued into the twentieth century, and kinsmen still frequently make visits across the border. During the nineteenth century Sik District was sparsely populated and new settlers had little difficulty finding unoccupied land on which to live and farm. In the absence of formal land titles, the presence of fruit trees, especially *durian*, in the middle of an area of jungle was sufficient to prove ownership by the family who had the locally recognized right to harvest such fruits. Similarly, ownership of rice land was based on previous and continuous usage.

During this period of Sik's history, subsistence production of wet rice dominated the economy, and the collection of various forest products for export down-river provided for the minimal import needs of the area. The value of hilly land was limited to the raising of livestock and the planting of fruit trees.

Settlements in the nineteenth century tended to cluster around the base of the hills adjoining the rice fields, and this pattern remains the most common today. Kampung Dusun follows this general settlement pattern, as seen in Map 4. One obvious reason for this is availability of well water, which, as noted, is a major seasonal problem. It is more convenient to build houses bordering the rice fields rather than further up the hill as the latter would necessitate either digging deep wells or physically carrying water up to the houses. In late 1977 piped water was provided to the village from the town of Sik, one mile away. Since the main pipe was laid for convenience to existing houses, and because the cost of running pipe to future houses is based on a per foot charge, it is unlikely that piped water supplies will seriously alter settlement patterns.

Near most houses is found a wide assortment of fruit trees which serve to shade and cool the surrounding area. In some cases the number and value of these fruit trees is considerable; in others, there are just enough trees to provide for the family's consumption. It is also common to find open spaces next to many homes. This land occasionally is planted with vegetables or cash crops such as

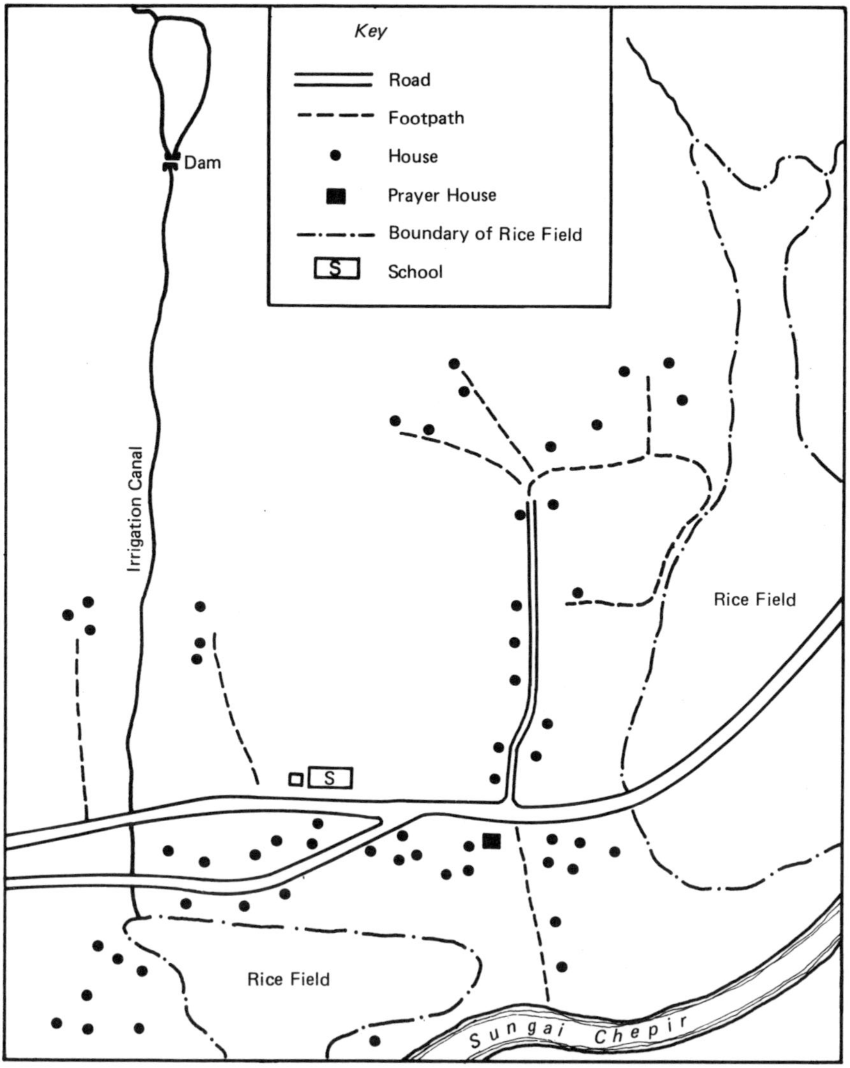

Map 4: Kampung Dusun

tobacco or groundnuts, but more commonly is grazed by livestock.

The houses in Kampung Dusun appear on the whole to be more substantial than those of Gong Guncil or Mangkok, the two communities studied in Besut, Trengganu. Virtually all the houses in Kampung Dusun are built of lumber, and galvanized metal roofs are equally common. Like Malay houses elsewhere, those in Kampung Dusun (and in Sik District generally) are raised off the ground on hardwood posts measuring 6 inches × 6 inches or thicker. Frequently, houses in Sik District are raised much higher than they are in Besut District, high enough to allow for the space under the houses to be used for work and leisure. Some families have laid concrete floors and enclosed part of this area for use as a kitchen and/or rest area; it is the coolest spot during the day.

In the context of rural Malay society, these are signs of prosperity, which are further confirmed by the presence in this village of 10 motor cycles and 2 television sets. Two cars owned by its residents are used for commercial purposes.

The relatively substantial houses of Kampung Dusun reflect a periodic prosperity brought by sudden high prices in the world rubber market. During such times rubber producers enjoy high earnings, and one of the first calls on these earnings is the construction or expansion of the family's home, though a sudden drop in the market price may force a family to delay completion of construction for years. Periodic cycles of prosperity and penury are the hallmark of an economy based on rubber production, and the relatively fine houses should be seen as major investments for the future (including future generations) which are made whenever the price of rubber permits.

The stands of rubber are located behind the houses and further up the hills. Occasionally some of this higher land is planted with fruit trees or various other crops for home consumption or sale. There also is a small amount of land that apparently is unproductive, usually because the owner is either too old or otherwise unable to cultivate the land. Such land will provide pasture for livestock and, unless it is fenced, becomes common grazing ground. Similarly, the rubber stands themselves provide important pasture, unless (as is often the case) the land is choked with inedible brush. Livestock is allowed to roam freely during the day in search of food and only brought home at night.

The main danger of allowing livestock to roam freely is that the animals may wander into the town of Sik. In the early 1970s the District Officer of Sik began enforcing a restriction on livestock within the town, subjecting the owners of errant animals to a fine. Within the village itself, allowing cattle to roam freely means that rice fields, household gardens, cash crops, or young fruit trees must be carefully fenced to prevent depredation.

The town of Sik is the administrative centre of Sik District. It is a small town of about 2,000 people which stretches perhaps one-quarter mile along the main road. Parallel to this road is a small river, the Sungai Chepir, on the other side of which are several shops and the weekly market. On the hill behind the town are various government offices, including the District Office, the Post Office, various other government agencies, an open building for weekly court hearings, and a Police Station, as well as the housing provided for many of the government officers who work in these offices. Further up the road from Sik, in the direction of Kampung Dusun, is a government Health Clinic which is being expanded into a District Hospital; beyond this is a Chinese-medium primary school and the district's secondary school, first opened in the mid-1960s. Another primary school is located within Kampung Dusun itself. In 1968, when the author first arrived in the village, this was an English-medium school, but by the mid-1970s the Malay language had been adopted in accordance with the national education policy.

There is a housing shortage in and around the town, primarily due to the large number of government employees who are now sent to Sik's offices and schools. Five families in Kampung Dusun have either built small rental houses adjacent to their own or expanded their homes to include separate living areas which can be rented out. The rents charged are substantially lower than in the town of Sik, and since piped water and electricity are available, there is a ready market for such lodgings. This provides a welcome source of income for the owners. A small village house can be rented for $40 per month.

The proximity of the town of Sik has other important consequences for the residents of Kampung Dusun. Access to government offices and services is a matter of a short walk or bicycle ride; the daily and weekly markets and the sundry goods and other shops in town are similarly convenient. Several men of Kampung Dusun are employed in the shops of licensed rubber dealers or as butchers and meat sellers at both the daily and weekly markets.

At the market fresh fish and vegetables are available on a daily basis, and meat is sold at least three times a week including Tuesday, the day of the weekly market. The Tuesday Market (*Pekan Selasa*) attracts merchants from a wide area who sell a broad range of goods including clothing, cloth, tools, kitchen utensils, spices, fruits, and other foodstuffs. There are also several stalls which serve beverages and local delicacies to refresh buyers and sellers.

ECONOMIC ROLES OF MEN AND WOMEN

DIFFERENCES AMONG RURAL MALAYS

The Tuesday Market attracts villagers from the entire district of Sik, but most of the buyers and sellers are men. On the East Coast women dominate the kind of small-scale trading represented by the Tuesday Market, and women also do the most of the family shopping. In every market-place this writer has visited on the East Coast women outnumber men, both in buying and selling; in Sik, however, women are conspicuous by their relative absence from the market-place.

Three factors may explain this phenomenon. On the West Coast, non-Malay merchants dominate much of the wholesale and retail trade, and most of these Chinese and Indian merchants are men. Malay traders also tend to be male, possibly because to obtain their goods they must deal with non-Malay men. The economic dominance of non-Malays is less complete on the East Coast, and the economy is more rural in nature compared to the more developed West Coast.

A second factor which may help to explain the difference between women of the East and West Coasts is subcultural variation between the Malays themselves. Those in the West Coast have been more directly influenced by Arab and Indian Muslims whose orthodoxy includes restrictions on the work and movement of women beyond the household. The Malay women of Sik District are not totally house-bound and are economically active within the village, but only infrequently do they venture beyond the village itself; even when walking to the weekly market in the town they typically go in groups. Women are much more sheltered in Sik District than in Besut District and are not encouraged to seek employment outside of the home village. Only two women from Kampung Dusun are employed outside the immediate village, as sales agents for a cloth merchant, but their husbands provide transport for them on the back of their motor cycles when they travel outside the village.

The third factor is related to certain constraints in the production of rubber. Many families in Kampung Dusun tap rubber 5 miles or more from home; one man travels by motor cycle to tap a planting 12 miles away. As noted, women generally are not encouraged to work far from home, especially if this means working in the physical isolation of a stand of rubber which may be heavily overgrown by brush. Cases of rape are not common, but neither are they unknown in the area, and newspaper reports indicate that throughout the country women working alone in a stand of rubber are vulnerable. In some cases husband and wife may tap together on land they own or share-crop away from the home village; more often, however, the amount of land worked can be managed by one person, which almost invariably will be, and for Kampung Dusun invariably is, the husband.

Women more frequently tap rubber within the immediate vicinity of the home village, but the amount of available land even for share-cropping is limited. Among the 27 families of Kampung Dusun who tap rubber, the women of 10 families do not tap, their economic roles being restricted to the home and, if the family plants some rice, to its rice lands. In some cases where the husband taps rubber in distant villages, the wife may tap on land closer to home. Though she may be assisted by her children, women typically tap fewer trees and collect less rubber than their husbands. In part this may be explained by the need to attend to domestic chores, including cooking the main midday meal and caring for children, and in part by the physical strength necessary to collect, process and transport large quantities of rubber. Moreover, much of the rubber stands in the vicinity of the village consists of older, less productive trees, many planted prior to World War II, and these are the trees most women tap.

Among the 27 families in Kampung Dusun who tap rubber there are 38 active tappers: 21 men and 17 women. In only 5 cases do husband and wife tap together; in 6 other cases both husband and wife tap but on separate parcels of land, and in 6 more, only the women tap. With one exception (an elderly husband), their husbands are employed full-time outside the village as watchmen, taxi drivers, or employees of a licensed rubber dealer.

Not included in these figures are the children who may assist their parents. Their assistance will vary depending on whether school is in session or, in the case of girls, according to the need for them to help care for younger siblings, cook meals, or attend to other domestic chores. Boys have less of these duties, but even after the completion of their schooling they may or may not contribute to the production of rubber, depending on the economic standing of their family. There seems to be a period during which male adolescent Malays become rather frivolous and irresponsible, when they prefer to 'hang out' with their contemporaries. This is not a universal phenomenon among Malays, but seems to be most common among offspring of relatively wealthy families; there are a number of families in this village whose adolescent sons fit this description. The boys refer to themselves as a '*geng*' and are given considerable freedom of movement, including periodic visits to major towns in the area. Their sisters are much more closely watched and chaperoned; virtue and a good reputation are important considerations when the family of a prospective groom comes to negotiate the dowry (*mas kahwin*) to be paid to the bride and her family.

Social prestige accrues to a family which can afford to remove from remunerative employment these potentially productive members. A wife who need not work, a son who can be indulged, and a daughter who can be protected from the rigours of work in the hot sun while being trained in the domestic arts, are hallmarks of a prosperous family. To some extent the same is true of the two communities studied in Besut District, but there the women are much more active in productive activities. The wives and children of fishermen are economically active, especially adolescent sons who go to sea and earn the share of a man. Few rice farming families can afford the luxury of unproductive women or children. The seasonal demands of rice cultivation dictate full mobilization of a family's labour.

DOMINANCE OF MEN IN RUBBER ECONOMY

In the production of rubber there is no sudden seasonal demand for labour and often, because of the limited size of a family's holdings, one tapper is sufficient; for reasons suggested above, this tapper often will be the husband. In those cases where both husband and wife tap or where only the wife taps, the marketing of their product will be carried out by the husband or an older son. Interviews with rubber dealers in the town of Sik and throughout Sik District indicate that only 5–10 per cent of those who sell rubber in their shops are women, and personal observation confirms this fact.

One reason why men dominate the marketing of rubber is the accumulated weight of several days' or a week's tapping which must be tied on to the back of a bicycle. This task is physically taxing and more easily managed by men. It is also significant that rubber dealers' shops are alien to women in the same way that coffee shops are predominantly male preserves: women may enter but do so hesitantly, conclude their business and depart; men, on the other hand, will hang around, drinking coffee or tea, discussing recent changes in the market, and greeting friends from other villages who also are in town to sell rubber.

Perhaps the most important difference in the economic roles of men on the East and West Coasts is in their control of family finances. The fishermen of Mangkok, for example, earned most of the income for most families, but with very few exceptions this income was handed over to their wives or, if unmarried, to their mothers. In Gong Guncil the men transported their rice to the rice dealers and received cash from the sale, but this income also was turned over to the women of the household for safekeeping. In Kampung Dusun, by way of contrast, the men control the family finances. There are a few exceptions to this rule, but they are based on the particular personalities of the men involved and serve to prove rather than disprove the rule. After selling their rubber in the town of Sik, the men purchase fish, vegetables, and other needs of the family. It is common for men to give their wives small amounts of money for the purchase of certain daily necessities that may be obtained in the small shop within the village, but major purchases almost always are made by men while in town. Since men regularly visit town anyway, it is logical and more efficient for them to do the marketing. The reason given by the men of Kampung Dusun is more basic than this: they consider that they are both guardians of the family and the primary income earners, and that it is their duty and their right to manage family finances.

PROBLEMS OF SMALLHOLDER PRODUCTIVITY

ESTATES AND SMALLHOLDINGS

Rubber production in Malaysia is divided almost equally between estates and smallholdings, the latter being defined as holdings of less than 100 acres. Though the approximately 2,700,000 acres of rubber smallholdings exceeds the 1,500,000 acres of estate holdings, it was only after 1972 that smallholders produced more rubber than estates (Rubber Industry Smallholders Development Authority, 1974). The productivity of the estate sector substantially exceeds that of the smallholding sector, primarily because it is in a position to take advantage of research carried out by the Rubber Research Institute of Malaysia (RRIM), especially the development of higher-yielding varieties. Estate managers have ready access to research reports published by the RRIM, which until recently were mainly in English. Due to their large size and capital resources, estates are able to replace older, less productive trees; by staggering their replanting schedule, the seven years it takes to clear land and bring newly planted trees into production presents relatively few problems.

During the colonial period, government policy actively discouraged smallholders from planting rubber and competing with estates (Lim, 1977; Rudner, 1975), and research efforts were explicitly directed towards the needs of the estate sector. Only after World War II were serious efforts made to apply research results to smallholders through the extension service of the RRIM. This function now is performed by the Rubber Industry Smallholders Development Authority, established in 1973. RISDA's field staff are among the most conscientious of government officials working in the rural areas. Yet though greater attention is now being focused on the particular problems of smallholders, these are so severe that it is unlikely that smallholdings will achieve the same level of productivity as the estate sector in the foreseeable future.

RUBBER REPLANTING SCHEME

The most important factor limiting productivity of smallholders is the continued tapping of trees whose yields are limited both by age and genetic potential. This in turn is related directly to the limited acreage of most smallholders, who can ill afford to remove even a small portion of their land from production for replanting. Though the definition of smallholder includes any holding of less than 100 acres, the vast majority of the approximately half a million smallholders own less than 10 acres, and nearly two-thirds own less than 5 acres (Pee and Ani bin Arope, 1976). For families dependent upon such limited acreages for their primary source of income, the felling of rubber trees, however old or unproductive, on even a minor portion of their land, means a loss of income that threatens an already precarious existence.

Replanting grants are available to assist smallholders willing to cut down older trees and plant more productive varieties. These grants, funded by a cess on rubber exported from Malaysia, are currently administered by RISDA. In June 1978 (shortly before the national elections held in July) the replanting grants were increased from $900 to $1,200 per acre. This sum is paid out at intervals, after deducting the cost of chemical fertilizers and planting materials, only after inspection by officials of RISDA to ensure proper maintenance of the new crop.

Replanting grants are designed to cover the expense of replanting, which is primarily the cost of labour to clear and prepare the land for planting, and to ensure weed-free maintenance of the newly planted stand of rubber. For the smallholder family which does this work on its own, the replanting grant provides some income until the new trees are in production. The work is strenuous but the return in increased productivity is substantial, often more than double the yield of the older, less productive rubber trees. During the first few years after clearing and replanting, the land may be intercropped with hill rice or other cash crops including pineapple, banana, ginger and cassava, which simultaneously serves to control weeds and to supplement the family's income. Production credit for cash crops is available through RISDA, the Department of Agriculture, and local Farmers' Cooperatives.

If a family is unable to do the work itself, e.g. due to age, infirmity, or conflicting occupations, it may hire someone else to do it. Some villagers specialize in this work and receive for their efforts the annual cash disbursements of the replanting grant. Usually those hired for clearing, replanting, and maintaining a parcel of land also have the right to plant and sell short-term cash crops, a feature which makes such employment especially attractive to landless families.

Although nationwide 63 per cent of individually owned smallholdings have been planted with improved varieties since the early

1950s (Pee and Ani bin Arope, 1976), this proportion includes material which may be only marginally more productive than the original varieties (Selvadurai, 1977). Only in the 1970s with the introduction of bud-grafted clones has the replanting programme led to major increases in smallholder productivity. Moreover, since the productive life of a rubber tree is limited to about 20 years, some of the replanted acreage is due for further replanting.

It is estimated by local RISDA officers and residents that less than one-quarter of Sik District's rubber land has been planted with high-yielding bud-grafted clones. Of the 190.5 *relong* (one *relong* is equal to seven-tenths of an acre) of rubber land owned by residents of Kampung Dusun, by 1978 only 5 *relong* of bud-grafted trees were in production; another 26.5 *relong* had been replanted but were still immature. Thus of the land owned by residents of the study area, only 16.5 per cent has been replanted with bud-grafted trees.

CONSTRAINTS TO REPLANTING

Now that replanting materials are significantly more productive, it is likely that the pace of replanting in the smallholder sector will increase. But there are a number of constraints which will limit full participation. Even with the replanting grant and the possibility of earning income by planting cash crops, many families are not in a position to remove from immediate production any part of their limited holdings of rubber. The first payment of a replanting grant is made only after successful completion of cutting and clearing, which takes at least several months. There will be a period, then, of several months before the first payment of the grant is made, and not all families are equally willing or able to limit their income for this length of time. Income from the cultivation of cash crops planted on the cleared land will come only after their harvest, usually a year or more later.

One alternative for a family owning limited acreage is to cut down part of the old stand, continue tapping the other part, and if possible enter into a share-cropping agreement with another landowner. Work on the land being replanted can be managed in the afternoons and during days when tapping is impossible due to the weather or the season. This is perhaps the most common manner in which smallholding families of limited means manage to replant their land. When the replanted trees are productive, the remainder of their land may be cleared and replanted as well.

This may be a workable strategy for a family in good health during its peak productive years. But for a couple in their fifties or sixties whose sons and daughters are otherwise or elsewhere employed and whose sole source of income is derived from a few *relong* of old rubber trees, replanting does not present such an attractive option. The strenuous work involved in replanting and the long interval before replanted land is back in production are strong factors inhibiting participation of such families in replanting schemes. Though it is possible to hire someone else to do the work, for a family of limited means this is not really a viable alternative. Replanting of such land is likely to be delayed until it is inherited by the succeeding generation.

Occasional squabbles may occur when several heirs inherit or claim a small parcel of land, which may delay its registration in the name of the new owner or owners. Until the land is registered, no replanting grant can be processed. If the inheritance is too small to support the several claimants, one heir may seek to buy out the others' shares. Alternatively, one or two heirs may tap the land and share the proceeds with the others in a modified share-cropping arrangement, or the entire parcel may be share-cropped by another family and the proceeds divided among the heirs.

Once legal ownership is established, the heir or heirs decide whether or not to replant. If the parcel is owned by several heirs, any decision will have to be made jointly. Unless all are equally interested in replanting, and unless they are able to agree on who should do the work, replanting may be delayed or neglected altogether. Similarly, any family tapping rubber land for which they do not have clear title will be unable to qualify for a replanting grant. Some families have been tapping rubber planted on State land for two generations, but because they do not have legal title to this land they are not eligible for replanting assistance.

The yield that may be expected from either older unselected rubber varieties or new clonal varieties such as RRIM 600 (the variety most commonly used for replanting in Sik District) will vary according to a number of factors, including soil fertility, prevalence of diseases, weather and rainfall patterns, and finally cultivation, fertilizer application and tapping practices.

It is estimated that unimproved rubber varieties produce approximately 500 lb. of dry rubber per acre, while a bud-grafted clone variety such as RRIM 600 may produce 1,800–2,000 lb. per acre (Williams, 1975; Selvadurai, 1977; Pee and Ani bin Arope, 1976; Haji Mohd. Johar bin Mohd. Rashid and Abdul Jalil bin Haji Yusof, 1976). These latter figures, however, were produced during the RRIM's trials and may not be replicable on smallholdings. Though supervision by RISDA during the replanting period assures proper management for the initial years, past experience indicates that the standard of field maintenance and the level of fertilizer application may be below optimal once this supervision ceases. Even the estate yields of 1,507 lb. is 15 per cent below the RRIM's trial yield of 1,772 lb. per acre for RRIM 600 (Pee and Ani bin Arope, 1976). Under these conditions it seems reasonable to discount the yield potential of 2,000 lb. per acre. To what extent yield potential will suffer under smallholder conditions must remain conjecture at this point as there are no available data, but the point is important, as actual performance under smallholder conditions will determine the degree of acceptance of the new clones.

Though the yield potential of RRIM 600 is substantial, maximum yields will not be obtained until perhaps the fifth year of tapping. During the RRIM trials, the first year of tapping yielded only 620 lb. per acre; the second, third, and fourth years yielded 1,070, 1,380, and 1,600 lb. per acre respectively (Haji Mohd. Johar bin Mohd. Rashid and Abdul Jalil bin Haji Yusof, 1976). Only in the fifth year did yields reach 2,060 lb. per acre. This means that in addition to seven years of lost production while waiting for the newly planted rubber to mature, the first year's yield is not markedly higher than that of the original unselected varieties.

If it is assumed that an existing stand of rubber produces 500 lb. per acre, there will be 3,500 lb. of lost production while waiting for the replanted rubber to mature, and some time will elapse before this lost production is recovered. In Table 5.1 a one-acre holding of an unimproved variety yeilding a constant 500 lb. per acre is compared to some possible yields from RRIM 600 based on 100 per cent, 80 per cent, and 60 per cent of the RRIM's experimental results.

Table 5.1 assumes that the older trees would continue to produce at the level of 500 lb. per acre, which may not be true in the case of very old trees, and that the productivity of RRIM 600 remains stable after 5 years (for which there are no available data). It also assumes that smallholder management practices are substantially inferior to that of the estates and RRIM experimental stations, though this may not be true in all cases; and that replanted trees will come into production after 7 years (that is, the beginning of the eighth year) from the time the original trees were cut down. Under estate conditions this time may be reduced by as much as a year, and the RRIM is experimenting with new varieties which will produce after only 4 or 5 years. Given present practices and materials, 7 full years seems a reasonable average for smallholders, though there will be some variation in either direction. Not considered in Table 5.1 is the income derived from the replanting grant itself or the production and sale of cash crops on the cleared land. Finally, the significance of lost production will depend on the price of rubber during this period. If the price has been high the relative loss in income will be greater than if the price levels generally were low.

TABLE 5.1

COMPARISON OF YIELD OF DRY RUBBER FOR
OLD RUBBER STANDS AND REPLANTED RUBBER STANDS
(lb./acre)

	Old Stand Production		*Replanted Stands of RRIM 600 at Varying Percentages of Trial Yields*					
			60%		*80%*		*100%*	
Year	*Annual*	*Cum.*	*Annual*	*Cum.*	*Annual*	*Cum.*	*Annual*	*Cum.*
1	500	500	–	–	–	–	–	–
2	500	1,000	–	–	–	–	–	–
3	500	1,500	–	–	–	–	–	–
4	500	2,000	–	–	–	–	–	–
5	500	2,500	–	–	–	–	–	–
6	500	3,000	–	–	–	–	–	–
7	500	3,500	–	–	–	–	–	–
8	500	4,000	372	372	496	496	620	620
9	500	4,500	642	1,014	856	1,352	1,070	1,690
10	500	5,000	828	1,842	1,104	2,456	1,380	3,070
11	500	5,500	960	2,802	1,280	3,736	1,600	4,670
12	500	6,000	1,236	4,038	1,648	5,384	2,060	6,730
13	500	6,500	1,236	5,274	1,648	7,032	2,060	8,790
14	500	7,000	1,236	6,510	1,648	8,680	2,060	10,850
15	500	7,500	1,236	7,746	1,648	10,328	2,060	12,910

Note: Figures underlined indicate approximate break-even point compared to unreplanted land.
Cum. = Cumulative

Despite these caveats, Table 5.1 is of more than passing interest. It shows that though only 7 years are lost to rubber production, because of the loss in earnings from the previous stand it takes anywhere from 12 to 15 years for the smallholder to show a 'profit', as measured by weight. Thereafter the benefits are substantial, but for many smallholders the delay may be daunting.

SMALLHOLDER RUBBER PRODUCTION

TAPPING

When a young rubber tree is first tapped the initial cut is made at an angle of approximately 30 degrees from top left to lower right and half way around the circumference of the tree. At the lower point a vertical cut of about 10 inches is made downwards. A tin spout is tacked on to the tree at the base of this vertical cut.

The initial spiral cut is shallow, with subsequent cuts moving deeper into the bark. The number of latex-bearing vessels increases further into the bark, and it is important to tap as close to the cambium as possible without cutting this tissue. Too shallow a cut will reduce yield, while too deep a cut, known as slaughter tapping, will give short-term increased latex production but will stunt the growth of the tree, increase its susceptibility to disease, and delay the formation of regenerated bark over the tapping panel, which can be tapped in the future. Slaughter tapping usually is done only to trees which are to be cut down for replanting as the practice quickly exhausts even full-grown trees.

The amount of bark removed by a tapper also is critical to the long-term productivity of the tree. As much as one-sixteenth inch of bark is consumed per tapping, and depending on the type of tree and the frequency of tapping, this means that a tapping panel will be consumed in 3–5 years. At this point the tapper begins tapping the other side of the tree, allowing the bark to regenerate where he has tapped before. If too much bark is consumed at too rapid a rate, there may not be enough time for it to be adequately restored before it is necessary to return to that tapping panel. Skill and care are essential in ensuring long-term productivity. Because of the potentially long productive life of a rubber tree, for smallholders often in excess of 20 years, proper care of the tree is of utmost importance.

Regardless of variety, the essential procedures for tapping rubber trees are the same. Tapping is done early in the morning while the air is cool and the latex vessels of the tree are at maximum turgor. The thin layer of coagulated latex or tree lace on the tapping groove and any small quantities of latex that may have flowed into the collection cup after the previous day's collection, known as cup-lump, are removed; they are sold as 'scrap' rubber. A common practice in Sik District is to leave scrap at the base of the tree and gather it for sale after several days of tapping.

The tapping itself is done with a grooved knife. A thin ribbon of bark is cut with short, careful strokes, beginning at the top and moving around the tree to the vertical cut. This vertical cut is left untapped, providing a channel for the flow of latex. After tapping, the latex begins to flow along the entire length of the fresh spiral cut and is carried by gravity down the spiral and vertical cuts and over the tin spout into the collection cup. This cup usually is attached to the tree by a wire holder secured around the trunk of the tree. Where the spout is quite low, the cup may be placed on the ground. The cup itself may be either a split coconut shell or an unfired clay cup. Clay cups and wire holders are inexpensive (together about $0.50) and in widespread use.

After tapping the latex will continue to flow for 4–5 hours, gradually ceasing as the tissue becomes clogged. Tappers begin work at dawn and tap for two hours or so, depending on the terrain and the number of trees to be worked, after which there is a break in the activity until the latex is ready to be collected. This time may be utilized for collection of scrap, clearing of undergrowth among the trees, or resting. If the tapper's home is nearby, he or she may return for a cup of tea and a snack. A woman tapper working near home may use this time to cook rice for the family's midday meal if there are no female children available to help with this, returning later to collect the latex. If the woman is tapping with her husband, she may let him collect the latex and carry it to the processing shed, where she may join him in pressing the latex into marketable sheet rubber.

COLLECTING

The contents of the collection cups are emptied into a bucket which is carried from tree to tree by hand. Typically the latex is then poured into a narrow-mouthed container strapped onto the back of a bicycle. This is heavy work if a large number of trees have been tapped; often more than 50 lb. of liquid must be moved to the processing site.

The main features of a processing site are two large mangles used to press coagulated latex into sheet form. There will be a clean, flat platform of wood, stone or concrete which is used for preliminary shaping of the sheets by hand. A source of water must be available nearby for cleaning the mangles and the trays used for coagulation of the latex. Finally there is likely to be a shed to protect the workers from the midday sun and the processing equipment from rain.

PROCESSING RIBBED SHEET RUBBER

When the latex has been collected and transported to the processing site, it is poured into shallow tin containers measuring approximately 14 × 20 inches. A filter is used to remove extraneous debris from the latex which otherwise would lower the price of the finished product. Sometimes a fine-mesh wire screen is used for this, but commonly the fibrous husk of a coconut is used, which removes the large pieces of foreign matter but probably replaces them with finer husk particles. Into the shallow pan of latex is poured an equal quantity of water and a small amount of formic acid, which hastens the coagulation of the latex. This mixture is stirred slowly several times for the first ten minutes or so to promote even mixing. Depending on the amount of acid used (one-half tablespoon diluted with some water is recommended), the latex should congeal within about half an hour. The slab of latex is then placed on a flat working surface and pressed out into a sheet with both hands until it has a uniform thickness of about one inch. The sheet is run through the first mangle, which has large, smooth steel rollers, as many as three times, each time with the rollers adjusted to produce progressively thinner sheets. It usually takes two people to operate this machine, one to turn the handle which, by means of gears, turns the heavy rollers, and the other to feed and stretch the latex sheet carefully through the machine. Ideally the sheet should be pressed down to one-eighth inch in thickness, though this is not always done. Sometimes the mangles are in poor condition and incapable of producing thin, high quality sheets; in other cases the processor may decide that the extra effort is not worth the difference in price offered for the thinner sheets.

After the sheet has been pressed by the smooth mangle it is passed once through a mangle that produces a ribbed pattern which increases the surface area of the sheet and hastens drying. After ribbing the sheets are hung to dry in the shade under fruit trees near the house or under the house itself.

Because tapping and collecting rubber can be managed by a single individual there is no necessity for any tapper to depend on another. It is even possible for one individual to operate the mangles by setting them into motion, feeding in the sheet, and then cranking the sheet through. Working alone precludes producing thin, quality sheet as the sheet cannot be stretched as it enters the mangle and hence the mangle would have to be adjusted to a thicker setting. In practice, however, several tappers usually share the use of one set of mangles and are able to help each other.

If several tappers are using the same set of mangles there may be some delay in pressing the sheets, but this usually is a minor factor in the time required for processing latex. More important will be the number of sheets to be processed and the number of people available for operating the mangles. Often, especially if the trees to be tapped are close to home, two members of the family will be available for pressing the latex into sheets. Because the mangles are driven by gears, a child of ten or twelve can crank the machines, and of course husband and wife may work together. The manual pressing of the latex before processing by the mangles requires more strength than such a young child is likely to possess, and at least one adult must be available for this step.

Not every tapping family owns its own mangles, and in some cases tappers must rent mangles owned by another family. The fee may be a straight cash payment of \$2 or \$3 for every *pikul* of dried sheets, or one sheet for every 20 or 25 sheets processed. The dried weight of a sheet will vary depending on the size of the pan in which the latex, water and acid were mixed, but generally is $1\frac{1}{2}$–2 *kati*.

ALTERNATIVES TO PROCESSING RIBBED SHEET RUBBER

In recent years there have been alternatives to processing the latex into sheets. In some areas smallholders are able to sell their unprocessed liquid latex at collection points either to private estates or to recently established government processing plants. This latex is processed into blocks of heveacrumb rubber which command a premium price on the world market. Another alternative which has gained increasing acceptance in the past few years is provided by a new process that makes use of scrap rubber to produce heveacrumb block suitable for the manufacture of tyres or other general uses. Rather than collecting the liquid latex or processing sheets, the tapper is able to tap the trees and let the latex coagulate in the cups. This process may be speeded up by the addition of minuscule quantities of formic acid to the collection cups, though this has the disadvantage that if at some point in the near future price fluctuations make the production of sheet rubber more attractive, the trace of acid in the cups will cause premature coagulation.

The advantage of selling scrap rubber is that by 9 a.m. or 10 a.m. the tapper is free for other activities or for leisure. Tappers selling liquid latex will have to stay for another hour until the latex has finished flowing, but they still save time by not having to process the latex into sheet rubber. For families who must rent mangles, by-passing this process means very real savings.

There are, of course, some disadvantages. In Sik District, liquid latex is bought by agents who receive franchises from a factory operated by the Malaysian Rubber Development Corporation (MARDEC), a government body established to process smallholder rubber and provide alternative marketing channels and higher prices for their product. In 1976 a MARDEC factory was opened 14 miles from the town of Sik. Tappers claim the agents sometimes fail to show up, leaving them with a heavy liquid load which they have with difficulty brought to the collection facility. This latex, if not sold, will have to be carried back to the mangles for processing into sheet or poured into containers and sold as scrap rubber.

The buying agents are licensed by MARDEC and are supposed to be on the job every tapping day. Often, however, the person with the licence from MARDEC will hire someone else to do the work, and the latter may be less diligent in his efforts. Problems also are posed by rain which may fall in one area but not another. When there is a heavy early morning or sustained late afternoon or evening rain at the MARDEC factory, it is sometimes assumed that no tapping was possible elsewhere. Hence, the purchasing agents are not informed of the day's price and, knowing that no transport will be sent to collect the latex, they are unable to buy latex from the producers. Though this may happen only a few times a year, the uncertainty, especially if combined with the irregular attendance of some agents, causes some tappers to market their rubber elsewhere.

In the past several efforts have been made to collect liquid latex from smallholders. In the late 1960s a large rubber estate outside the district of Sik sent private purchasing agents into some parts of the district to buy latex for processing into heveacrumb. This effort foundered because the sellers felt they were being cheated by the buyers. This may or may not have been the case, but it is easy to see how cheating can take place in the marketing of liquid latex.

The procedure then as now is to measure the dry rubber content (DRC) of the latex by means of a hydrometer. Depending on the season and the variety of tree tapped, the DRC of latex is about 30 per cent of the weight of a given quantity of latex. Weighing the latex presents few problems as the scales are read easily by buyer and seller alike. Reading the hydrometer, however, presents some problems. The hydrometer is slightly larger than an oral thermometer and is allowed to bob in a sample of the latex. This simple hydrometer is fairly accurate but, because of its small size, reading the scale requires close and careful examination. The buyer will probably be more familiar than the seller with the hydrometer's markings and may make a calculated error of one or two degrees, giving him a higher profit.

This apparently is what happened in the late 1960s and resulted in the tappers returning to the production of sheet rubber when the lower price they received no longer justified the reduced effort of selling liquid latex. During 1978 the author heard no claims of such cheating, which may be because the actual buyers were hired men from a local village who received a fixed daily wage and who would not benefit from cheating their customers. Using these men, however, has presented some problems as noted above, which may be resolved in time as the MARDEC staff gains experience and several vacant supervisory positions are filled.

Cheating in the sale of liquid latex is not altogether one-sided, however. It is common practice in Sik District to add water to the liquid latex collected from the trees to increase its gross weight; though this will reduce the DRC percentage, many tappers seem to think that a judicious addition of as much as a gallon of water will affect the weight more than the DRC reading of the hydrometer.

Some tappers also claim that adding hot water to their liquid latex has a favourable effect on the DRC readings.

Because there are only 23 latex collection stations in the district of Sik, for many tappers selling liquid latex would entail transporting the heavy liquid for several miles. The importance of liquid latex marketing also is reduced during the dry season (January to March) when rubber trees in Sik lose most of their leaves (the so-called 'wintering effect') and only a limited amount of latex is produced. Moreover, the dry weight content of the latex is reduced during this season, lowering the price paid to tappers for liquid latex. Under these circumstances most tappers prefer to produce sheet or scrap rubber, and all the liquid latex collection centres close down temporarily.

Scrap has none of the disadvantages of liquid latex, but it does have some of its own. Scrap is easily transported and finds a ready market at any licensed rubber dealer. Because the scrap must be ground up and the heveacrumb produced is of a lower quality than that produced from liquid latex, the price of scrap is somewhat lower. It also is lower than for good quality sheet rubber, but the difference is not substantial. One tapper reported selling one day's production of dried sheet for $9.80, and one day's production of scrap from the same land for $9.40. Other tappers report similar differences. With this minimal difference in price many tappers valued their three-plus hours more than the extra $0.40, while for those tappers who found it necessary to rent mangles, the difference in actual cash income may favour the production of scrap.

Producing scrap during the dry season presents little difficulty, but during the rest of the year there is a danger that rain in the morning or early afternoon may wash away the latex before it has congealed in the cups. For the most part rains in Sik District are caused by the building up of heat over the day, resulting in brief though sometimes heavy and violent thunderstorms late in the afternoon. If rains hold off until the afternoon there is little or no danger to the latex in the cup, but a midday rain is likely to cause a total loss of the day's production. During the rainy season tappers are more likely to sell liquid latex or process it into sheet.

LAND-OWNERSHIP AND SHARE-CROPPING

DIFFICULTIES IN COLLECTING DATA

Collecting accurate information on land-ownership in an area of rubber smallholdings is most difficult. Unlike rice land, which is on level ground and demarcated by clearly visible bunds, rubber land typically is hilly and one's view is obstructed by the trees themselves. By walking through rice fields with a reliable informant it is possible to learn what land is owned by whom, but for rubber smallholdings this is insufficient. Though most of the land in the immediate vicinity of Kampung Dusun is owned by its residents, it represents less than half of the total amount of rubber land owned by the households interviewed. Most of the land owned by the people of Kampung Dusun is several miles away, and in some cases more than 5 miles away.

As a consequence it was necessary to rely heavily on information gathered during interviews. As noted previously in Chapter 3 this presents certain problems of reliability, especially with owners of larger acreages. It was impossible personally to check on the information provided during interviews, though an attempt was made to confirm these data with reliable informants. In many cases, however, informants could contribute little in this regard. The scattered nature of rubber holdings effectively limits knowledge within a community of the exact acreages owned by individual families. Despite these limitations, it is possible that the information provided during interviews was reasonably accurate. The author's previous long-term residence in the community (1968–71 and part of 1974) allowed not only for rapport and trust, but for a certain level of knowledge prior to interviews which may have lessened the tendency of those interviewed to misstate the information requested.

DISTRIBUTION OF RUBBER LAND OWNERSHIP

Of the 190.5 *relong* of rubber land owned by residents of Kampung Dusun, seven families own 109, and five of these families own 87 *relong*. The distribution of ownership of rubber land in Kampung Dusun is significantly more skewed than was the case with either rice or rubber land in Gong Guncil, as may be seen by comparing Table 5.2 with Table 3.2. Though this sample of only 25 families which actually own rubber land is small, the author would offer the judgement that the distribution of land-ownership is roughly representative for Sik District as a whole. A number of local residents were farsighted enough to obtain title to 10, 20, or more *relong* when rubber was first introduced into Sik District in the early twentieth century, a time when land was still plentiful, but later migrants and the offspring of families which previously obtained grants to small areas have found it difficult to obtain title to additional land. Though there are no large-scale estates within Sik District, there are a few families who own land exceeding 100 acres, which is the official point separating smallholders from non-smallholders.

Though some land in Sik District is still available, the process of

TABLE 5.2

DISTRIBUTION OF RUBBER LAND OWNERSHIP AMONG FAMILIES ACTIVE IN THE RUBBER ECONOMY (N = 35)

Area (relong)	*No. of Families*
0	10
< 1	1
1– 1.9	1
2– 2.9	2
3– 3.9	2
4– 4.9	2
5– 5.9	5
6– 6.9	2
7– 7.9	1
8– 8.9	1
9– 9.9	1
10–14.9	2
15–19.9	4
> 20	1

Note: 1 *relong* = 0.7 acre.

obtaining a land title may take years. This is especially so if there are several applicants for a single piece of land, and if there are traditional claims based on previous occupation or locally recognized rights to the fruits of *durian* or other trees on the land. Moreover, what land remains available typically is on rough terrain and far from any road.

Though no longer plentiful, rubber land does not have the same scarcity value as rice land. Neither do families attach the same emotional ties to rubber land that they do to rice land, which provides for their food needs. Though the market in rubber land in Sik District is not highly active, its transfer through sale is more common than rice land in Kampung Dusun or Gong Guncil. Rubber land is more nearly an exchangeable economic commodity, but exchangeability depends on meeting the market price. A number of factors affect the price of rubber land, including age and quality of the trees, access to roads, and roughness of terrain. Land with a gentle slope, easy access to a road, and planted with old trees may cost $1,000 per *relong* ($1,430 per acre), while the same land planted with high-yielding varieties may attract three times this sum.

Rarely is only one *relong* bought or sold unless this land is contiguous to land which the buyer already owns, because such a holding could not provide an adequate return to the investment of time and effort spent in tapping; more frequently a sale will involve 3–4 *relong*. Unlike rice farmers who can cultivate different plots by staggering the timing of planting and harvesting, rubber tappers tap all their trees each day. Tapping separate stands of rubber is inconvenient at best and unless the stands are quite close to each other the amount of time spent in moving from one to another will preclude timely tapping and complicate the collection of latex.

While a rice farmer can purchase land in parcels as small as one acre at a time, this option is not available to most rubber tappers. At least 3–4 *relong* (2.1–2.8 acres) are necessary for efficient use of time and effort, and to produce an adequate income. For these reasons, a landless family seeking to buy rubber land will need to accumulate substantial capital resources in order to purchase even land planted with older, less productive trees. One family, which moved into Kampung Dusun in the late 1960s and had three members share-cropping land owned by others, was able to buy 4 *relong* of old trees of their own after 10 years of effort.

It is far easier for families who already own land, or who earn regular cash incomes, to purchase what land does enter the market. A family owning 10 *relong* may find it relatively easy to expand its holdings or to improve its holdings through replanting. Government officers, including teachers, also have ready cash or access to channels of credit which may allow them quickly to take advantage of a sale of land. To these people, rubber land is both a hedge against inflation and a source of income, especially after retirement.

Though there is a market for rubber land, for most families in villages such as Kampung Dusun the most important means of access to land is inheritance. Within any family the pattern may vary, but as a general rule male and female heirs are treated equally. If a daughter has married a man who already owns land, her portion of the inheritance of land may be divided among the other heirs. Similarly, if a son has found employment outside the village, e.g. in the police or army, his share may be divided among his siblings, especially if the amount of land concerned is small.

As with the case of Gong Guncil, division of a family's land among heirs usually does not proceed beyond a point where a holding is deemed uneconomic. The definition of an uneconomic holding by village standards may not correspond to that of agricultural economists, as it will include issues of equity among the heirs. Though it may take 4 *relong* of rubber land to adequately provide for a family, several heirs may divide a holding of this size. Rarely, however, will holdings be fragmented into units of one *relong* or less, and division into units of less than 2 *relong* also appears to be uncommon. Two *relong* of rubber may provide for the minimal needs of a family, but a smaller holding than this may make tapping not worth the effort unless additional land in the immediate area is available for share-cropping.

Of the 35 families directly involved in the rubber economy,[1] 10 own no land and share-crop land owned by others. Of the remaining 25 families which own land, 8 leased all their land to share-croppers. There are, then, 27 families in Kampung Dusun which are active tappers. Table 5.3 indicates the distribution of families by tenure category.

TABLE 5.3

LAND TENURE STATUS OF ACTIVE TAPPING FAMILIES IN KAMPUNG DUSUN (N = 27)

Category	*Number of Families*
Owner—operator	15
Owner—tenant	2
Tenant	10

Tenancy relationships are much more complicated than Table 5.3 indicates. Included under the category 'Owner—tenant' is one family which owns land in a distant village and lets it out to a tapper there, and in turn share-crops land located closer to home. Among the 15 'Owners—operators', only 7 families tap all the land they own; the others tap only a part of their land and let out the rest to share-croppers. Due to the distance between Kampung Dusun and some of these holdings, it generally is more practical to hire a share-cropper who lives close to the holding itself.

SHARE-CROPPING

In Sik District the share-cropping of rubber is based on the equal division of production, or *bagi dua*, within which system there are a number of variations. The cost of purchased inputs is not significant for rubber, and most production costs are borne by the owner, including planting and maintaining the rubber stand and the provision of collection cups and holders. If ribbed sheet rubber is produced, the cost of formic acid ($1—2 per month) may be shared or the acid may be provided by the owner. More significant is the

[1]An additional ten households in the study area are not involved in the rubber economy. These include several families whose male members are carpenters as well as several which depend on employment in the town of Sik.

cost associated with the use of the mangles for pressing and ribbing the sheets. Mangles may be provided at no cost by an owner whose land is tapped by a tenant, especially if he has a number of tenants working in the same area. Some owners, however, charge their tenants a rent of up to $3 per *pikul* of sheet produced. If the mangles used are owned by a third party, a land-owner may either share the rent with his tenant, make the tenant pay the rent, or pay it himself.

In cases where a land-owning family is not significantly more wealthy than its tenants, sharing the cost of using the mangles is reasonable and does not antagonize the tenants; in cases of wealthy land-owners, however, local sentiment applauds the owner who provides free access to mangles and criticizes the owner who does not.

The actual marketing of the rubber may be undertaken by either the owner or the share-cropper. If the owner does not live nearby but there is a licensed rubber dealer in the vicinity, his tenants may sell the total production and, with receipt in hand, share the proceeds with him. Alternatively the owner may collect the rubber and pay the share-cropping family after it has been sold. In some cases the production is divided by weight and each party sells its own share. In most cases who sells the rubber is based on convenience, but in some cases, especially when the owner and share-cropper are from different villages, convenience is replaced by concern on the part of the owner that he or she may be cheated by the share-cropper, who may either withhold some of the total production or, if ribbed sheet rubber is being produced, engage in practices which increase the proportion of scrap to sheet rubber.

When rubber is processed into ribbed sheets, the tenant tapper is allowed to collect and sell the usually small quantities of scrap, i.e. the tree lace and cuplump. One study estimated that 18 per cent of the incomes of smallholders who produced sheet rubber was derived from the sale of such scrap (Cheam, 1971). A share-cropper seeking to increase his or her share of the production may do so by collecting latex soon after tapping, thereby gaining a larger quantity of cuplump for sale as scrap. Because the yield of rubber varies from year to year and from season to season, the owner may not be aware of such cheating on the basis of sales receipts alone, but regular checks of the rubber stand itself would indicate if excessive latex was being collected as cuplump.

Regular checks by owners also are made to ensure that the tapper does not remove the bark at too rapid a rate and cut too deeply into the trees. Some tappers, especially transient families which move into an area to share-crop rubber, will slaughter tap for a short period of time before moving on to another area. This problem is especially serious in some of the more remote parts of Sik District where few local residents are available to share-crop and where the owner does not regularly check on the work of the tappers. Many tenant tappers in these remote areas are short-term residents, young men and women from other villages or other districts who seek temporary cash employment. For them a reputation as a careless tapper is unimportant; they can move on and find employment elsewhere. In some cases tenants slaughter tap trees for several days or even weeks and leave the area without warning, taking the rubber and leaving the owner with injured trees which are lost to production for as long as a year. Consequently, whenever possible, land-owners seek to hire local people to work their land.

If the rubber is sold as liquid latex the tenant also receives any scrap collected. If the rubber is sold as scrap, however, all the production is divided equally between the owner and tapper. It might be expected that tenant tappers would prefer to produce sheet rubber and oppose the marketing of rubber in scrap form as an infringement of their rights, but such does not appear to be the case, and tenant tappers appear to have readily adopted the sale of scrap because of the time saved compared to producing ribbed sheet rubber.

MARKETING

LOCAL AND URBAN RUBBER DEALERS

Trade in rubber is closely regulated by the government, which collects a substantial revenue from rubber exports. Only licensed rubber dealers are permitted to buy rubber and their accounts are frequently checked by government officials. The price paid to producers, however, is established by the individual dealers and is not subject to government control. Primary purchasers of rubber, such as those found in the town of Sik and in other parts of the district, in turn sell their rubber to purchasers located in major urban areas near the ports from which rubber is exported. It is from these major dealers/exporters that the primary purchasers obtain daily (and sometimes even more frequent) price quotations. The relationship between primary purchasers and the major urban dealers usually is long-lasting and mutually beneficial. An urban dealer may offer credit facilities or cash advances and will cushion the consequences if a sudden drop in price occurs between the purchase from the tapper and delivery to the urban dealer; having to fulfil export contracts, he is keenly interested in ensuring steady sources of supply.

RELATIONS BETWEEN LOCAL DEALERS AND RUBBER TAPPERS

Primary purchasers of rubber are no less interested than the urban dealers in a steady source of rubber and employ a number of tactics to attract regular customers. Producers typically sell to the same dealer on a regular basis, unless there is a significant difference in price. The prices offered by rubber dealers are posted and may be readily compared by the sellers. There usually is little variation among the five shops in the town of Sik, where the majority of Kampung Dusun's tappers sell their product. (A few villagers sell their rubber to shops near where they tap; while the price may be slightly lower than that offered in Sik, the trouble and expense of transporting the rubber makes the difference insignificant.) Producers keep informed of price trends through regular radio broadcasts which announce prices paid at the major urban marketing and export centres.

Dealers in the town of Sik report that sellers have become increasingly aware of even minor price differentials and will look for the best price before they sell. This may be so, but there are some factors which limit such 'shopping around'. Often sellers of ribbed sheet rubber will bring a week's production with them tied on to the back of a bicycle, and though the town itself is not large, the shops of the rubber dealers are not centrally located; it is easy to understand why sellers usually go directly to their regular dealer rather than peddle their heavy load from shop to shop. Producers from distant villages who use taxis and buses to bring their product to town for sale are even more constrained since it is impossible to have their transport stop at several shops. Residents of distant villages generally will choose to bring their rubber to Sik only if they are planning a trip anyway, e.g. to attend the weekly market; unless they have a large quantity to sell, the expense of transport would make the price differential between the dealers in the town and those closer to their home villages less tempting.

A rubber producer may decide to sell to one dealer instead of any other out of habit or because of personally friendly relations with that dealer or one of his workers. This decision may be made on the basis of other economic dealings. This is especially the case with those producers selling to a particular shop which handles the largest volume in the district of Sik. In addition to his business as a rubber dealer, the owner of this shop also is one of the two local retailers of lumber and other construction materials. He is willing to sell these materials on credit to those rubber producers who regularly sell to him; either in expectation of future credit needs or in gratitude for past dealings, a large clientele has been established. This dealer also owns the only rubber smokehouse in the area, and because he is able to make a profit on the increased value of the smoked ribbed sheet rubber he sells, his competitive position is quite strong. Smoking of ribbed sheet rubber completes the drying process and prevents the growth of mould; for this reason ribbed sheet rubber must be smoked before it is exported from Malaysia. Though all the licensed rubber dealers offer limited credit to regular customers, this dealer probably accounts for the largest share of outstanding credit.

There does not appear to be a price differential between sellers tied to a particular dealer through credit and those without such ties. Rather, credit is used to establish a lasting relationship between buyer and seller. In addition to assured supply from tappers, purchasing from regular customers makes grading the rubber brought to the shop a matter of common understanding since the quality of the product is constant and known. A new customer is more likely to question the grade or quality assigned to his rubber, whereas a regular customer knows what to expect.

Of the 5 licensed rubber dealers in the town of Sik, 4 are run by Chinese and only one by a Malay. In two cases the licence is held in the name of a Malay who has leased his licence to a Chinese buyer. The decision as to which dealer to patronize does not appear to be influenced by considerations of ethnic origin, and the largest rubber dealer in Sik District is Chinese. All the dealers buy both ribbed sheet rubber and scrap, though one dealer seems to specialize in scrap. According to him, he can make a better profit from buying and selling this product, because sellers are less aware of the prices paid for scrap at varying degrees of dryness, and if a seller brings him several days' production including some that is drier than the rest, he will be able to pay the going price for fresh scrap. The difference to any single seller may be small, but cumulatively this dealer feels he can make a better profit on scrap based on his fuller knowledge of this commodity.

Scrap rubber must undergo further processing before use or export. Only dry scrap can be processed, and dealers usually will dry the scrap in front of their shops for several days (the odour is distinctive, a sickly-sweet aroma which is not altogether displeasing). Every few days the accumulated scrap is gathered and loaded on to a small lorry and sent to a processing plant to be ground and recombined with latex and some unsmoked ribbed sheet rubber to produce heveacrumb. Most of the scrap produced in Sik District is processed at the local MARDEC factory, but some is sent to private processors as far as 70 miles away. Two grades of heveacrumb are made from scrap rubber, SMR 20 and SMR 50. Compared with other lighter coloured and more expensive grades of

Standard Malaysian Rubber (SMR) which are made exclusively from liquid latex, SMR 20 and SMR 50 are more attractive to manufacturers of tyres and other products where colour is unimportant. Malaysia first began to produce heveacrumb rubber in 1965, but it is only since the early 1970s that export demand for these grades of rubber has had the effect of raising the price paid for scrap relative to other types of rubber. As late as 1974 in the district of Sik, the production of scrap was limited to tree lace and small quantities of cuplump; by 1978 scrap had come to occupy a position of importance equal to that of ribbed sheet rubber, especially during the drier months of the year.

INCOME FROM RUBBER TAPPING

THE EFFECT OF FLUCTUATING PRICE LEVELS

The price paid for rubber fluctuates widely, as may be seen in Figure 5.1. When the price of rubber is $0.70 per *kati* and above, most rubber tapping families earn incomes adequate for their consumption needs and may be able to afford such minor luxuries as a new bicycle or a radio, but when it falls to $0.40 per *kati* or lower, they are hard pressed to meet even basic consumption requirements. Obviously the point at which a life of relative plenty turns to one of hardship will depend on the amount of land and the quality of the trees worked, as well as the existence of secondary economic activities which would soften the effect of lowered income from rubber production.

As noted previously, collecting data on extent of land-ownership presents many problems, and this affects information on the amount of land worked by each household of active rubber tappers. Even if an accurate figure is obtained, there are so many qualitative variables to be considered (productivity of trees, number of trees per *relong*, type and quality of product) that this alone would be insufficient to provide adequate information on household incomes. The best guide to incomes earned is to ask each informant how much (in weight) is produced per day. But even this introduces an unknown variable, as the number of days tapped per year or month varies according to weather and competing social activities.

Depending on terrain, one tapper should be able to work up to 4 *relong* per day if producing ribbed sheet rubber, or up to 6 *relong* if scrap is being produced. The overwhelming majority of households in Kampung Dusun which depend primarily upon rubber tapping work 3–5 *relong* of land. The only exceptions to this are a number of households in which the women tap rubber to earn an income supplementary to that of their husbands and one other household

FIGURE 5.1

PRICE PAID PER *KATI* FOR NO. 5 UNSMOKED SHEET RUBBER, JANUARY 1970–MAY 1978, SIK, KEDAH

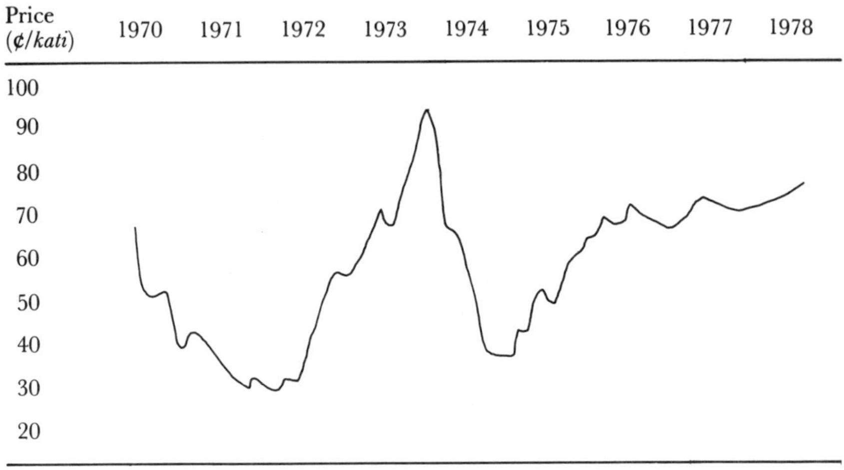

which has three active tappers share-cropping 10 *relong*. In most cases the trees tapped are old and relatively unproductive, and over the course of the years several trees may have died or fallen over during a storm, further reducing the yield of the holding on a per *relong* basis.

One *relong* of old rubber trees may produce between 4 and 5 *kati* (between 5.3 and 6.7 lb.) of dry ribbed sheet rubber per day, whereas more highly productive grafted trees may produce 12 *kati* (16 lb.) per *relong*. If a family taps 4 *relong* of old trees capable of producing 5 *kati* of dried ribbed sheet rubber per *relong*, the daily production would be 20 *kati*. The same amount of land planted to more highly productive grafted trees would produce 48 *kati*. If the price per *kati* is $0.80, the daily income would be $16 and $38.40 respectively. If a family is able to tap 20 days per month, its monthly income would be $320 and $768 respectively. Even the lower of the two incomes is substantially higher than the incomes earned by the rice farmers of Gong Guncil or the fishermen of Mangkok.

As may be seen from Figure 5.1, $0.80 per *kati* is an optimistic figure. If the price falls to $0.30, as it did for a 6-month period from late 1971 until the middle of 1972, a family tapping 4 *relong* of older trees would be able to earn only $6 per day, or $120 per month, assuming that the family owns the land and trees; if they are share-cropping, the income would be halved. As noted previously, a substantial proportion of tappers in the community studied, and in the district of Sik as a whole, are share-croppers.

These figures assume that trees could be tapped 20 days per month. In fact, the period of low prices during 1971/2 included some of the best tapping months, the period from October until January when the trees are at full strength and tapping usually is not seriously affected by rains. But following this peak tapping period is a dry season of 2–3 months when rubber trees lose most of their leaves and the flow of latex is seriously reduced. Though tapping is not restricted by rain, heavy tapping of trees during this drought may have serious long-term consequences on the trees themselves. During the rainy season of March–April, much of the trees' resources is devoted to developing new leaves, and latex yields continue to be low; moreover, heavy rains may allow only 10 days of tapping per month.

After this prolonged period of low prices, the world market recovered in mid-1972, reaching a high of $0.90 per *kati* in January 1974. At this point a precipitous slide began with prices once again approaching the $0.30 mark. But this time the problem was much more serious, because since 1972 the price of milled rice had risen from $1.60 to almost $3.00 per *gantang*. For many families rice is the major item of the household budget, and as noted in the preceding chapters, a family of six will consume as much as one *gantang* of milled rice in a day. A family of share-croppers tapping 4 *relong* of land planted with old trees and who need one *gantang* of milled rice for consumption each day would barely be able to meet this single expense at a market price of $0.40 per *kati* of rubber, assuming a yield of 20 *kati* and 20 days' tapping. This would give a gross total of $160 to be divided with the owner, leaving the tapping family with $80 per month. The cheapest quality of rice available at the time sold for $2.60 per *gantang*, i.e. $78 for a 30-day month. As may be seen from Figure 5.1, the prevailing price hovered near the $0.40 mark for about 4 months before beginning the current generally rising trend.

POVERTY AND PROTEST

It was under these conditions that two major demonstrations demanding that the government raise the price paid for rubber took place in Kedah in 1974. In the town of Sik itself an estimated 5,000 demonstrators gathered in front of the District Office, some villagers having marched up the main road from as far as 12 miles away. The demonstration in Sik was peaceful, but in the neighbouring district of Baling 10,000 demonstrators were dispersed by tear gas. Demonstrations of sympathy and solidarity were held at two national universities and led to the arrest of a number of prominent student and faculty leaders.

These demonstrations by rural Malays were touched off by widespread economic hardship among rubber smallholders. Many families were unable to earn enough money from rubber tapping to buy sufficient food, and while there was no starvation, many families were reduced to finding alternative and less nutritious foods, e.g. cassava, to their beloved rice.

Not all families were hit equally hard by the rapid drop in prices in 1974. Those families which employed several tappers to work their land certainly suffered a drop in income, but not one which threatened their existence. Other families were able to fall back on secondary economic activities to tide them through the worst, and families which owned a little rice land were somewhat cushioned by the grain they themselves grew.

SECONDARY ECONOMIC ACTIVITIES

Secondary economic activities serve two functions in a volatile economy such as that based on rubber: increasing income and reducing economic vulnerability by diversifying sources of income.

The most common productive activity other than rubber tapping is the planting of rice. Almost half (20 out of 45) of the households in Kampung Dusun own and cultivate small rice fields—rarely more than 2 *relong* and more usually half this size. In addition, another 6 households share-crop or rent rice land. Yields in the study area are low and, with the exception of one field of 20 acres, only one crop is grown per year. (Since mid-1977 even this field has yielded only one crop due to improper construction of a new road through the village which blocked an irrigation canal.) One family claimed to obtain yields comparable with the rice farmers of Gong Guncil (300 *gantang* per acre), but most families' yields are as low as 100 *gantang* per *relong* (less than 150 *gantang* per acre). In the absence of effective water control under rain-fed conditions, little investment is made in chemical fertilizers. A mixture of fertilizer-responsive and traditional varieties of rice are planted, the former being harvested by threshing and the latter with a *ketam*. Small plots and low yields mean that less than half of those families cultivating rice are self-sufficient in this staple for an entire year. Rice is produced solely for home consumption, and it is common practice for the grain to be stored rather than eaten if the income from rubber tapping or other employment enables the family to purchase rice. The habit of storing grain as a hedge against economic hard times helped some families weather low rubber prices in 1971/2 and 1974.

In Gong Guncil where rice cultivation is the primary economic activity, those families which also tap rubber cease tapping during peak periods of labour demand for rice. In Kampung Dusun this is not the case. Even during the transplanting and harvest seasons the small size of rice plots operated by most families allows adequate time, during the afternoons or those mornings when rain prevents tapping, to get the crop in or out of the field. Labour also is saved by the almost universal use of contract tractor ploughing, which as recently as 1968 was a novel practice; by 1978 virtually every family cultivating more than one *relong* used this service. Some with even smaller plots also used tractors.

One major effect of the increased use of contract ploughing services has been the reduction in the water-buffalo population in the community. Although no data were collected during previous periods of residence in this community, the author recalls very clearly that these animals were in common use for land preparation, and that many families owned water-buffalo. By 1978, however, only two families owned 2 and 3 water-buffalo respectively, and three of these animals were still calves. Since all the mature male water-buffalo in the village had been sold off, the opportunity for these two families to increase the size of their herds was limited.

Artificial insemination of water-buffalo is still in the experimental stage, and under village conditions a bull water-buffalo may require three years before it is mature enough for natural breeding (Camoens, 1976). There are bull water-buffalo in villages several miles away, but even though no stud fees are charged, both of the owners in Kampung Dusun expressed hesitancy about either taking their cows to stay with the bull until mated or borrowing a stud bull. Detecting the period of a female water-buffalo's oestrus is more difficult than with other ruminants, and considerable time may elapse before she is successfully bred. Both families mentioned fear of theft as a deterrent to borrowing a stud bull for the animal is worth at least $1,000, which they would be unable to repay.

Besides the ubiquitous chicken, by far the most important animals in Kampung Dusun are cattle. Just over half the households in Kampung Dusun (23 out of 45) own cattle. Most of these households raise 1–4 animals, though 2 households own 14 and 16 cattle respectively. Goats are conspicuous by their relative absence; only 2 families own these voracious animals. Livestock is allowed to roam freely during the day. Goats are much more difficult to control, e.g. by fencing, than are cattle. An owner is responsible for his animal, and goats are more likely to be the cause of troublesome disputes than are cattle or water-buffalo, for unlike in Mangkok, where vegetable gardening and other agricultural pursuits are impossible, in Kampung Dusun these pursuits are more common.

The importance of livestock in the household economy of Kampung Dusun is similar to the case of Gong Guncil. Cattle function as capital on the hoof, an asset that may be turned into cash at short notice. Usually cattle are sold to meet major expenses, such as the construction of or a major addition to the family house, further education for a child, the purchase of land, or to finance a religious pilgrimage. In some cases a family will sell off all of its mature cattle at one time, gradually building up the number of its livestock again either from young animals retained, or by taking over the care and raising of another family's cow, from which it receives a share in the ensuing offspring under the *pawah* system similar to that found in Gong Guncil.

Goats also may be sold to meet household expenses, though because the value of a goat is so much less than that of a cow, its sale is not likely to contribute greatly to the major expenses and investments noted above. Unlike cattle and water-buffalo, which usually are sold to butchers who provide meat to the daily and weekly markets in Sik, most of the goats are sold to fellow villagers or slaughtered by the family itself when minor feasts are held to celebrate a rite of passage such as the circumcision of a son. Major feasts, such as typically are held for a wedding, usually will entail the slaughtering of a cow or even a water-buffalo to feed the guests.

Rice production and raising livestock are the two most common sources of income after rubber tapping. Beyond this are a number of other occupations and activities which may serve to diversify a family's income, including cultivating vegetables or growing tobacco. Most families at one time or another do grow some vegetables, but usually these are for home consumption with minimal surplus for sale within the village itself. The daily and weekly markets in the town of Sik are supplied by vegetable producers outside Sik District, who specialize in vegetable cultivation and are able to ensure a steady supply to the retail sellers in the local market. There is some room for improvement in the local production of vegetable crops, though the problem of steady supply to the market would require further study. There also is limited absorptive capacity in Sik's town market due to the small population.

Tobacco cultivation presents a broader opportunity, though there are marketing problems in this commodity as well. Tobacco is a high-value, labour-intensive crop which requires relatively little land. Under favourable conditions and careful management practices, one *relong* of tobacco may yield a cash income of as much as $500 over a 4-month period. Unlike vegetable production, there is less of a problem of oversupply as the market served is not local. In the early 1970s a licensed tobacco processing facility was opened in a nearby village. A number of residents of Kampung Dusun grew tobacco for this processor, but for only one season. The reason given for this is that the processor offered a price lower than justified by the quality of the leaf, and in some cases delayed payment for several months. Allegations of unfairness in grading were supported by a young man from Kampung Dusun whom the author has known intimately for over ten years. This man, the son of the man who was the author's 'adoptive father' when he first lived in Kampung Dusun, was trained by the government's National Tobacco Board as a tobacco grader and was employed for a short time by this processor. As a consequence of alleged unfair practices, no tobacco was grown in Kampung Dusun after the initial season and production in other villages in the area was so reduced that the processing facility was closed for two years. Though it has re-opened, as of 1978 no one in Kampung Dusun had taken up tobacco cultivation, though several families were again considering the possibility.

One crop that has taken on increasing importance in recent years is cassava. Unlike tobacco, which matures in a short time and is intensive both in labour and land usage, cassava takes at least a year to reach maturity and requires less intensive labour but more extensive land to obtain comparable income. Also unlike tobacco, whose price is established by the National Tobacco Board, the price of cassava is subject to wide fluctuations; cassava grown for commercial purposes is sold to buyers representing factories which process the tubers into flour and animal feed. High prices in 1977 and early 1978 encouraged many farmers to plant cassava but by mid-1978 the price per *pikul* had dropped from \$4 to \$2.80. Cassava planting often takes place on land cleared for rubber planting or replanting, a practice encouraged by Farmers' Cooperatives which offer production credit for this crop. RISDA provides production credit for interplanting of crops other than cassava but does not approve of cassava cultivation on land to be planted to rubber because of the possibility that its root system, left behind in the soil when the tubers are harvested, may pick up and transmit certain root diseases to young rubber trees.

Besides these agricultural activities which supplement income from rubber production, a number of families in Kampung Dusun are engaged in non-agricultural occupations. Members of 4 families make cement bricks and post supports on which the raised pilings of village houses rest. These materials are made in their spare time at home, using homemade moulds. Their production is sold under contract to a local lumber merchant, who supplies the raw materials and collects the completed product in his small lorry. Most of the work is done by the women of these closely related families. One of these women is a widow, while the husbands of the other three are regularly employed as carpenters.

The husbands of three women who tap rubber are employed in the town of Sik as helpers in the shops of rubber dealers, earning $5 per day. Until recently two other men worked three days a week as butchers and meat sellers in the daily and weekly markets. (One of these men died in 1975 and the other has 'retired', living off the proceeds of his land that is being share-cropped and from the rental of a small house he built next to his own.) The wives of two men who tap rubber earn income from selling cloth in villages throughout the district. One family owns and operates a small sundry goods store in the village, and another family operates the canteen at the primary school in the village.

Though there is a wide range of possible secondary sources of income available to the residents of Kampung Dusun, the economy of the village as a whole is tied closely to the production and sale of rubber. In the chapters which follow the rubber-based economy of Kampung Dusun will be compared to the economies of rice farming and fishing. They differ in important respects concerning the organization of labour and productive resources, and these differences have important implications for the organization of social life in these three communities.

6 The Material Context of Production: Natural and Technological Resources

INTRODUCTION

As should be clear from Chapters 3, 4, and 5, the production processes of rice farming, fishing, and rubber tapping differ in a number of important respects. The different natural and technological resources utilized by the residents of the three communities studied provide the material context in which production processes and relationships take place. The availability of and means of access to natural and technological resources affect a wide range of economic and non-economic social relationships and determine the relative rigidity of social and economic stratification in each of the three communities studied. While the vast majority of Malaysia's rural Malays live at or near subsistence level, a small minority is significantly better off. This economic stratification is significantly more rigid among rice farmers and rubber tappers than among fishermen. Fishermen are more easily upwardly mobile than are rice farmers or rubber tappers, but even for these latter groups there are strategies of capital accumulation through which some families successfully improve their economic standing.

The two land-based economies of rice farming and rubber tapping have more in common with each other than either of them do with the economy of fishing. There are, nonetheless, significant differences between these two land-based economies, and of course between them and the fishing economy.

The differences found among the three communities studied, interesting in their own right, have practical implications for the design of rural development policies and programmes. The introduction of new technologies and the increased commercialization of the rural economy have led to new material opportunities. However, the benefits of development may be shared unequally and may exacerbate existing inequalities.

GONG GUNCIL

In the rice farming village of Gong Guncil, the most important natural resource is land. At the turn of this century land in the Gong Guncil area was plentiful compared to the more crowded rice producing areas of Kelantan. Gradual migration from Kelantan combined with natural population increase has led to a situation where all available land has been claimed for private ownership. Over the past decade, the purchase price of land escalated rapidly, partly due to the introduction of irrigation facilities which increased the productivity of rice land, and partly to general inflationary pressures which have made rice land an attractive speculative investment. Rice land is priced at at least $3,000 per acre, and in surrounding villages even up to $4,000. The value of land unsuited to rice cultivation also has increased. Land planted with rubber trees in the vicinity of Gong Guncil varies in worth depending on the type and ages of trees, with a range of $2,000–3,000 per acre. Land on which houses and fruit orchards are situated is of similar value.

Land of any kind rarely is offered for sale. The most common reasons for selling land are a family moving away from the area or heirs being unable to agree on the distribution of inherited land. Even with the current high market value of land, few families are willing to sell, realizing that once their holdings are sold they will be unable to replace them in the future. This especially is important for rice land, the key to a family's subsistence needs. A family dependent on share-cropping arrangements for access to land must expend twice the labour to obtain the same yields as a family which owns its own land. As tenant farmers its members would have little hope of producing a surplus of rice beyond their immediate consumption needs.

Rice land is valued primarily as a subsistence resource and only secondarily as a source of cash income. A farm family's rice land not only provides its members their daily sustenance, but did so for their ancestors and is expected to do so for their descendants. As such, it has a high subjective value, and this emotional attachment to the land is one reason why rice land rarely enters the market.

A second reason why rice land rarely is sold is that once sold it would be difficult to replace. This is so not only because the market in rice land is relatively inactive, but because the price of any type of land is rising rapidly, putting it beyond the reach of many families. The current high price of rice land has little to do with either the land's subjective value or an objective value based on its income producing potential (see Table 3.8). Rather, the most important factor accounting for the rise in price of rice land is its value as a scarce commodity. This in turn has made rice land attractive to non-farmers with cash to invest. Within the study universe of Gong Guncil, all purchases of rice land made in the past decade save one are reported by local informants to have been made by teachers who live or work nearby. The one exception is a farm family which sold its rice land in Kelantan (where land values are even higher) and moved to Gong Guncil, using the proceeds from the sale to purchase new land. The amount of land that has changed ownership in the past decade is small, totalling less than 15 acres. Farmers are not being displaced from their land in a wholesale fashion, but as the market value of land continues to rise, future sales are likely to be made to non-farmers, confirming a disturbing pattern which has been noted elsewhere (see especially Swift, 1967).

Rubber land differs from rice land in having lower subjective and scarcity values. Rubber production is a source of variable cash income and of secondary importance to most farm families of Gong Guncil. Most of the rubber land in the area is planted with old trees of limited productivity. Unlike rice, rubber is a purely commercial crop, is not eaten, and is not shared among families. Neither is rubber land as scarce as rice land. New rubber stands are being planted further inland within a radius of 10 miles, and within the village itself land thinly planted with fruit trees mixed with secondary undergrowth could be put under rubber.

Land used for housing (*tanah kampung*) and land planted with fruit trees (*tanah dusun*) carry greater subjective value than rubber land. Fruit trees which a man planted in his youth, or which his or his wife's father or even grandfather planted, lend a certain emotional appeal to *tanah dusun* and make a family reluctant to part with this land. The land upon which a family has built its house also is likely to have been occupied by either the husband's or the wife's forebears. In a village where there are numerous close kinsmen, a family will have no difficulty in finding a spot to locate its house and, if it chooses, plant a small garden or a few trees. It is common to find several closely related households living on the same piece of land without any rent being paid to the owner. Even non-kinsmen are allowed to build their houses on *tanah kampung*, and if any rent is charged the sum will be nominal, e.g. $5.00 per year. Neither *tanah kampung* nor *tanah dusun* can be considered scarce in the sense that rice land is scarce.

INHERITANCE AND LAND FRAGMENTATION

As a consequence of the high market and scarcity values of rice land, inheritance is the most prevalent means by which a farming family gains access to this resource. One consequence of inheritance among rice farmers is the gradual fragmentation of holdings from one generation to the next. This process is modified, however, by practical limitations. Holdings of rice land rarely are subdivided below a certain threshold, in practice set at about one acre; below this level a household would be unable to produce enough rice to assure its basic subsistence needs. A farm family owning 2 acres of rice land is unlikely to divide this small holding among several offspring. Often a child or two will marry spouses who own or have access to land or who are otherwise economically established. A son, or less commonly a daughter, may migrate to a town or another rural area looking for employment if economic opportunity near the home village is limited. By the time the inheritance is divided, it is likely that several siblings will have moved away or become economically independent. Though each sibling has an equal share in the inheritance, individual needs are not likely to be equal, and the distribution ideally (and in practice usually) takes into consideration such needs. One heir may receive the family home and livestock, another the family's orchards or rubber land, and a third the rice land.

A farm family with larger than average landholdings, e.g. 5–10 acres, may be able to provide an inheritance of land to all or most of the children sufficient to produce enough rice for subsistence needs, though again relative need may determine the specifics of the distribution. The fragmentation of such larger than average landholdings has a levelling effect within a community, ultimately bringing most families to or near subsistence level.

The process of land fragmentation through inheritance may be modified as a result of any one of a number of factors. A couple may have only one surviving child, natural or adopted, in which case the family's land remains undivided. Alternatively, all but one of this couple's children may continue their schooling at the secondary or even tertiary level and find employment outside the village; their relatively high salaries make them less dependent upon an inheritance, and those of their siblings who remain in the home village are then likely to inherit control over most or all of the family's land. Finally, the process of land fragmentation for relatively wealthy farm families may be modified by their ability to purchase land.

Families which already possess larger than average holdings are more likely to be in a position to buy land when it becomes available, and to take advantage of technological innovations which require greater investment of production capital (and the associated risks), but which also may provide significant increases in production. By combining larger farm size with greater productivity per unit of land, these families generate large rice surpluses for sale. Villagers who have regular cash incomes from wage employment as labourers and non-villagers such as schoolteachers and government clerks with substantial cash reserves and access to institutional credit also are advantageously placed to purchase land.

In discussing land fragmentation through inheritance it was assumed there was something to divide. Yet one-quarter of the households in Gong Guncil are landless tenant farmers. Their heirs are likely to remain landless, and depend upon share-cropping and rental agreements to obtain access to rice land.

ACCUMULATING CAPITAL: *PAJAK* AND *GADAI*

This scenario of the rich effectively maintaining their economic position while the poor struggle to maintain a subsistence base is accurate in general, but there also are possibilities for a family with limited material assets to accumulate capital and acquire land. A family with little or no land can obtain access to land through *gadai* or *pajak*. A land-owner who is in need of immediate cash will lease his land to another who is able to provide cash on short notice. Typically it is the owner of smaller holdings who will need to avail himself of such credit rather than the owner of relatively extensive holdings, whose production surpluses are adequate to cover most immediate cash needs. The relatively wealthy villagers also are likely to be the ones who have ready cash and often are approached by others in need of this form of credit, usually for consumption purposes. There also are farm families of more limited means which use lease agreements to increase their effective farm size. The sums of money involved usually are small, between $200 and $300 per acre, and can be accumulated by a family of modest means.

Lease agreements are not considered to be exploitative, though as noted in Chapter 3 the return to the investment of a leaseholder is quite attractive. In Gong Guncil lease agreements provide the land-owner with immediate cash and the leaseholder with temporary rights to the use of the land. Under *pajak* a certain time is stipulated (often a year or two) after which the land-owner regains effective possession of the land. *Pajak* essentially is an extended rental, the leaseholder paying rent in advance, usually at a substantial discount compared to seasonal rents which are paid at the end of each harvest. *Gadai*, on the other hand, is an open-ended lease whereby the legal owner of the land regains effective control of the land only after the loan has been repaid in full; the leaseholder may gain little if the loan is repaid after only one season but stands to gain more the longer the loan remains unpaid.

Gadai is the more prevalent form of lease arrangement, and because often it takes several years for the owners to repay their loan, the leaseholder retains control over the land for an extended period. As noted in Chapter 3, it is common practice for the leaseholder to allow the legal owner to continue cultivating his or her land under a share-cropping agreement which returns one-third of the harvest to the leaseholder (*bagi tiga*). This especially is common when the farm family holding the lease is relatively wealthy and is not trying to increase the amount of land farmed. An owner who wishes to continue working his own land usually will be able to do so by approaching such a creditor. Sometimes, however, the owner may prefer to allow the leaseholder to cultivate the land. If this is the case, the owner will lease the land to a farm family wishing to increase its effective farm size.

Through leasing, a farm family of limited means is able to increase its effective farm size at a cost lower than share-cropping or rental arrangements, and thus produce a larger surplus of rice for sale. The accumulated profits from such sales then can be used for other leases or the purchase of land that comes onto the market. This is an effective though long-term strategy for increasing a family's landed wealth, and one which requires years of hard work and frugality to acquire enough capital to purchase even one acre of land.

ACCUMULATING CAPITAL: LIVESTOCK

A more common method of capital accumulation adopted by families of limited means is raising livestock for sale, especially cattle and to a lesser extent water-buffalo and goats. Meat is a luxury food only rarely consumed in a village. Cattle and water-buffalo usually are sold to specialized traders who frequently pass through the village and who in turn sell the animals to urban abattoirs. The sale of a five-year-old cow will bring a farm family at least $500; a water-buffalo of the same age will sell for even more. Older, larger water-buffalo may sell for over $1,000.

Since the introduction of double-cropping, the number of livestock raised in the Gong Guncil area has declined, primarily due to the difficulty of providing adequate grazing grounds for these animals. The pressures of double-cropping also have decreased reliance upon the use of workstock for land preparation. These factors have affected the water-buffalo population more seriously than the cattle population. Water-buffalo have been replaced by the use of tractors for land preparation and also require more grazing land for their maintenance than do cattle. Moreover, unlike cattle which can be looked after by younger children, water-buffalo require the attention of an adult male member of a household.

For these reasons cattle are the most prevalent livestock raised in Gong Guncil. They are taken from their corrals early in the morning and tethered wherever grass is available. They usually are moved to new grazing spots several times during the day; sometimes additional fodder is cut for them. No grain is provided either to cattle or water-buffalo, and the only cost in their rearing is that of the labour involved. Rarely do families purchase either young animals to rear or older animals as breeding stock. If a farm family has not inherited livestock, or has sold what livestock it owned, it is able to re-establish its herd by means of *pawah* arrangements with fellow villagers, with no expense other than time and labour.

Livestock represents a walking capital fund which quickly may be turned into cash to meet extraordinary expenses—a wedding or other feast, a pilgrimage to Mecca, advanced secular or religious education for children, building a new house, or repairs and extensions to an existing house. Usually the cost of such expenditures will be met by the sale of one or two animals. Proceeds from the sale of livestock also may be used for the purchase of rice land, but unless a family has an extensive herd this sum is unlikely to be sufficient to purchase even one acre. Among rice farmers, the majority of whom are unable to produce large surpluses of grain for sale, raising livestock is probably the most important means of accumulating capital. Though the proceeds from the sale of livestock may be insufficient to buy land, the sale of three or four mature cattle may cover half or more of the price of an acre of land; if the family already owns one or two acres it may be able to earn part of the balance of funds needed by leasing out this land (i.e. *gadai*) to another family.

A hard-working, frugal family of limited means may gradually accumulate enough cash to purchase small amounts of land, but this is likely to take many years. Raising livestock is a relatively effortless and inexpensive means of acquiring capital, but it will only be one part of an overall strategy of capital accumulation. Leasing the land of fellow villagers allows for the production of surplus rice which may be sold. Money also can be earned by growing a cash crop such as tobacco, pedalling a trishaw, or working in the construction industry in Singapore. There is, then, some chance for upward mobility even for poor families, but the process is slow. However, if land values continue to escalate the ability of a family of limited means to afford even one acre of rice land will decrease.

KAMPUNG DUSUN

With its land-based economy, Kampung Dusun is more directly comparable with Gong Guncil than with Mangkok. For rubber tappers, the primary natural resource, land, is expensive and in limited supply. Inheritance provides the single most important source of land for most families, and the offspring of landless families are likely to remain landless. There are, however, important differences to be highlighted between the situation in Kampung Dusun and that in Gong Guncil.

The rice farmers in Gong Guncil tend to cultivate land near their houses, a practice which limits their available land resource to the immediate vicinity of their home village. Rice farmers visit their fields irregularly once the crop is established, but during certain critical periods, e.g. when seed-beds are being established and immediately after transplanting, constant watch is maintained. If the rice fields are distant, these tasks are more difficult. After harvest a heavy and bulky crop needs to be carried home. Moreover, a crop of rice ready to harvest is vulnerable to the depredations of birds and to theft, and farmers understandably prefer to have their fields closer to home to guard against these dangers.

Rubber tappers prefer to work land near their homes, but they are less constrained than rice farmers in this regard. With a bicycle a tapper easily can travel 5 miles or more to his rubber stand, and a small motor cycle allows an even wider range. The ability to work land outside the immediate confines of the village greatly expands the available land resource for families in Kampung Dusun, and for rubber tappers generally.

Kampung Dusun and other villages in the vicinity of the town of Sik are long established and relatively more densely populated than those in Sik District's interior. Kampung Dusun is served by piped water and electricity, the only one of the three communities studied which has these amenities. In Kampung Dusun land suitable for housing is worth more than $5,000 per *relong* ($7,000 per acre), a price which reflects the close proximity of the town.

Bordering the village is a small area suitable for rice cultivation; this land virtually never changes ownership except through inheritance. Though the yields are small, those families which own rice land place a very high value on their ability to produce at least some part of their consumption requirements. The volatile nature of the rubber market and the extreme scarcity of rice land in this hilly area serve to explain the importance of rice land to its owners.

Rubber land is the primary natural resource from which most

families of Kampung Dusun earn their living. Rubber land in the immediate vicinity of the village has a higher market value than rubber land with trees of comparable quality which is located further inland. In Kampung Dusun rubber land may cost more than $3,000 per *relong* even if planted with older, less productive trees; further inland a comparable planting may cost $2,000 or less per *relong*, depending on terrain and access to a road. Land planted with younger, high-yielding trees will bring a premium price of perhaps $1,000 per *relong* more than land planted with older trees. This is an estimate supplied by informants; such land is offered for sale even less frequently than other rubber land, and the author was unable to collect precise data on such sales.

The higher value of land in and around Kampung Dusun reflects the higher population density in this area compared to the interior of Sik District, and also the obvious convenience of working land close to home. The scarcity value of rubber land is limited, however, by the availability of land further inland and by the tappers' mobility, which allows them to exploit land miles from their home village without necessitating a move from that village.

Three-quarters of Sik District's 636 square miles is covered with primary and secondary jungle under Forest Reserve. This extensive area is not at present legally available for cultivation, but its existence would seem to mitigate against subjective feelings of land hunger. Though many families are landless, the presence of hundreds of square miles of land suitable for rubber gives local residents hope that in the future the government will alienate blocks of land for cultivation, as was done in the 1950s and 1960s. At that time land with easy access to roads was still available for the price of administrative and surveying costs, although the process of applying for title to this land required several years to complete.

A few scattered parcels which can be claimed for private ownership still remain, but without exception they are located far from existing roads and often on steep terrain. At present, the government appears to have no further plans for alienating Forest Reserve land for private ownership. Nonetheless, many landless families appropriate parts of this Forest Reserve for their own use and plant fruit and rubber trees. (A few wealthy and politically well-connected families cleared larger areas, in one case reportedly 200 *relong*, which then was planted with rubber.) Many of these illegal holdings exist for decades without government interference; in other cases squatters are moved out by government authorities soon after they are discovered.

During 1977, in two separate incidents in Sik District, the government evicted squatters and cut down their fruit and rubber trees. In one case the land had been in use by the squatters since before World War II; in another the settlement had existed for at least 5 years. In both cases the settlers, through public demonstrations, effectively pressured the government into officially recognizing their rights to own and operate the land.

Through legal or extra-legal means, land in Sik District suitable for rubber cultivation is in relatively abundant supply when compared to the rice land available to farmers of Gong Guncil. Though land near Kampung Dusun itself can be considered scarce, further inland it is less so, and is more frequently offered for sale. Though the market in rubber land in Sik District cannot be characterized as being highly active, it is when compared to the market in rice land in Gong Guncil. In part this is due to the relatively abundant supply of land and in part to the fact that there is less emotional attachment to rubber land than there is to rice land.

For centuries rice cultivation has been the primary occupation of rural Malays. Rice is more than simply a staple food; it is inextricably bound up with Malay cultural identity. Rice is central to Malay customs and ceremonies, and though many of the pre-Islamic practices associated with rice cultivation (e.g. propitiation of the rice spirits) have fallen into disuse, rice and rice cultivation have meaning beyond the food provided.

Unlike rice land, from which a family draws direct sustenance, rubber land is a purely commercial commodity. Introduced early in the twentieth century, rubber tapping has not accumulated a comparable set of ceremonies and beliefs and requires none of the complex forms of labour organization found in rice farming and fishing. In the smallholder sector, rubber is a cash crop produced by the labour of an individual family which, unlike the families of rice farmers and fishermen, does not share the fruits of its labour with fellow villagers. Rubber land is a capital asset which provides for a family's cash needs, but it is not the basis of a broad range of cooperative relationships within a village.

Sik District's relatively active market in rubber land means that a landless family could purchase land. As tenant tappers their production must be shared with the land-owner, but if both the yield of the trees and the price for rubber are high, they will be able to put extra money aside. These savings are likely to be supplemented by raising livestock, as in Gong Guncil. Unlike Gong Guncil, leasing land is not a viable strategy for gaining access to this resource in Kampung Dusun: there are no lease arrangements among rubber tappers comparable to those among rice farmers. A family leasing out rubber land for a stipulated sum risks the very real threat of having its trees slaughter tapped by the leaseholder, who will seek to maximize immediate yields at the expense of the trees' long-term productivity; the trees are likely to be seriously damaged and, in extreme cases, may have to be cut down and replanted. The owner of a rice field risks comparatively little; the leaseholder may neglect to fertilize the fields and may not maintain the bunds, but there is not likely to be significant damage to the soil.

The ability of a landless or near landless family to buy rubber land is limited by a production regimen which make holdings of only one or 2 *relong* uneconomic. Often families in Gong Guncil will own or farm several small, separate plots located in different fields, which may reduce the risk of loss through disease or insect infestation. Since different fields are often on a slightly different planting schedule, farming separate plots also facilitates the allocation of a family's labour. Because rice fields typically are within a mile or so of the family home, the time spent in travelling between the different plots is not a major problem. In rubber tapping, however, fragmentation of land into separate small plots presents major difficulties. Daily tapping is carried out in the early morning hours, and working separate plots of land would seriously reduce labour efficiency, both in tapping and in collecting the latex.

Depending on topography and type of tree tapped, a tapper can effectively work 4 or 5 *relong* of land. Though some people tap holdings of as little as 1–2 *relong*, this most commonly is done by an elderly tapper or by the wife of a man who taps (or is employed) elsewhere. If their economic activities were confined to rubber tapping, such a small holding would provide insufficient income for most families, and would be an inefficient use of their time.

A family of rice farmers might consider the effort of cultivating one acre (or even less) worthwhile and would be able to schedule alternative employment strategies around the limited seasonal labour requirements of rice cultivation. Rubber tapping, in contrast, requires a certain daily input of time and labour which varies little whether one or 4 *relong* of land is worked. The production of scrap rubber modifies this regimen somewhat as the tapper producing scrap is not required to wait for the latex to flow or process the latex into ribbed sheet. Scrap production, however, is risky during periods of heavy rain, which may wash away the latex before it coagulates.

Since a parcel of 1–2 *relong* of rubber land is insufficient to support a family and is inefficient in terms of labour utilization, a landless family seeking to buy rubber land would need to purchase at least 3–4 *relong*. Even if relatively inexpensive rubber land is available (e.g., less than $2,000 per *relong*), the cost of an economic holding is prohibitive for most families. A family of rice farmers may purchase one acre ($3,000) or less, and gradually increase the size of its holdings over a period of years. Rubber tappers are less likely to purchase land in such small increments, and consequently require a larger sum of money for any single purchase.

The necessity of maintaining an economic holding for rubber production directly affects matters of inheritance. A man or woman owning 4 *relong* and having four potential heirs is unlikely simply to divide the land equally among them. As in Gong Guncil, the division of the family property will be influenced by the status and need of the various heirs, in order to keep the rubber holding to an economic size, but in practice questions of inheritance are not resolved so easily. The heirs may disagree on the distribution and decide that the only way to settle the dispute is to sell the land. Alternatively the holding may be fragmented even though the resulting parcels are uneconomic in size. If a young husband or wife inherits an uneconomic holding, the wife may tap this land while the husband works as a share-cropper on the land of another family. Alternatively, the small parcel may be leased out for share-cropping to a family working on a contiguous parcel of land, or the couple may share-crop the land adjacent to their inheritance in order to make it a more economic holding.

Over time this young family may inherit additional rubber land which, if contiguous or nearly so, may make up an economic holding. If the two parcels of land are too distant from each other to be operated effectively, both parcels of land may be share-cropped by others while the owners in turn share-crop a larger holding. Alternatively, they may decide to sell the two parcels and buy one single, larger plot.

The necessity of purchasing land in blocks of several *relong* at a time rather than in smaller increments (as is possible for rice farmers) limits the ability of landless families to acquire land, the relatively active market in land notwithstanding. As in Gong Guncil, the relatively wealthy families of Kampung Dusun can afford to purchase land more easily than can their less fortunate neighbours. Rubber land is an attractive investment for these families as well as non-villagers, providing a hedge against inflation and a source of cash income. In Gong Guncil the ability of wealthy farm families and non-villagers to purchase rice land is limited by the infrequency of sales. For reasons stated above, rubber land in Sik District is a more active commodity. Moreover, families which can afford to postpone immediate cash income and consider rubber land a long-term investment are more likely to take advantage of the government's replanting grants than are families whose primary source of cash income must be derived from one small holding.

Data collected indicate greater inequality in the distribution of land-ownership in Kampung Dusun than in Gong Guncil (compare Tables 5.2 and 3.2). Moreover, these data do not reflect the very sizeable holdings of rubber land controlled by several wealthy families in Sik District, some of which are in excess of 100 *relong*. Though there will be a tendency for large holdings to become fragmented from one generation to the next, the levelling effect of inheritance is mitigated by marriage alliances between similarly wealthy families, and as stated previously, by their ability to purchase land on the open market. It is likely that this pattern of inequality not only will continue, but will worsen in the future, especially as those families which can afford to replant their land with high-yielding rubber trees do so and begin to obtain significantly greater yields.

MANGKOK

The fishing economy of Mangkok differs in important respects from the land-based economies of Gong Guncil and Kampung Dusun. Land is a secondary economic asset for most families of Mangkok. The sandy soils support little vegetation other than coconuts and a thin ground cover of grass which quickly withers in the absence of rain. The sparse vegetation severely limits livestock raising to goats and a few usually hungry-looking cattle. Animal husbandry is not a viable strategy for capital accumulation in Mangkok. Neither is coconut production, which is limited by climatic features discussed in Chapter 4 and by the fact that most of Mangkok's coconut trees are old and past their prime. A few families earn several hundred dollars a year through the sale of fresh coconut and copra, but the majority must be content with production for household consumption only.

Land within Mangkok is valued primarily for housing, though a family with no land will find little difficulty in gaining permission to build a house on a kinsman's land. Most land is valued at $700 per acre, significantly lower than land in either Gong Guncil or Kampung Dusun. The market value of land reflects its limited productive potential and the absence of any scarcity value attached to it. A family may have emotional attachment to land it has inherited, but this attachment has little to do with basic subsistence needs. Unlike the other two communities studied, in Mangkok non-villagers speculatively investing in land are conspicuously absent.

Land is a relatively unattractive investment to fishermen whose primary productive assets are boats, engines, and nets. Unlike land, which is a finite resource with clear and enforceable restrictions on access, the primary resource of fishermen is the fish in the sea. Though there are legal restrictions on the operation of trawlers close to shore, and there are specific fishing grounds which can be marked off for exclusive use through the erection of traps or shelters, the sea essentially is open to all fishermen. The technology for catching fish is similarly open ended. Additional boats and nets may be added and only a marked reduction in the catch is likely to interrupt this process. In recent years this unrestricted access to fishing grounds has led to concern that fish stocks may be overexploited (Marr, 1976). In Mangkok, fishermen express the same concerns and lay blame on the proliferation of trawlers which illegally operate close to shore and whose fine-mesh nets capture the small fish upon which the primarily carnivorous commercial species feed, as well as capturing the fry of these commercial species. While trawlers may be responsible in large part for the decline in fish stocks in Malaysia's coastal waters, the ease with which fishermen operating traditional gears expand the number of boats and nets operating in a given area no doubt is another contributing factor.

As noted in Chapter 4, a young fisherman may buy an old boat and a used net and become an owner—operator. The investment required may be as little as $1,000. He may depend on his parents, grandparents, or in-laws to lend part or even the entire amount necessary. While he lives in his parents' home, most of his income will be turned over to his mother. Any subsequent loan from his parents may be considered not so much a matter of inheritance or cross-generational assistance as recognition of past contributions to the family which in this manner are being repaid. Usually such a purchase will be made only after this son has worked at sea for a number of years, often including employment as captain on another person's boat.

As the years pass the young fisherman may sell his original boat and buy a newer, more seaworthy craft. In the meantime new sections of netting will be added, gradually replacing those that have worn out, and perhaps the total length of the net will be increased. Unlike rice farming and rubber tapping families, ownership of productive resources is available to many if not most fishermen and further investments may be made incrementally. As some fishermen and their families trade up to newer boats, other fishermen provide a market for the used boats. Not all fishermen make such investments: some prefer the lesser responsibilities of working as crewmen, or are engaged in secondary economic activities which keep them from being full-time fishermen. Others are less frugal, less diligent, or less lucky at fishing and are unable to accumulate the capital required to become a boat owner. Nonetheless, it is obvious that fishermen have greater opportunity to own the means of their production than either rice farmers or rubber tappers.

Boats and nets depreciate and deteriorate over time and require constant maintenance, part of which may require only an investment in labour, but there also are a number of expenses which require cash payment. Boats need to be painted at least once a year, preferably twice a year, and there are occasional minor engine breakdowns which require new parts. Less frequently, major engine breakdowns may put a boat out of action for an extended period of time and cost several hundred dollars for repairs. A net requires constant maintenance and regular replacement of worn out sections if its efficiency is to be sustained. The need for such constant reinvestment is recognized by specifying a particular share for both the boat and the net from the total proceeds of the catch.

In a situation where the primary natural resource is open to all and the technology for exploiting this resource is available to many if not to all, the importance of inheritance is reduced. In Mangkok the only permanent rights over a fixed resource to be transmitted from one generation to the next are rights over land, a commodity of limited utility. If a family owns a boat or net these are likely to be of greater value and of greater income-producing potential. In common with rural Malay society in general, the villagers of Mangkok feel that both sons and daughters should be treated equally in terms of inheritance. In practice, however, sons are more likely to inherit a family's boat and/or net, while daughters tend to inherit the family's house, land, coconut trees, and any livestock.

Unlike the land-based economies of Gong Guncil and Kampung Dusun, in Mangkok the most important assets—boats and nets—are divisible only through sale. If there are several heirs, it is not possible to fragment such a holding among them. Therefore if a family owns a boat and net there are several options: the boat and net may be sold and the proceeds divided among the heirs; alternatively, one of the heirs may inherit the boat (and usually the net as well) and the other heirs divide the remainder of the family's assets.

The decision will hinge on several factors. If the father, the probable owner of the boat and net, dies intestate, the heirs must collectively agree upon the distribution of the inheritance. They may agree that only one of them will inherit the boat and net, but more commonly these assets will be sold and the cash distributed. If the father decides to retire from active fishing, he and his wife may decide to hand over ownership to one of their sons or even a grandson, with the understanding that the son or grandson will support them in their old age. By the time a fisherman retires, often in his sixties, several or even all of his sons already will be established as owners and captains of their own boats or be otherwise employed.

Because the father is likely to continue fishing long after his sons have gone to sea, they have no immediate prospect of taking over his boat; by the time he retires, the hull and net may have worn out, leaving little of value to inherit. He also may decide to sell his boat and net and use the proceeds to support himself and his wife in their old age. Alternatively, the boat and net may be handed over to another fisherman to operate, the family then receiving the boat and net shares as income.

In Mangkok, children grow up with the understanding that the most important material assets owned by the family are impermanent. If a son desires to become a boat owner, he either must wait until his father retires from fishing (which may not be for another 15 or 20 years) or buy a used boat of his own. Because of the uncertainties associated with the first strategy, it usually is the latter which is adopted.

In a fishing village the transmission of wealth from one generation to the next is an important but not a crucial factor in the economic success of individual families. A young family with relatively wealthy kinsmen may more easily borrow the money necessary to purchase a boat and net, but even one of limited means without such ready credit may become the owner of these productive assets. In land-based economies, inheritance to a large extent determines the economic standing of succeeding generations. In a fishing economy, economic success is determined to a much greater extent by the skill, diligence and luck of individual fishermen and the careful management of their household economy by their wives. Consequently, economic stratification in a fishing community such as Mangkok is less rigid than in the two land-based economies represented by Gong Guncil and Kampung Dusun.

An important caveat should be noted concerning this portrayal of a relatively egalitarian situation. Future technological changes in the direction of larger boats and more expensive gear may lead to distributional changes which favour owners as opposed to crewmen. In the neighbouring villages of Kuala Baru and Penarek the crewmen of large purse-seiners earn incomes comparable to and sometimes higher than the drift netters of Mangkok, but the captains and the owners of these boats earn considerably more. Where such capital-intensive fishing takes place, the owners have significantly higher incomes and assets to pass to their heirs, and in this situation economic inequalities are more likely to persist from generation to generation.

CONCLUSIONS

One of the most important differences between the three communities studied concerns the availability of natural resources. The economies of rice farming and rubber tapping are based on a finite natural resource, the land, to which access is limited by clear and enforceable rights of ownership. In contrast, the natural resource exploited by fishermen, the sea, is freely available to all.

This major difference makes inheritance a more important determinant of economic standing in rice farming and rubber tapping communities than it is in a fishing economy. As a scarce and highly valued commodity, land rarely is offered for sale, and when it is, its price is so high that most farm families not fortunate enough to have inherited land are likely to remain landless. Inheritance in a fishing economy also is important, but to a lesser extent because the transferable assets (boats and nets) deteriorate and depreciate over time. In contrast, land holds or increases its value and is a more permanent asset which can be passed from generation to generation. As a consequence, economic inequalities are more likely to be persistent from generation to generation among rice farmers and rubber tappers than among fishermen.

Variations in the availability of and access to natural resources are paralleled by similar differences which affect the use of technological resources. Fishermen enjoy unimpeded access to the sea, and an active market in used boats and nets makes it possible for most fishermen who so choose to become owners of the means of their production. The technological resources available to rice farmers and rubber tappers, including new varieties of seed, planting materials, and chemical fertilizers, also in principle are available to all; in practice, however, technological innovations which promise increases in productivity have not been adopted uniformly. Only farmers and tappers in a position to accept the costs and risks associated with these innovations have benefited from the new agricultural technologies. Rice farmers operating at or near a subsistence level of production have been reluctant to maximize their yields by increasing the application of chemical fertilizers for fear of a crop loss, which then would threaten not only their subsistence but their limited working capital as well. Farm families which own larger than average acreages of rice land from which a substantial surplus can be produced are in a better position to take advantage of the new rice technology. Similarly, rubber tappers who own larger than average acreages of rubber land are able to take advantage of the government's replanting scheme and replace older, less productive trees with high-yielding varieties. Their less fortunate neighbours can less easily afford the 7 years of lost production entailed in replanting, and are more likely to continue tapping less productive trees.

In this chapter we have seen that important differences exist in access to and control over natural and technological resources among Malay rice farmers, fishermen, and rubber tappers. These differences in turn affect a wide range of social relationships, a theme that is explored at greater length in the chapter which follows.

7 Social Consequences of Economic Organization

THIS study has concentrated on production processes and the social relationships which these processes engender. In so doing it has identified major differences within rural Malay society based on the differing economic adaptations of rice farming, fishing, and rubber tapping. The central tenet of this study is that production processes and relationships affect many aspects of social life. Indeed, the distinction between economic and non-economic aspects of life often is blurred. Virtually every aspect of social life can be seen to be affected by the economic context in which social relationships exist. Many social relationships are influenced by the nature of the relationships between owners and non-owners of productive resources. Relations among kinsmen and patterns of local leadership are directly influenced by the exigencies of economic life. The character and tone of a community are influenced by the necessity (or lack thereof) for its members to cooperate in production-oriented activities. The discussion which follows will consider each of the three communities studied and will focus on the issues introduced above: relations between owners and non-owners, relations among kinsmen, local leadership patterns, and the social consequences of reciprocal exchanges of labour.

GONG GUNCIL

INTERDEPENDENCE OF RICE FARMERS

Rice farmers depend on their neighbours and kinsmen both for supplementary labour during peak seasons of labour demand and for coordination of the planting schedule. In order to achicve optimum water, pest, and disease control, successful rice cultivation in a given field requires roughly simultaneous land preparation, seeding, transplanting, and harvesting. The crop of a farm family planting prior to others in a particular field is likely to attract the attention of birds and various insect pests which will seriously damage the earlier ripening crop. A family late in planting risks similar losses, and in addition will suffer if draining of contiguous parcels begins before its rice crop is fully developed. If the parcels of each individual family planting rice in a given field develop and ripen simultaneously, the risk of loss is substantially reduced for all. It is for this reason that prior to each season farm families in Gong Guncil meet informally, both in their fields and in their homes, to exchange information on which variety they intend to plant and when they intend to begin seeding. Consequently, all the plots within a field tend to be planted simultaneously, with a limited number of rice varieties which have roughly comparable maturation rates. There is no formal mechanism to achieve this cooperation. Rather, the decisions are made through an informal consensus based on mutual interests.

At one time or another, most farm families in Gong Guncil depend on the assistance of others during the transplanting season. When their rice seeds are sown a family is committed to transplanting the seedlings in a relatively short period of a week to ten days. Some families avoid this problem by making successive sowings or sowing their seed in separate seed-beds for each of their plots. This may reduce some of the pressure of transplanting, but in any given season a number of families will require additional help beyond their own labour resources. They may hire labour on a cash basis, or engage in reciprocal exchanges of labour either with a limited circle of kinsmen and friends (*tolong-menolong*), or through a call upon a large number of helpers (*pinjam orang*). If a limited amount of assistance is required, hired help or labour mobilized through *tolong-menolong* will be used; if there is a great amount of work to be done, however, *pinjam orang* often is the only practical option available.

The number of helpers called upon for *pinjam orang* depends on a number of factors, including the amount of work that needs to be done and the number of people whom the family has helped in the past. Using *pinjam orang* establishes an obligation to reciprocate in the future. Most farm families consider it in their interest to participate in *pinjam orang* activities even if no immediate need to call upon such labour is foreseen. If they do not assist others, no one would come to help them in time of need, e.g. when sudden illness, injury, or recent or imminent childbirth reduces a family's ability to plant a crop. The majority of farm families at one time or another are subject to such problems, creating the need for mutual interdependence. The result of this interdependency of farm families is a web of reciprocal labour obligations which have great importance not only in rice production but in other aspects of social life as well.

Only members of the local economic élite are isolated from this interdependence and the associated reciprocal labour obligations. Their labour needs are met through hired labour brought in from distant villages where rice either is not grown or is grown on a different schedule. Other families in the Gong Guncil area requiring hired help without exception hire members of the local community, providing an important source of employment and income.

THE *KETUA PINJAM ORANG*

Effective utilization of Gong Guncil's labour resources during critical periods such as transplanting requires effective coordination. To accomplish this each community has one or two recognized labour organizers, known as *ketua pinjam orang*. Gong Guncil has two such persons. A family wishing to utilize *pinjam orang* will call upon one or both of these men, stating how much work needs to be done in which field on what day. By channelling requests through these men, the problem of several families attempting to use *pinjam orang* on the same day is avoided. The family needing the help also is saved the time and difficulty of informing a large number of people as the organizers undertake the task of spreading the word, either by hailing people as they pass by, visiting them in their homes, or sending messages via children.

The organizers act as more than a simple clearing-house for families seeking assistance through *pinjam orang*. Intimate knowledge of reciprocal obligations incurred in the past enables them to make accurate estimates of the number of helpers a family is likely to attract for an afternoon's work. It is clear that those who have assisted others in the past are able to attract large numbers of helpers through *pinjam orang*, while those who did not participate are unable to obtain such help. It might be thought that the decision as to whether or not to help would be made by the individual family whose assistance is requested. In the final analysis this is true, but the *ketua pinjam orang* is in a position to exert considerable influence in this matter. In this he acts not only as a coordinator but as an organizer and enforcer.

Whenever a *ketua pinjam orang* agrees to help a family mobilize labour he puts his prestige and reputation for effectiveness on the line. If he promises a family that forty workers will arrive on a given afternoon and significantly less turn out, it will be embarrassing for all concerned; if this occurs repeatedly he will lose his position. In practice, however, an effective *ketua pinjam orang* is able to estimate how many people are willing to help a particular family, and he will not agree to call out an unrealizable number. Those asked to help a particular family are likely to do so not only to discharge reciprocal labour obligations but also with an eye to staying in the *ketua pinjam orang*'s favour. A family informed that others need help on a certain day is bound to send at least one of its members. If a family failed to help another family without good reason, the *ketua pinjam orang* might refuse to assist it in the future. Thus, reciprocal labour obligations are buttressed not only by the norm of reciprocity but by the person of the *ketua pinjam orang*.

The willingness of families to turn out whenever a *ketua pinjam orang* requests their assistance carries over into matters not directly related to rice production. Because a majority of farm families are beholden or potentially beholden to this man, calls to contribute labour for community projects such as the clearing of small irrigation canals or maintenance of the local mosque or cemetery are not likely to be ignored.

A *ketua pinjam orang* also mobilizes cooperative labour beyond the confines of the immediate village. Moving a large house may require more manpower than is available within a single community. As many as 300 men may be needed to move a large house, requiring the cooperative effort of men from half a dozen or more communities. A family in need of such help will approach a *ketua pinjam orang* in their community, and together an estimation will be made of the number of men required for the task. If labour beyond the immediate community is required, this *ketua pinjam orang* will visit his counterparts in neighbouring communities to enlist assistance. Each of these *ketua pinjam orang* will be asked to provide a certain number of men on the appointed day. From a community the size of Gong Guncil the assistance of as many as 30 men may be requested. There is no payment for this work other than food, which will vary from local cakes and coffee or tea if a house is moved a short distance, to a full meal if the move requires several hours of work. Individuals who turn out to help move a house in another community do so not in expectation of obtaining commensurate assistance for themselves; rather they do so out of a general sense of social responsibility, because such gatherings are entertaining social activities, and because the *ketua pinjam orang* requested their assistance.

THE EFFECTIVE SOURCE OF LEADERSHIP IN GONG GUNCIL

In Gong Guncil the two *ketua pinjam orang* appeared to be very effective in mobilizing labour. One of these men is employed full-time as a labourer by the Drainage and Irrigation Department, though he and his family continue to plant 2 acres of rice on their own land. The other, Tok Wan, is the more influential. Landless and with two wives, he occasionally helps them in the fields, but it would be an exaggeration to call him a farmer. Self-educated, he is widely respected for his religious learning and piety. He is gifted with a particularly sonorous voice and as muezzin (*bilal*, a formal position at a mosque) gives the Friday call to prayer. He earns a small income from services as circumciser of boys entering manhood, and from making handles and scabbards for the heavy choppers used for clearing brush and the somewhat smaller knives used for slaughtering and butchering animals. Though he is not a rich man, he finds ample time in his daily schedule to attend to various community needs. He initiated a programme of religious instruction for young children, adolescents, and adults, the last of which meets two or three nights a week, except during the transplanting and harvest seasons. Tok Wan also is the person to whom people turn for mediating local disputes. No doubt his effectiveness as a mediator in part is due to his position as *ketua pinjam orang*; a family who refuses to abide by his recommended solution to a dispute may find Tok Wan less than enthusiastic about helping them with future needs.

Tok Wan is the most influential person in the Gong Guncil area, although he is not the formal village headman. The position of *ketua kampung* is held by a member of the local economic élite, the nephew of the previous *ketua kampung*. Though he was chosen for this position by the men of the community over ten years ago, he is not an active leader; indeed, he is regarded with considerable dislike by many. It was his alleged unfair treatment of local residents hired to work his land that led to the boycott of his fields and those of several of his close relatives. His unpopularity is compounded by the commonly held notion that he channelled most of the benefits of various government projects (e.g., the Veterinary Department's *pawah* scheme) to himself and to his immediate kinsmen.

CLASS POLARIZATION

Traditionally it was expected that members of the local economic élite would use their wealth for social purposes, e.g., gifts, loans, feasts, etc. As the rural economy has become increasingly commercialized, however, these traditional expectations are no longer met. Whereas previously the rural economy operated at a subsistence level, at present there are both possibilities for earning cash incomes and opportunities for spending such incomes. Instead of being redistributed throughout the community, wealth now tends to be used for private consumption.

This commercialization of the rural economy has altered the relationship between the majority of the rural population and the local economic élite. Increasingly one finds that the élite deviate from traditional expectations regarding their role as people of wealth and disassociate themselves from involvement in reciprocal exchanges of labour. It also is significant that they are broadening their contacts with non-villagers through advanced education and employment outside the village and through marriage alliances which unite them with other élite groups, especially teachers or other government employees.

There are different economic interests in virtually every Malay village, and relationships between owners and non-owners of productive resources are prone to tension. This was found to be true in each of the three communities studied. However, despite the important exception of the labour boycott metioned above, the rice farmers of Gong Guncil were less affected by such tensions than were the fishermen of Mangkok or the rubber tappers of Kampung Dusun. Other than the few families which comprised the local economic élite, virtually all other families, despite differences in wealth and income, needed to work together on the timing and cultivation of their fields.

MANGKOK

COOPERATION AMONG FISHERMEN

The residents of the fishing village of Mangkok, like those of the rice farming community of Gong Guncil, need to cooperate in the course of productive activities. However, compared to rice farmers, fishermen are able to operate much more independently of one another. Indeed, their occupation calls for independence of judgement and operation. Their interdependence is limited to their small crews of two or three men, and the composition of these crews is itself constantly changing.

Large-scale labour mobilization comparable to that in rice production is unnecessary. The only time that labour beyond that of the crew itself is required is when a new net has been purchased and the numerous component sections need to be sewn together. However, fishermen rarely purchase a completely new net, but rather replace sections of old netting as required. The labour necessary for this task is provided by the crew itself.

At sea, fishermen depend upon their fellow crew members, and indeed generally cannot put to sea until their small crew assembles. The rice farmers of Gong Guncil depend upon the help of others only during certain periods of the crop cycle. In contrast, fishermen are dependent upon their fellow crewmen during every productive day. The nature of this dependence, and the manner of its expression, however, varies greatly from the example of Gong Guncil presented above. In rice production, the need to work together carries over from year to year, and cooperative relationships tend to be long-lasting. The cooperation between individual fishermen, in contrast, is less permanent due to frequent changes in the composition of boat crews.

SOURCES OF CONFLICT

Within Mangkok itself there are numerous boats on which a fisherman can work. A fisherman who is unhappy with the success of one boat or has an argument with the boat's captain, owner, or another crew member is quite free to throw in his lot with another boat. Similarly, if a boat captain is unhappy with a crewman, he may force the crewman to find another boat on which to work. Disputes at sea are common. A crewman and a captain may disagree over where or how many times to cast the net. There also may be disagreements on the manner or price at which the catch is sold or on the maintenance of the boat and net. Most commonly of all, the generosity of the boat captain in sharing the *bahagian bawa* is called into question.

In Chapter 3 it was noted that the right to a subsistence in rice was considered to be basic and incontrovertible among the farm families of Gong Guncil. In the fishing economy of Mangkok the recognition of this right is limited by practical considerations. Fishing essentially is a commercial venture and the capture of fish requires a substantial investment in depreciable equipment. A small amount of fish is reserved for home consumption, but the bulk of the catch is destined to be sold. Fishermen receive their share of the catch in cash, a more impersonal medium than rice standing in a field. The distribution of this cash between boat and net shares and the shares of fishermen allows less room for flexibility than the division of a rice crop. Owners and crewmen alike recognize that a substantial share of the gross income must be retained to meet regular maintenance expenses and the irreversible process of deterioration. Seeing the larger share given to the owners often leads crewmen to ask owners for small loans during periods of poor fishing. The owners are reluctant to do so, however, because there is little likelihood that such loans will be repaid, and their own limited cash reserves must be saved to meet the possible expense of an emergency repair, and for maintaining or improving their equipment.

Tensions also arise in the marketing of fish. Fish buyers, for the most part local men, seek to buy fish cheaply, while their neighbours and kinsmen who caught the fish want to sell dear. Despite the fact that most of the fishermen and buyers operating in

Mangkok are kinsmen, their economic relationships are full of tension and distrust. Fishermen fear that buyers may collectively agree to manipulate the local market to their disadvantage. This distrust was dramatically illustrated when in early 1978 the buyers forced a change in the commonly accepted sale by Dutch auction in favour of buying by weight at standard prices set by the buyers. The buyers claimed that this was the easiest and fairest marketing system, but virtually every fisherman questioned by the author voiced concern that the buyers would fix the prices and unfairly gain from this arrangement.

This new marketing arrangement did not last long, however, as the buyers' solid front itself broke down when several of them began to offer higher prices than the others. With the sale of fish no longer going to the highest bid at auction, several of the buyers were able to call upon economic, kinship, or friendship relationships to obtain sole access to the catch of a particular boat (see Table 4.4). This placed the other buyers at a disadvantage, and they found themselves with hardly any fish to buy and sell. Furthermore, two buyers were able to offer higher prices than the others because they had direct links to the major urban markets, which gave them a larger profit margin than their competitors who sold fish to middlemen in Kuala Trengganu.

PATTERNS OF LOCAL LEADERSHIP

An important consequence of the absence of regular and large-scale cooperative labour exchanges is the absence of any local leadership roles related to matters of production. As in Gong Guncil, Mangkok has a village headman formally recognized by the government, but unlike the one in Gong Guncil, the *ketua kampung* of Mangkok is a popular member of the community. The extent of his power is quite limited, however, for though he is responsible for settling local disputes, in practice he shares this task with several other members of the community, including the *imam* of the local mosque, the head of the Fishermen's Cooperative, and the locally born headmaster of Mangkok's primary school.

The chairman of the Fishermen's Cooperative is in fact the most important leader within Mangkok. Interestingly, he is not a fisherman, nor has he ever worked as one. He and his wife operate a small sundry goods store in Mangkok and he earns a steady cash income as caretaker of the local school. The fishermen of Mangkok elected him chairman of the Fishermen's Cooperative because of his educational background, which included both secular and religious instruction at the secondary school level. This education enables him to keep the Cooperative's books and effectively deal with government officers. He is not, however, a leader in the active sense of the word.

As a community, Mangkok is divided by the competing economic interests of owners, captains, crewmen, and buyers, which contribute to the relative weakness of leadership roles in this community. Mangkok's fishermen lack the kind of solidarity imposed upon the rice farmers of Gong Guncil by the necessities of production. Due to the absence of a comparable need for large-scale cooperative action, in Mangkok there are neither reciprocal labour obligations nor leadership positions which enforce such obligations.

Despite the presence of competing economic interests, the fishermen are spared the deeper divisions based on economic inequalities found among the rice farmers of Gong Guncil. Though there are inequalities of wealth and income in Mangkok, these are not based upon permanent rights over limited resources. As noted in Chapter 6, the sea is a resource open to all, and most fishermen who so choose are able to become owners of their own boats and nets. Economic stratification is less rigid in Mangkok and neither the relationship between owners and non-owners of productive resources nor the competing interests of fishermen and buyers have ossified into class polarization.

KAMPUNG DUSUN

RUBBER TAPPING

The production of rubber requires little or no cooperative labour outside the immediate family. Unlike rice cultivation, there are no periods of peak labour demand. A tapper normally taps and collects latex from several hundred trees without assistance, unless accompanied by a spouse or child. The routine of tapping, collecting, and processing into ribbed sheets occupies the period from daybreak until about noon, day in and day out, weather permitting. There are no advantages to be gained in mobilizing a group of helpers in the course of rubber production. Sometimes, while waiting for the latex to flow after tapping, several tappers will rest and talk together, and they may meet again later if they share the same mangles for pressing ribbed sheet rubber. In some cases they may even help each other operate the mangles, though apart from this they operate independently.

The only time when labour resources beyond the immediate family may be required is when an old stand of rubber trees or a patch of jungle is cleared in preparation for planting new rubber trees, or when an established stand of rubber is cleared of accumulated undergrowth. In practice, however, these tasks usually are managed by a single household which, if necessary, supplements its own labour with hired help. Often the cutting of old rubber trees is contracted to a man owning a powered chain-saw. Clearing the felled trees and planting new trees requires months of work. A close friend or kinsman may offer to help for a few days, but this is rare and in terms of the overall task is of limited importance.

Tappers from separate households rarely work together, even when clearing undergrowth from an established rubber holding. A stand of rubber can be maintained free of weeds by one man, who either clears the undergrowth little by little or who concentrates his effort once or twice a year. Occasionally men from several households join together in small cooperative groups and work on each other's land in rotation. This, it is said, seems to speed up the work and makes the task an enjoyable social activity.

Interestingly, such groups working together to clear rubber stands were found to be more common in Gong Guncil than in Kampung Dusun. In Gong Guncil the tradition of cooperative labour is solidly entrenched, while in Kampung Dusun no comparable tradition exists. In addition to their relative lack of experience in working together, there are two other factors which limit the use of cooperative labour by the residents of this community: the scattered nature of rubber holdings; and the fact that many owners prefer to pay others to complete this task.

In many cases the parcels of land tapped by the people of Kampung Dusun are not contiguous but are scattered across a wide area. Often their land is several miles away from Kampung Dusun, and it is difficult to organize a group of men from the home village to travel such distances. It also would be difficult to organize a group of men from households which tap contiguous rubber stands, as it is likely that such a group would include residents from several villages, some of them miles apart.

The cash-oriented relationship between owners and share-tappers also discourages the formation of such cooperative groups. It is not the responsibility of the tenant to clear the rubber stand of undergrowth. If the owner wants his stand of rubber cleared he must do it himself or hire someone else (usually the share-tapper) to do the work. When the share-tapper is hired, the work is done on the basis of a cash payment. It is of little importance to the owner if the share-tapper does the work himself or arranges to have it done through a cooperative effort. In practice, however, when a person is paid for a given amount of work, others are unlikely to assist him, even if the amount of work they would contribute is reciprocated in full. Work which is paid for in cash is differentiated from work done on one's own behalf; the latter is a suitable situation for cooperative endeavours, but the former is not.

SHARE-CROPPING RELATIONSHIPS

It may be recalled that of the 27 families from Kampung Dusun which tap rubber, 10 own no land and are share-tappers. In a large majority of these cases, they are not related by kinship to the owners of the land they share-tap; often they do not even reside in the same village. Because of this, their social interaction often is limited to the narrow concerns of rubber production.

Tenancy relationships are affected by the commercial nature of rubber production. The rubber economy is based on cash, not on the production of a subsistence food item. An owner of rice land in Gong Guncil is not able to strictly enforce a tenancy agreement if it threatens the subsistence needs of a tenant family. However, unlike yields from rice cultivation, which are prone to loss through natural causes, the income from rubber production is less likely to be affected by natural calamity than by fluctuations in the market price. Also unlike rice farming, rubber production is a commercial proposition unencumbered by a traditional norm of distributive equity between owners and tenants. Lowered income affects the ability of tenant tappers to meet their consumption requirements just as much as a crop loss threatens the subsistence needs of a tenant family cultivating rice, but even when the price of rubber falls, the owner expects to follow the agreed division of production. The product shared by owner and tenant is valued in cash terms, and as such is not directly related (at least from the standpoint of the owner) to the subsistence needs of the tenant family. The commercial nature of rubber, the impersonal workings of the international rubber market, and the fact that owners and tenants often are neither kinsmen nor even residents of the same community are factors which differentiate land tenure relationships between rubber producers and rice farmers.

LOCAL LEADERS

The rubber tappers of Kampung Dusun have no need to cooperate while working, and have no leadership role comparable to that of the *ketua pinjam orang*, or even to the more limited role of boat captain. The leadership roles found in Kampung Dusun are of limited importance in the day-to-day lives of the villagers. The man recognized as the *ketua kampung* has operated a licensed rubber shop in a village almost ten miles away since 1971; six days a week he is away from the village from early morning until the evening. He is a respected member of the community, but his regular absence precludes his acting as an effective leader. Like his neighbours, he is taking care of his own business. In so far as a local leader can be identified, a more likely candidate would be a younger man, a skilled carpenter who heads the Village Development Committee. In recent years, however, this man has been in poor health and unable to spend much time on community affairs.

As in Gong Guncil and Mangkok, formal leadership positions based on government recognition are an insufficient basis in themselves for effective local leadership. In the case of Kampung Dusun's *ketua kampung*, even official recognition is lacking: the position of *ketua kampung* was formally abolished in Kedah in 1950s, and though the title still is used in villages, it is devoid of official sanction or power. The Village Development Committee is recognized officially, but in most cases where it exists at all, it acts as a forum for requesting government assistance rather than as an institution for mobilizing local energies to carry out local projects. These Committees provide little more than the appearance of popular participation in rural development programmes, and in most cases exist only on paper.

The lack of effective leadership within Kampung Dusun, however, cannot be understood on the basis of conflicting business interests, poor health, or lack of official support of existing leaders. Rather, the most significant cause would appear to be the lack of any functional requirement for such leadership. There is no need to mobilize labour on a regular basis for work on rubber holdings as each family operates independently of its neighbours. There is no strong tradition of cooperative action in Kampung Dusun, and it is difficult to call together members of a community who work in scattered locations throughout the district. Rather than actively leading, in the sense of mobilizing the community's energies, its leaders, like those of Mangkok, limit their concerns to the mediation of local disputes and other efforts designed to foster community harmony.

ECONOMIC INEQUALITY

Economic inequalities among rubber producers are more extreme than those among rice farmers primarily because of the more unequal distribution of rubber land ownership. This certainly is true in a comparison of Kampung Dusun and Gong Guncil (Tables 5.2 and 3.2), and probably holds true in general. Rubber land always has been an attractive investment for tappers and non-tappers alike. Some families were fortunate or farsighted enough to obtain legal title to relatively large acreages of such land when it could be easily acquired in the early twentieth century, but through the process of inheritance these holdings are being fragmented. A counter to this, however, is the ability of relatively wealthy landowners to utilize their income from the sale of rubber to purchase additional land. Moreover, the possession of larger than average holdings of rubber land enables owners to cut down older, less productive trees on part of their land and by stages replant with more productive trees. As a consequence of these advantages, economic inequalities among rubber tappers are likely to persist, and indeed become even more extreme in the future.

CONCLUSIONS

THE NATURE OF RURAL MALAY COMMUNITIES

In this chapter and in Chapter 6 a number of important differences between rural Malay communities have been summarized and related to the three most important economic adaptations in which rural Malays are engaged—rice farming, fishing, and rubber tapping. These differences have a direct effect on the character of rural life. In the final analysis, social relationships are basically interactions between individuals and no theoretical framework can fully account for the diversity of such relationships. Nonetheless, the systematic and structural differences pointed out in this study allow us to understand a significant cause of diversity within rural Malay society and provide a framework for understanding the widely divergent character of various rural Malay communities.

The existence and significance of this diversity appears to have been overlooked both in the available academic literature and by those responsible for the planning and implementation of rural development programmes. For the most part, previous research efforts have been limited to case studies of individual communities. These studies contain important information but, lacking a comparative perspective, they have been unable to provide an understanding of major differences within rural Malay society. Similarly, many government officers consider the rural population to be an undifferentiated whole and do not realize that much of the subcultural variation pointed out in this study is relevant to their work.

Government officers and students of rural Malay society alike often hold the rather romantic notion that rural Malay communities possess an inherent cohesiveness that enables and encourages members of these communities to work together for the common good. Many government programmes based on this misconception seek to mobilize supposedly pre-existing local energies and resources for development projects. Eliciting popular participation in development is a worthy goal, but a number of serious obstacles must be recognized and dealt with.

Virtually all rural Malay communities work cooperatively at one time or another, but the regularity and importance of such cooperative effort varies significantly: as shown in this study, only rice farmers have a recurring need to work together; rubber tappers and fishermen have neither organizational experience comparable to that of rice farmers nor leadership roles comparable to the *ketua pinjam orang*. The well-developed capacity of rice farmers to cooperate actively with one another is a direct result of production processes and relationships which place a premium on coordination of the planting schedule and mobilization of the community's labour during the transplanting and harvest seasons. These reciprocal labour obligations and the organizational ability to mobilize rice farmers for cooperative efforts have no counterparts among rubber tappers or fishermen. Cooperative activities among fishermen and rubber tappers are likely to be limited to such matters as preparations for wedding feasts. These activities certainly are important, but they occur sporadically and do not provide an organizational framework for other types of cooperative endeavours.

The willingness of rice farmers to work together presents a valuable opportunity for mobilizing their efforts and encouraging their active participation in development programmes. Coordinating the efforts of fishermen and rubber tappers and encouraging their collective participation in rural development programmes presents more challenging problems.

Cooperation in production and participation in development programmes are both complex phenomenon. They are related, however, in so far as popular participation in development programmes calls for the mobilization of the collective energies of a community, whether it be for deciding local priorities or organizing people to construct and maintain roads, bridges, irrigation canals, or other infrastructural developments. However, efforts to organize the rural population have done little to encourage active participation in planning and implementing development programmes. This is due to the government's somewhat paternalistic 'top-down' approach to rural development, and the tendency for members of local economic élites to be selected as leaders of the various organizations established in the rural areas.

ECONOMIC STRATIFICATION AND LOCAL LEADERSHIP

Rural Malay communities often are divided by competing economic interests and increasing polarization along what essentially are class lines. There is conflict or the potential for conflict between those who control productive resources and those who do not. In fishing communities, competing economic interests are readily apparent and affect the everyday lives of the people involved. Among rubber tappers, conflict between land-owners and their tenants is evidenced by the slaughter tapping of trees and the concerted efforts of land-owners to discourage this and other harmful practices. Even among rice farmers, where the need for coordination and cooperation is crucial, and where land-owners to some extent protect their tenants during times of crop loss, there is evidence that the commercialization of rice production results in conflict between owners and non-owners.

A second misconception commonly held by government officers is that local leaders such as the *ketua kampung* are representative members and effective leaders of their communities. Often government officers working in rural areas channel their efforts through these formal leaders. However, as should be clear from the example of the *ketua kampung* of Gong Guncil, formal leaders may be neither the most effective leaders of their community nor representative of their community. This presents problems in so far as these leaders are in a position to divert the benefits of certain government programmes so as to assist a restricted number of families. These local élites, further strengthened by their contacts with political and administrative élites at the local, state, and national levels, are able to gain disproportionate advantage from development programmes.

ECONOMIC ATTITUDES AND DEVELOPMENTAL CHANGE

A third misconception involving rural Malays concerns their willingness to adopt new production processes and technologies and thereby improve their material standard of living. The persistence of traditional practices has convinced many government officers that rural Malays are unwilling to change the ways of the past and are content to live at or near the margin of subsistence. This misconception fits in with the image of the 'lazy village Malay' fostered by the British during the colonial period, and has been the focus of an interesting debate among academicians (see, for example, the conflicting views of Parkinson, 1967, and Wilder, 1968).

In any population it is possible to find individuals who exemplify a given stereotype. Among rural Malays one may meet those who claim that as long as they have enough to eat they are happy ('*cukup makan, sudah*'). This characterization of rural Malays is not accurate. For the most part, rural Malays work hard within the context of their available resources. The fact that they live at or near the margin of subsistence has less to do with indolence or contentedness with their lot in life than with the limited opportunities available to them. This is most clearly illustrated by the case of Malay rice farmers, who are reluctant to adopt new varieties and production practices due to their limited financial resources. Though the new rice technology promises increased yields, it also entails new risks. Given the small size of most family farms, even optimum yields would not provide income sufficient to maintain a farm family. Consequently, most farm families in Gong Guncil have adopted a more conservative approach to rice production than that recommended by government extension agents. Rather than invest the majority of their time and working capital in rice production alone, most farm families engage in a multiplicity of economic activities which reduce their dependence upon any single source of income, and indeed provides them with higher incomes than would be possible through rice farming alone.

The decision on whether or not, or to what extent, to adopt a new production process is made on economic terms, but using different criteria from those of the government's development officers. The latter tend to be specialists who focus their attention on only one crop or activity, seeking to obtain optimal results in their particular speciality. The people with whom they work, however, engage in a broader economy in which maximization of income from any one source often results in a loss in other important economic activities, either through constraints on time, land, or available funds. Moreover, where there is a threat of crop loss or other uncertainty in production or marketing, economic specialization leads to unacceptable vulnerability. Diversification of risk and income is a rational economic strategy for most rural Malays.

Far from being resistant to change, rural Malays are inveterate experimenters, and willingly adopt new methods of proven utility. Early in the twentieth century rubber production replaced subsistence farming in areas suitable for the cultivation of rubber trees. Indeed, Malay smallholders were so successful in competing with large foreign-owned rubber estates that during the colonial period a number of official policies were established to discourage rural Malays from this endeavour.

Rice farmers constantly are trying new rice varieties, including not only those recommended by extension officers, but those in use by farmers in other areas. For example, farmers in the Gong Guncil area have introduced new rice varieties from Kedah and Kelantan, including those not yet officially released by the government. Demonstration plots planted by government agricultural scientists are carefully observed, and in at least one instance farmers have been known to enter a fenced-in experimental station at night and abscond with the ripened grain of a variety which attracted their attention (M. L. Barnett, personal communication). Malay fishermen also have proven their willingness to change by quickly adopting diesel engines once they became available, thus reducing their dependence on wind power. This enables them to operate at night and to fish farther away from their home villages. The rapid adoption of the *pukat tansi*, requiring a rapid mobilization of capital, is another case in point.

The need to improve levels of productivity in the rural areas is beyond dispute. The knowledge and technology to do so is available. What is lacking is the clear recognition that not all rural Malays are equally able to take advantage of the opportunities provided by the new technologies. This has led to frustration and misunderstanding on the part of government officers, and problems in the design and implementation of development programmes.

The existence of socio-cultural diversity based on differing economic and environmental adaptations must be taken into account in the design of rural development programmes. Not all rural Malays have the same organizational experience or leadership roles as those that were found among the rice farmers of Gong Guncil. The production processes and relationships of fishing and rubber tapping require no comparable organizational forms or leadership roles, and to mobilize the energies of these groups will require greater efforts than among rice farmers. Rice farmers are able to act collectively because there are good and practical reasons why they should. Fishermen and rubber tappers have no comparable needs during the course of their day-to-day activities. This does not mean that fishermen or rubber tappers lack the ability to organize themselves; they will be able to do so if allowed the opportunity to share in the design and implementation of rural development programmes which serve their interests—that is, if there are good and practical reasons for cooperation.

By focusing on production processes and the relationships these processes engender, social scientists can contribute to the design of development policies and programmes tailored to the differing needs and capacities of rural populations. It has been shown in this study that a careful analysis of differing economic and environmental adaptations allows for the identification of a systematic source of socio-cultural variation. The comparative framework presented here is considered useful not only for understanding social and cultural processes, but for its practical application to issues of rural development in Malaysia and, by logical extension, to other developing nations.

Glossary

Alor: A low-lying natural drainage channel of importance for draining rice fields and as wallowing grounds for water-buffalo.

Ani-ani: The small hand-scythe used for harvesting traditional rice varieties, more commonly known in Malaysia as the *ketam*.

Air jernih: Literally 'clear water', used here to refer to the calm and clear seas between the north-east and south-west monsoons.

Air keroh: Literally 'turbid water', used here to refer to the turbid conditions of the sea during the north-east monsoon when the water contains high levels of suspended matter.

Bagi dua: Literally 'equal division', a system of share-cropping used by both rice farmers and rubber tappers whereby both owners and tenants equally share the production.

Bagi tiga: A share-cropping system used by rice farmers which divides the production into three parts, one part each going to the owner and the tenant, and the third part going to whichever party pays for production costs (e.g., fertilizers, etc.).

Bahagian bawa: The extra share of the catch which a boat captain earns for the added work and responsibility of managing the boat and net and selling the catch. In Mangkok, this extra share amounts to 20 per cent of the owner's share.

Bangsal bilis: The processing shed where small shrimp, *ikan bilis*, and other fish are processed and dried; located near the beach.

Barisan Nasional: National Front, the ruling national coalition of political parties.

Belacan: A thick paste of shrimp and salt used as a spice in cooking, or eaten as a condiment together with rice.

Beli: The root of the verb 'to buy'.

Beras: Milled rice.

Berderau: A form of labour organization whereby a group of women hire themselves out as a group to transplant rice; most common in Kedah.

Beris: A sandy soil type common near the coast, especially on the East Coast of Peninsular Malaysia, and of limited agricultural potential.

Bilal: A mosque official who gives the Friday call to prayer.

Borong: A form of auction used for selling fish whereby the seller starts with a high price, gradually lowering this price until it is acceptable to one of the buyers.

Budu: A sauce made from fermented *ikan bilis*.

Bukit: Hill.

Cabut semai: The pulling of rice seedlings from the seed-bed before transplanting.

Cedung: The transplanting of rice seedlings from seed-bed to field.

'*Cukup makan, sudah*': Literally 'enough to eat, that's it', but used to imply an economic orientation where sufficiency of food is more highly valued than a striving for improved yields, with the attendant risks.

Dagangan: Intermediate buyer who assures fishermen of a final buyer and for this and other services obtains a part of the sale as a commission. Rarely used in the Mangkok area.

Durian: A large fruit with a spine-covered shell whose unique taste is highly prized by most Malaysians.

Dusun: Literally 'orchard'.

Gadai: A form of lease whereby the leaseholder retains use of the land that serves as collateral until the sum of money advanced to the owner is repaid.

Gantang: A volumetric unit equivalent to one Imperial gallon (1.2 US gallons).

Gelam: A type of tree (*Melaleuca leucadendron*) found on poorly drained coastal soils and used primarily for making charcoal.

Gemai: A bundle of rice formed after harvesting a traditional rice variety; the grain is left on the panicle and the panicles are tied together with rice straw.

Geng: 'Gang'.

Gong: Word used in reference to a small rise in elevation, typically near rice fields, where houses are usually concentrated; Kelantan and Trengganu dialect.

Haj: The pilgrimage to Mecca.

Haji: The honorific title of a man who has made the pilgrimage to Mecca.

Hajjah: The honorific title given to a woman who has made the pilgrimage to Mecca.

Ikan bilis: The anchovy (*Stolephorus spp.*).

Imam: The leader of the congregation at a Muslim mosque, and the top official of the mosque. In Malaysia, *imam* are confirmed in their position and paid a small salary by the government.

Jala: A type of circular net cast by one person. The net is weighted by lead sinkers and is normally used close to the shore.

Jambu golok: The cashew nut (*Anacardium occidentale*).

Jawatan Kuasa Kemajuan Kampung: Village Development Committee.

Jeragang: This term refers to boat captains of small fishing boats.

Kampung: Village.

Kati: A measure of weight equal to 1.33 lb.

Kawah: A large cooking pot with sides which slope to a deep centre, like a *wok*. *Kawah* are used for preparation of food for feasts and for the cooking of *ikan bilis* and trash fish in *bangsal bilis*.

Kebun getah: This term literally means 'rubber stand'.

Kelam: The term used to refer to a fishing period, and literally meaning dark or obscure. One *kelam* (*sekelam*) usually includes approximately twenty nights of fishing; only when the moon is at its brightest does fishing cease. Occasionally if rough seas break up a fishing period there may be two or more *kelam* per lunar month.

Keping: Used here to refer to rice land within bunds which control water in the rice fields. There may be as many as seven or eight *keping* per acre.

Kercut: A type of sedge (*Scirpus mucronatus*) found in coastal swamps. The long slender leaves are collected, pounded, and woven into mats and baskets.

Kesin: The rice bug (*Leptocorisa acuta*), the most serious insect pest in the Gong Guncil area up to and during the period of research.

Ketam: A small hand-scythe used for harvesting traditional rice varieties.

Ketua kampung: The formal village headman, usually a government recognized position.

Ketua pinjam orang: Leader and organizer of cooperative labour groups; see *pinjam orang*.

Kolek: A small boat powered by sail or paddle and usually capable of carrying one or two fishermen. Now for the most part displaced by powered boats.

Kongsi: A partnership or cooperative association. The word is of Chinese origin, and most commonly used on the East Coast of Peninsular Malaysia to refer to joint ownership of boats and nets.

Kueh: A traditional type of small sail boat used on the East Coast; now mostly displaced by powered boats.

Madrassa: A typically small building for religious instruction and worship.

Mas kahwin: Literally 'wedding gold', the bride-price paid by the groom.

Nipah: A type of palm (*Nypa fruticans*) used for a wide variety of purposes, most notably as roofing material.

Padi: This is the origin of the English word 'paddy', or unmilled rice.

Pajak: A form of lease whereby the leaseholder pays a land-owner in return for use of land, usually for several years at a time.

Pantat potong: This term refers to the 'square-sterned' boats most commonly used in the Mangkok area.

Partai Islam: Literally, the 'Islamic Party', the most important competitor of the ruling UMNO.

Pawah: A term which refers to the arrangement between the owner of a cow and the person who takes over responsibility of raising and feeding the animal. The latter party thus obtains a half-share in the ensuing progeny, and in this way may begin to increase his own herd.

Pekan Selasa: Weekly market held on Tuesdays.

Penghulu: A government official who acts as headman of a sub-district.

Perahu: A general term used for various small boats powered by sail or paddle.

Pikul: A measure of weight equivalent to 133.33 lb.; 16.8 *pikul* is equal to 1 ton.

Pinang: The areca nut (*Areca catechu*).

Pinjam orang: Literally 'borrow people', this term refers to a type of reciprocal exchange of labour whereby a farm family may mobilize a large number of helpers for one afternoon, usually to help with transplanting.

Praih moto: Operators of small motor cycles who buy fish from fishermen and sell it in other villages.

Praih van: Fish buyers who operate on a larger scale than the *praih moto*, transporting fish they purchase to urban markets in small pick-up trucks.

Pukat dalam: A type of net used to encircle schools of fish which are then frightened and become enmeshed in the net when they attempt to swim out of the trap.

Pukat hanyut: Literally the 'drift net', this net is the most common in Mangkok. The net is as long as 1,000 yards and typically has mesh sizes ranging from $2\frac{1}{4}$ to 3 inches.

Pukat hijau: A type of drift net with a larger mesh size than the *pukat hanyut* (usually 4 inches). This net takes its name from the typically green coloration of the netting; also known as the *pukat tenggiri*.

Pukat jerut bilis: A purse-seine net used to capture *ikan bilis*.

Pukat jerut udang baring: A small purse-seine net used to capture the small shrimp known as *udang baring*.

Pukat kilat: A large purse-seine net which uses a powered winch to close the 'purse' at the bottom of the net.

Pukat kokoh: A small trawl net towed behind boats powered by small diesel engines of 6 to 8 horsepower and used to capture trash fish.

Pukat tangkol: A lift net previously used by fishermen in the Mangkok area.

Pukat tansi: A drift net made of clear monofilament nylon. In Mangkok this net recently was adopted for use during and immediately after the north-east monsoon. Unlike the *pukat hanyut*, which hangs just below the surface, the bottom edge of the *pukat tansi* is weighted with lead sinkers and drifts at the bottom.

Pukat tenggiri: A synonym for the *pukat hijau*.

Pukat tiga lapis: A trammel net used to capture large marine prawn. The name (*tiga lapis*) indicates that this net has three different mesh sizes.

Pukul padi: Literally 'striking paddy', or threshing rice.

Raga: The large baskets of woven split bamboo used for hauling fish and *udang baring*.

Rambutan: A fruit (*Nephelium lappaceum*) whose outer skin is covered with hair-like follicles. The skin is usually red when ripe, though there also are yellow varieties. The flesh is soft and juicy and there is a large pit in the centre.

Relong: A unit of areal measurement equivalent to 0.7 acre.

Remis: A small edible bivalve shellfish found along the coast.

Ru: The casuarina tree (*Casuarina equisetifolia*), which grows along Malaysia's coastlines.

Rumah padi: The 'rice house' or granary used for storing

unmilled rice. It is usually a separate structure from the family's house.

Sauk: A scoop net used by one person to capture small fish in the shallow waters along the coast.

Sekelam: One fishing period; see *kelam*.

Semoh bendang: A propitiatory rite in the past used to ensure a good harvest of rice.

Sireh: The betel vine (*Piper betle*) which is chewed together with the areca nut.

Sungai: River.

Surau: A building devoted to religious meetings and worship by Muslims, but which is smaller than a mosque.

Tajak: A large and heavy tool somewhere between a hoe and a scythe used for preparing weedy and waterlogged soils for rice cultivation.

Tanah dusun: Literally 'orchard land'.

Tanah kampung: Literally 'village land', this term refers to land around a family's house upon which typically there are planted a number of fruit trees and vegetables.

Tanah padi: Literally 'rice land'.

Teksi: A colloquial term used on the East Coast for trishaw.

Tolong-monolong: A form of reciprocal exchange of labour which typically is used to mobilize a few friends and kinsmen, e.g., for transplanting rice.

Tuai: A synonym for the *ketam*.

Tuntong: A type of large river turtle (*Callagur picta*).

Udang baring: A type of small shrimp (*Acetes spp.*) used for making *belacan* or which is dried and sold.

Unting: A bundle of rice seedlings; 400 *unting* are enough to transplant one acre.

Upah: The term for wage labour or piece-rate work.

Wakaf: This refers to the roadside shelters which are especially prevalent on the East Coast.

Wayang kulit: The 'shadow play' which uses puppets behind an illuminated screen. Stories often are based on the Hindu epics of the Mahabharatha and Ramayana, but with local embellishments.

Bibliography

Abdullah bin Sepien (1976), *Benefits of Economies of Scale in the Marketing of Smallholders' Rubber*, Kuala Lumpur: Rubber Research Institute of Malaysia.

Affifudin Haji Omar (1972), *A Study of Leadership Pattern, Activities, and Behaviour among Leaders of Farmers' Association within the Muda Scheme*, Telok Chengai, Kedah: Muda Agricultural Development Authority.

Agarwal, M. C. (1965), 'Rural Cooperative Credit—A Malaysian Case Study', *Kajian Ekonomi Malaysia*, Vol. II, No. 2 (December), pp. 10–23.

Ahmad Hussein, S. (1974), 'Kampung Elites and Rural Development: Case Studies in Penang and Kedah', M.A. Thesis, Universiti Sains Malaysia, School of Social Sciences.

Ahmad Yunus and B. Balasubramaniam (1975), *Major Crop Pests in Peninsular Malaysia*, Kuala Lumpur: Ministry of Agriculture.

Bailey, Conner (1976), *Broker, Mediator, Patron, and Kinsman: An Historical Analysis of Key Leadership Roles in a Rural Malaysian District*, Athens, Ohio: Ohio University Center for International Studies.

____ (1977), 'Padi Production in Besut, Trengganu: Social and Agronomic Factors Affecting Development', mimeo.

____ (1979), 'The Myth of Subsistence Farming: Rice Farming in Besut, Trengganu', Paper presented at the Symposium on the Malay World, 3–5 May 1979, Ohio University.

Banks, David J. (1969), 'Malay Kinship', Ph.D. dissertation, University of Chicago, Department of Anthropology.

____ (1972), 'Changing Kinship in North Malaya', *American Anthropologist*, Vol. 74, No. 5, pp. 1254–75.

____ (1974), 'Malay Kinship Terms and Morgan's Malayan Terminology: The Complexity of Simplicity', *Bijdragen tot de Taal-, Land- en Volkenkunde*, Vol. 130, Pt. 1, pp. 44–68.

Barlow, Colin (1978), *The Natural Rubber Industry; Its Development, Technology, and Economy in Malaysia*, Kuala Lumpur: Oxford University Press.

Barnard, Rosemary E. (1970), 'Organization of Production in a

Kedah Rice-Farming Village', Ph.D. dissertation, The Australian National University.

Barth, Fredrik (1956), 'Ecologic Relationships of Ethnic Groups in Swat, North Pakistan', *American Anthropologist*, Vol. 58, pp. 1079–89.

Baum, Gerhard A. (1975), 'Kuala Besut II—A Supplementary Report', Working Paper, South China Sea Fisheries Development and Coordinating Programme, Manila.

Bennett, John W. (1969), *Northern Plainsmen: Adaptive Strategy and Agrarian Life*, Chicago: Aldine Publishing Company.

Bisco, Barbara (1973), 'Constraints on Development: A Case Study of the Thai Rubber Industry', Ph.D. dissertation, Cornell University, Department of Economics.

Boudon, R. G. *et al.* (1970), *Report on Costs and Earnings Survey of Malaysian Trawl Fisheries, 1966–70*, Kuala Lumpur: Ministry of Agriculture.

Brown, David. W. (1960), 'A Reconnaissance Study of Farming Organization in a Coastal Area of West Johore (A Preliminary Report)', mimeo.

Burridge, Kenelm O. L. (1956), 'The Malay Composition of a Village in Johore', *Journal of the Malayan Branch, Royal Asiatic Society*, Vol. XXIX, Pt. 3, pp. 60–77.

Camoens, J. K. (1976), *The Buffalo in Malaysia*, Kuala Lumpur: Ministry of Agriculture.

Castillo, Gelia (1975), *All in a Grain of Rice*, Los Banos, Philippines: South-East Asian Regional Center for Graduate Study and Research in Agriculture.

Chandler, Robert F., Jr. (1979), *Rice in the Tropics: A Guide to the Development of National Programs*, Boulder, Colorado: Westview Press.

Chang, H. T. (1975), 'Non-Cash Technology in Rice Production', mimeo.

Cheam Soon Tee (1971), *A Study of the Marketing of Smallholders' Lower Grade Rubber*, Kuala Lumpur: Rubber Research Institute of Malaysia.

Chee, Stephen (1974), *Local Institutions and Rural Development in Malaysia*, Ithaca, New York: Cornell University Center for International Studies, Rural Development Committee.

Childs, Stephen Murray (1977), 'Political Correlates of Socioeconomic Change in Rural Society: A Study of Three Malay Communities', Ph.D. dissertation, State University of New York at Albany, Department of Anthropology.

Cho, Freddie (n.d.), 'Fishing Industry in West Malaysia', mimeo.

Coulson, N. (1929), 'System of Land Tenure in Kelantan', *Malayan Agricultural Journal*, Vol. 16, pp. 118–26.

Craig, J. A. (1933), 'Dry Padi in Kelantan', *Malayan Agricultural Journal*, Vol. 21, pp. 664–6.

____ (1935), 'Agriculture in Kelantan', *Malayan Agricultural Journal*, Vol. 23, pp. 369–74.

Devendra, C. and S. Thamutaram (eds.) (1976), *Proceedings of the Symposium on Smallholder Livestock Production and Development*, Kuala Lumpur: Ministry of Agriculture.

Djamour, Judith (1959), *Malay Kinship and Marriage in Singapore*, London: Athlone Press.

Dobby, E. H. G. (1951), 'The Kelantan Delta', *Geographical Review*, Vol. 41, pp. 226–55.

____ (1957), 'Padi Landscapes of Malaya, Part I: Daerah Tanjong Pauh', *Malayan Journal of Tropical Geography*, Vol. 10, pp. 3–41.

Downs, R. E. (1967), 'A Kelantanese Village in Malaya', in J. H. Steward (ed.), *Contemporary Change in Traditional Societies*, Vol. II, Urbana: University of Illinois Press, pp. 105–86.

Duewel, John and Hj. Osman Mohd. Noor (1971), *Socio-Economic Survey of Tenancy Patterns in Trengganu Padi Production*, Kuala Trengganu: State Agriculture Office, Trengganu.

Elliston, G. R. (n.d.), 'A Critique of the Kuala Linggi Scheme', mimeo.

____ (1967), 'The Role of Middlemen in the Fishing Industry of West Malaysia', *Review of Agricultural Economics-Malaysia*, Vol. 1, No. 2 (December), pp. 1–18.

____ (1978), 'Problems in Assessing the Costs and Earnings of Mechanized Fishing Boats', Paper presented at the Regional Conference on Technology for Rural Development, Kuala Lumpur, 24–29 April 1978.

Esman, Milton J. (1972), *Administration and Development in Malaya*, Ithaca, New York: Cornell University Press.

Firth, Raymond W. (1950), 'The Peasantry of Southeast Asia', *International Affairs*, Vol. 26 (October), pp. 503–14.

____ (1952), *Elements of Social Organization*, London: Watts & Co., p. 122.

____ (1966), *Malay Fishermen: Their Peasant Economy*, Hamden, Conn.: Archon Books.

____ (1969), 'Social Structure and Peasant Economy: The Influence of Social Structure upon Peasant Economies', in Clifton R. Wharton, Jr. (ed.), *Subsistence Agriculture and Economic Development*, Chicago: Aldine Publishing Co., pp. 23–37.

____ (1974), 'Relations between Personal Kin (Waris) among Kelantan Malays', in R. J. Smith (ed.), *Social Organization and the Applications of Anthropology; Essays Presented to Laurison Sharp*, Ithaca, New York: Cornell University Press, pp. 23–61.

Firth, Rosemary (1966), *Housekeeping among Malay Peasants*, London: Athlone Press.

Forde, C. Daryll (1934), *Habitat, Economy and Society*, London: Methuen & Co. Ltd.

Fraser, Thomas (1960), *Rusembilan: A Malay Fishing Village*, Ithaca, New York: Cornell University Press.

Fujimoto, Akimi (1974), 'A Case Study of Human Resources in Peasant Paddy Farming in Kelantan', *Southeast Asian Studies*, Vol. 12, No. 3 (December), pp. 350–64.

—— (1976), 'On the Effects of Farming Techniques on Rice Yield: A Case Study in Kelantan, Malaysia', mimeo.

Geertz, Clifford (1963), *Agricultural Involution; The Process of Ecological Change in Indonesia*, Berkeley: University of California Press.

Gibbons, David (1976), 'Public Policy towards Fisheries Development in Peninsular Malaysia: A Critical Review Emphasizing Penang and Kedah', *Kajian Ekonomi Malaysia*, Vol. XIII, Nos. 1 & 2 (June–December), pp. 89–121.

Gimlette, John D. (1971), *Malay Poisons and Charm Cures*, Kuala Lumpur: Oxford University Press.

Gullick, J. M. (1965), *Indigenous Political Systems of Western Malaya*, London: Athlone Press.

Gunawan, Basuki and Gustaaf W. von Liebenstein (n.d.), 'The Plight of the Kelantanese Peasant; Some Observations in the Bachok District', mimeo.

Hanks, Lucien M. (1972), *Rice and Man: Agricultural Ecology in Southeast Asia*, Chicago: Aldine-Atherton Press.

Harris, Marvin (1979), *Cultural Materialism*, New York: Random House (1st edition).

Hawley, Amos H. (1950), *Human Ecology; A Theory of Community Structure*, New York: The Ronald Press Company.

Hill, A. H. (1951), 'Kelantan Padi Planting', *Journal of the Malayan Branch of the Royal Asiatic Society*, Vol. 24, Pt. 1, pp. 56–76.

Hirschman, Charles (1975), *Ethnic and Social Stratification in Peninsular Malaysia*, Washington, D.C.: American Sociological Association.

Huang, Yukon (1975), 'Tenancy Patterns, Productivity, and Rentals in Malaysia', *Economic Development and Cultural Change*, Vol. 23, No. 4 (July), pp. 703–18.

Huntington, Ellsworth (1927), *The Human Habitat*, New York: D. Van Nostrand Co.

Husin Ali, S. (1964), *Social Stratification in Kampong Bagan; A Study of Class, Status, Conflict and Mobility in a Rural Malay Community*, Singapore: Malaysian Branch of the Royal Asiatic Society.

—— (1968), 'Patterns of Rural Leadership in Malaya', *Journal of the*

Malaysian Branch of the Royal Asiatic Society, Vol. 41, Pt. 1, pp. 95–145.

____ (1973), 'Political Functionaries in Rural Malaysia: Leaders or Middlemen?', Paper presented at the Ninth International Congress of Anthropological and Ethnological Sciences, Chicago, USA, August–September 1973.

____ (1975), *Malay Peasant Society and Leadership*, Kuala Lumpur: Oxford University Press.

Hussein Alatas, S. (1968), 'The Grading of Occupational Prestige amongst the Malays of Malaysia', *Journal of the Malaysian Branch of the Royal Asiatic Society*, Vol. 41, Pt. 1, pp. 146–56.

Jack, H. W. (1928), 'Brief Notes on Agricultural Conditions on the East Coast of Malaya', *Malayan Agricultural Journal*, Vol. 16, pp. 88–91.

Jahara Yahaya (1978), 'The Trawl Fishery of Peninsular Malaysia: Its Origin, Development and Present Status', mimeo.

Jay, Robert R. (1964), 'Local and National Politics in a Rural Malay Community', Paper presented to the Association for Asian Studies, Washington, D.C., 26 March 1964.

Johnson, H. (1976), 'East Coast Malaysia Artisanal Fisheries Development-Investment Opportunities', Working Paper, South China Seas Fisheries Development and Coordinating Programme, Manila.

Johnson, Willard I. Twig (1977), 'Work among Portuguese Fishermen: Towards a Model of Social Production', Ph.D. dissertation, Columbia University, Department of Anthropology.

Josselin de Jong, P. E. de (1952), *Minangkabau and Negri Sembilan*, The Hague: M. Nijhoff.

Jothy, A. A. *et al.* (1975), *Demersal Fish Resources in Malaysian Waters*, Kuala Lumpur: Ministry of Agriculture.

Kessler, Clive S. (1978), *Islam and Politics in a Malay State*, Ithaca, New York: Cornell University Press.

Kuchiba, Masuo and Yoshihiro Tsubouchi (1968), 'Paddy Farming and Social Structure in a Malay Village', *Review of Agricultural Economics—Malaysia*, Vol. 2, No. 1 (June), pp. 9–34.

Kuchiba, Masuo, Yoshihiro Tsubouchi, and Narifumi Maeda (1979), *Three Malay Villages: A Sociology of Paddy Growers in West Malaysia*, Honolulu: University of Hawaii Press, translated by Peter and Stephanie Hawkes.

Lambert, Donald Harley (1981), 'Diversified Farming and Ecological Change in a Pahang Malay Neighborhood', Ph.D. dissertation, University of California at Berkeley, Department of Anthropology.

Larsson, S. O. R. and G. C. A. Van Noort (1975), 'A Report on

Artisanal Fisheries of Peninsular Malaysia with Particular Reference to Kuala Besut', Working Paper, South China Sea Fisheries Development and Coordinating Programme, Manila.

Lim Teck Ghee (1977), *Peasants and Their Agricultural Economy in Colonial Malaya, 1874–1941*, Kuala Lumpur: Oxford University Press.

Ling Shao-Wen (1977), *Aquaculture in Southeast Asia; An Historical Overview*, Seattle: University of Washington Press.

Lockwood, Brian and Kenneth Ruddle (eds.) (1977), *Small Scale Fisheries Development; Social Science Contribution*, Honolulu, Hawaii: East-West Food Institute, East-West Center.

Low Wan Kim (1968), 'The Supply and Demand Prospects for Fish in West Malaysia', *Review of Agricultural Economics—Malaysia*, Vol. 2, No. 2 (December), pp. 45–59.

Malaysia, Ministry of Agriculture, Besut Agricultural Development Project (1970), *Summarized Project Description and Appraisal* (May 1970).

Malaysia, Ministry of Agriculture, Department of Fisheries (1971), 'The Role and Function of Fishermen's Associations', mimeo.

____ (1977), *Annual Fisheries Statistics for 1976*.

____ (1979), *Senarai Motobot-Motobot Dan Perahu-Perahu Menangkap Ikan Yang Dilesenkan Dalam Tahun 1978, Negeri Trengganu* (List of Powered and Un-Powered Fishing Boats Licensed in 1978 in Trengganu State).

Malaysia, Prime Minister's Department (1976), *Third Malaysia Plan, 1976–1980*.

Malaysia, Prime Minister's Department, Malaysian Centre for Development Studies (1976), *Value Orientations of the Rural Population towards Change in Peninsular Malaysia*.

Marr, John C. (1976), *Fishery and Resource Management in Southeast Asia*, Washington, D.C.: Resources for the Future.

Mohd. Johar bin Mohd. Rashid, Haji, and Abdul Jalil bin Haji Yusof (1976), *Buku Panduan Getah* (A Guide Book to Rubber), Kuala Lumpur: Rubber Research Institute of Malaysia.

Mohd. Shaari bin Sam Abdul Latif, Chang Boo Jock, and D. Pathansali (1976), *Assessment of Marine Fisheries Resources of Malaysia*, Kuala Lumpur: Ministry of Agriculture.

Mokhtar Tamin and N. Hashim Mustapha (1975), 'Kelantan, West Malaysia', in *Changes in Rice Farming in Selected Areas of Asia*, Los Banos, Philippines: International Rice Research Institute.

Narendran, Vasantha Malliha (1977), 'The Women of Perupok: An Economic Study', M.A. thesis, Universiti Sains Malaysia, School of Social Sciences.

____ (1978), 'The Market as an Articulator of the Integrated Economy: An Anthropological Case of Pasir Mas, Malaysia', Ph.D. dissertation, Cornell University, Department of Anthropology.

Nash, Manning (1966), 'Tradition in Tension in Kelantan', *Journal of Asian and African Studies*, Vol. 1, pp. 310–14.

____ (1974), *Peasant Citizens: Politics, Religion, and Modernization in Kelantan, Malaysia*, Athens, Ohio: Ohio University Center for International Studies.

Ness, Gayl D. (1967), *Bureaucracy and Rural Development in Malaysia*, Berkeley: University of California Press.

Ouchi, Tsutomu, *et al.* (1977), *Farmer and Village in West Malaysia*, Tokyo: University of Tokyo Press.

Panton, W. P. (n.d.), 'Reconnaissance Soil Survey of the Marang, Ajil, and Bukit Payong Areas', Kuala Lumpur: Department of Agriculture.

Parkinson, B. K. (1967), 'Non-economic Factors in the Economic Retardation of the Rural Malays', *Modern Asian Studies*, Vol. I, No. 1, pp. 31–46.

Pee Teck Yew and Ani bin Arope (1976), *Rubber Owners' Manual 1976; Economics and Management in Production and Marketing*, Kuala Lumpur: Rubber Research Institute of Malaysia.

Purcal, J. T. (1971), *Rice Economy; A Study of Four Villages in West Malaysia*, Kuala Lumpur: University of Malaya Press.

Roff, William R. (ed.) (1974), *Kelantan: Religion, Society and Politics in a Malay State*, Kuala Lumpur: Oxford University Press.

Rogers, Marvin L. (1974), 'Village Leadership and National Development in Malaysia', Paper presented to the Association for Asian Studies, Boston, 1–3 April 1974.

____ (1975), 'The Politicization of Malay Villagers: National Integration or Disintegration?', *Comparative Politics*, Vol. 7, No. 2 (January), pp. 205–26.

____ (1977), *Sungai Raya: A Sociopolitical Study of a Rural Malay Community*, Berkeley: University of California Center for South and Southeast Asian Studies.

Rudner, Martin (1975), *Nationalism, Planning, and Economic Modernization in Malaysia: The Politics of Beginning Development*, London: Sage Publications.

Scott, James C. (1972), 'The Erosion of Patron–Client Bonds and Social Change in Rural Southeast Asia', *Journal of Asian Studies*, Vol. XXXII, No. 1 (November), pp. 5–37.

____ (1976), *The Moral Economy of the Peasant; Rebellion and Subsistence in Southeast Asia*, New Haven: Yale University Press.

Selvadurai, S. (1972), *Padi Farming in West Malaysia*, Kuala Lumpur: Ministry of Agriculture.

____ (1975), *Survey of Rubber Smallholdings in Parit*, Kuala Lumpur:

Ministry of Agriculture.

—— (1977), 'Agriculture in Peninsular Malaysia' (draft), Kuala Lumpur: Planning and Development Division, Ministry of Agriculture.

Smelser, Neil J. (1963), *The Sociology of Economic Life*, Englewood Cliffs, New Jersey: Prentice-Hall.

Smith, Philip E. L. (1976), *Food Production and Its Consequences*, London: Cummings Publishing Company.

Sutherland, Heather (1978), 'Taming of the Trengganu Elite', in Ruth T. McVey (ed.), *Southeast Asian Transitions*, New Haven: Yale University Press, pp. 32–85.

Swift, M. G. (1965), *Malay Peasant Society in Jelebu*, London: Athlone Press.

—— (1966), 'Capital, Saving and Credit in a Malay Peasant Economy', in Raymond Firth and B. S. Yamey (eds.), *Capital, Saving and Credit in Peasant Societies*, Chicago: Aldine Publishing Company, pp. 133–56.

—— (1967), 'Economic Concentration and Malay Peasant Society', in Maurice Freedman (ed.), *Social Organization: Essays Presented to Raymond Firth*, London: Frank Cass and Co., pp. 241–69.

Uphoff, Norman T. and Milton J. Esman (1974), *Local Organization for Rural Development: Analysis of Asian Experience*, Ithaca, New York: Cornell University Center for International Studies, Rural Development Committee.

Wharton, Clifton R., Jr. (1966), 'Malay Rice and Rubber Smallholders', Paper presented at the Association for Asian Studies, 4 April 1966.

Wilder, William (1968), 'Islam, Other Factors and Malay Backwardness: Comments on an Argument', *Modern Asian Studies*, Vol. II, No. 2, pp. 155–64.

Williams, C. N. (1975), *The Agronomy of the Major Tropical Crops*, Kuala Lumpur: Oxford University Press.

Wilson, Peter (1967), *A Malay Village and Malaysia*, New Haven: Human Relations Area Files Press.

Wilson, T. B. (1958), *The Economics of Padi Production in North Malaya, Part I: Land Tenure, Rents, Land Use and Fragmentation*, Kuala Lumpur: Department of Agriculture.

Winzeler, Robert L. (1974), 'The Social Organization of Islam in Kelantan', in Roff (ed.), *Kelantan: Religion, Society and Politics in a Malay State*. Kuala Lumpur: Oxford University Press.

Yap Lim Lian and John A. Dixon (1972), *Socio-Economic Study of Padi Farms in the Besut Project Area of Trengganu*, Besut, Trengganu: Besut Agricultural Development Project.

Index

ABSCONDERS, 203
Achinese, 9
Administration of loans, 72
Agricultural labourer, 32; *see also* Wage labour
Air jernih, 87, 204
Air keroh, 87, 204
Alor, 204
Anchovies, 75; *see also Ikan bilis*
Ani-ani, 204
Animal husbandry, 74, 89, 165, 174, 181
Artificial insemination, 165; *see also* Animal husbandry
Asian Development Bank, 22

Bagi Dua, 77, 156, 204
Bagi tiga, 174, 204
Bahagia, 51
Bahagian bawa, 104, 105, 193, 204
Baling, 10
Baling demonstrations, 163–4
Banana, 22, 142
Bangsal bilis, 124, 128, 129–31, 204
Bank Pertanian, 26, 72–4
Barisan Nasional, 11, 204; *see also* National Front
Baruh Kual, 27, 31, 34, 63, 76
Batu Rakit, 118
Beach economy, 122–30
Belacan, 123, 205
Beras, 67
Beris, 20, 205
Besut Agricultural Development Project, 4, 21, 32–3, 42, 52, 68, 70, 71, 74–5
Bilal, 191, 205; *see also* Muezzin
Birds, 53, 176; *see also* Pests
Boat designs, 94–5
Borong, 113, 114, 118; *see also* Dutch auction
Bud-grafted clones, 143
Budu, 75, 205
Buffalo: advantages and disadvantages of ploughing with, 48–51; care of, 49; decrease in population of, 49, 165, 174
Bugis, 9
Bunds, 54; *see also* Rice

Cabut Semai, 56–7, 205
Capital: accumulation of, 173–5; mobilization of, 203; *see also Gadai*; Livestock; *Pajak*
Capital on the hoof, 166; *see also* Cattle
Cartel, 194; *see also* Price cartel
Case studies, 7
Cash crops, 69, 134, 142–3, 145, 167, 175
Cash employment, 158; *see also* Hired labour; Wage labour
Cash income, 130, 152
Cash inputs, 62
Cash orientated relationships, 196; *see also* Wage labour
Cashew nut, 89; *see also Jambu golok*
Cassava, 142, 167; *see also* Cash crops
Cattle, 165, 174, 181
Cedung, 57, 205
Cempedak, 25
Charcoal, 5, 91
Cheating, 101, 151, 158
Chemical fertilizers, 42–3, 52, 71, 74, 89, 164, 185; *see also* Fertilizers
Chempaka series, 21
Chickens, 67, 165
Chinese: in wholesale and retail trade, 9, 138; fish buyers, 129
Circumcisions, 28
Class differentiation, 29
Class polarization, 191–2, 195
Coagulated latex, 148

Coconuts, 5, 22, 89, 181; *see also* Cash crops
Coffee, 58
Commercialization, 6, 169, 191
Community: definition, 14; labour, 58, 190, 200; *see also* Social life
Comparative approach, 6–8
Competition, 114; among fish buyers, 194
Conflict between fishermen and fish buyers, 113
Constraints to rubber replanting, 143–6
Construction: labour, 75–6; of Malay house, 13
Contract tractor ploughing, 165; *see also* Ploughing; Tractors
Cooperative labour, 188, 192, 196, 200; *see also* Community labour; *Pinjam orang*; *Tolong-menolong*
Copra, 89
Cottage industry, 90; *see also* Women
Credit facilities, 42, 72, 130, 155, 158–60, 173; *see also* *Gadai*; Loans; Local Credit Centres; *Pajak*
Crop failure, 47; *see also* Crop loss
Crop loss, 53, 201; *see also* Share-cropping
Crop management, 74–5
Crop rotation, 20
Cuplump, 147, 157

Dagangan, 116, 205
Dam, 21, 133; *see also* Besut Agricultural Development Project
Department of Agriculture, 142
Depreciation, 128, 182
Development programmes, 200; *see also* Besut Agricultural Development Project; Kemubu Agricultural Development Authority; Muda Agricultural Development Authority
Diseases, 12, 55, 71, 89, 144, 187
Disputes, 193; *see also* Conflict between fishermen and fish buyers
Distribution of fertilizers, 72
Distribution of rubber land ownership, 153–6
District Hospital, 137
District Office, 14, 136
Diversity of rural Malay communities, 199
Division of labour, 56; *see also* Community labour; Family labour
Divorce, 17
Dock, 108
Double-cropping, effect on cattle population, 49, 174; *see also* Share-cropping; Share-tapping
Dowry, 139; *see also* Marriage; *Mas kahwin*
Drainage and Irrigation Department, 34–5, 42, 75, 190
Draught animals, 48; *see also* Buffalo; Oxen
Drift net, 5, 95; *see also* *Pukat hanyut*
Dry rubber content (DRC), 151–2
Duku, 25
Dusun, 25, 205; *see also* *Tanah dusun*
Dutch auction, 113–15, 118

ECONOMIC ATTITUDES, 201–3
Economic cooperation, 6
Economic diversification, 202; *see also* Income
Economic inequality, 198–9
Economic roles of men and women, 137–41; *see also* Women
Economic specialization, 202
Economic stratification, 169, 184, 195, 200–1
Education, 16, 18
Élite, 29; *see also* Gong Tanah Merah
Employment of women, 5, 90; *see also* Non-farm employment; Women
Endogamous marriages, 92
Ethnic identity, 10–11
Ethnic solidarity, 11, 19; *see also* Partai Islam Sa-Malaysia; United Malays National Organization
Exchange of information, 188; *see also* Marketing
Exogamous marriages, 92
Exploitation, 123, 182
Extended rental, 173; *see also* *Gadai*
Extension services, 42, 47, 202; *see also* Development programmes
Extractive economy, 9

FAMILY LABOUR, 54, 57, 142, 149, 179; *see also* Labour; Women
Family structure, 92–4
Farm: size, 31, 34; management of élite, 41

Farmers' Associations, 72; *see also* Farmers' Cooperatives
Farmers' Cooperatives, 72–3, 142, 167; *see also* Marketing; Rice; Rubber
Farmers' response to double-cropping, 46; *see also* Double-cropping
Federal Ministry of Education, 14
Fertilizers, 55, 62, 69, 89, 144; *see also* Chemical fertilizers
Fikri, 84
Fish processing: drying, 109; of *ikan bilis*, 125; and effect on price, 126–7; disincentives for investment in, 129–31
Fishermen's attitude to change, 203
Fishermen's Cooperative, 97, 108, 118, 194
Fishing: seasons, 85–7; boats, 94; nets, 94–9; distribution of catch, 102–4; marketing of fish, 102, 108–22; value of catch, 105; relationship between catch, distribution, and income, 106–7; fish vendors, 109, 121; effect of seasonality on fish buyers, 119; relationship between fishermen and buyers, 120; role of women in, 130–2; as a commercial venture, 193
Fixed daily wage, 151; *see also* Wage labour
Fodder, 49; *see also* Cattle
Forest Reserve, 133, 177
Formic acid, 148, 156
Fragmentation, 31, 171–3, 179, 199; *see also* Inheritance; Land
Frequency of tapping, 161; *see also* Rubber

Gadai, 37–9, 173–5; *see also* Credit facilities
Gantang, definition, 21, 206
Gelam tree, 5, 90, 206
Gemai, 46, 65, 206
Gifts, 64
Gill net, 97; *see also Pukat tansi*
Ginger, 142; *see also* Cash crops
Goats, 174; *see also* Animal husbandry
Gong Guncil: location, 4, 20; land use, 4; topography, 20; economic activities, 20
Gong Guncil Village: local environment, 22; diet of villagers, 24–5; economic activities, 24; land use patterns, 24–5
Gong Tanah Merah, 26–9, 31, 34, 41, 62–3, 67, 76; *see also* Social life; Wealth
Government processing plants, 150
Groundnuts, 134; *see also* Cash crops

Haj, 13, 206
Haji, 13, 206
Hajjah, 13, 206
Harvesting, 64; *see also Pinjam orang*; *Tolong-menolong*
Health Clinic, 137
Herbology, 11
Heveacrumb, 151–2, 160; *see also* Rubber
Hired labour, 62, 64, 189, 192; *see also* Wage labour
Hospital, 137
Housing, 135; shortage of, 137
Hydrometer, 150; *see also* Dry rubber content

ICE, 112, 118–19; *see also* Fishing
Ikan bilis, 117, 123–30; *see also* Anchovies; *Bangsal bilis*
Imam, 194, 206
Income: cash, 4; supplementary, 4; subsistence level of, 12; unequal distribution of, 12–13; from sale of rubber, 157; diversifying sources of, 164; from fishing, 105; distribution (fishing), 193; inequalities of wealth and, 195; maximization of, 202
Indians: on plantations, 9; in wholesale and retail trade, 138
Inheritance: division according to needs, 17–19; and acquisition of breeding livestock, 24; as a means of acquiring land, 155; of land, 171–3; and the necessity to prevent fragmentation, 180, 181–5, 199; *see also* Fragmentation; Rice; Rubber; Wealth
Insecticides, 40
Insects, 53, 187; *see also Kesin*; Pests
Intermarriage, 29
Investment: in housing, 136; in boats, engines, and nets, 181–2; *see also* Land; Inheritance
Irrigation facilities, 4, 12, 21, 22, 41–2, 50, 54, 133, 170; *see also* Water control
Islam, 11; *see also* Malays

Islamic practices associated with rice cultivation, 178

Jala, 92, 206
Jambu golok, 89, 206
Javanese, 9
Jeragang, 96, 102, 206
Jerteh, 25–6, 65
Johor Bahru, 112

KAMPUNG AMIR, 26
Kampung Buluh, 82, 84, 91
Kampung Dusun: location, 5; land use, 5–6
Kampung Mandul, 133
Kampung Raja, 26
Kawah, 125, 206
Kayu Kelat, 46
Kebun getah, 25, 206
Kelam, 97, 207
Kemubu Agricultural Development Authority, 22
Keping, 30–1, 207
Kercut, 5, 90, 130, 207; *see also* Weaving
Kesin, 53, 74, 207; *see also* Pests
Ketam, 46, 64–5, 164, 207
Ketua kampung, 14, 15, 26, 63, 191, 194, 197–8, 207
Ketua pinjam orang, 58–61, 189, 197, 200, 207
Kinship, obligations of, 16; *see also* Family labour; Reciprocal exchanges of labour
Kolek, 94, 207
Kongsi, 110, 207; *see also* Tenaga Baru
Kota Bharu, 126, 129
Kuala Baru, 100, 101, 115, 117, 118, 123, 184
Kuala Besut, 75, 118
Kuala Dungun, 88
Kuala Lumpur, 112–13
Kuala Trengganu, 84, 100, 112–13, 118–19, 123, 126, 129, 194
Kuantan, 88, 112
Kubang Pasu, 10
Kueh, 94, 207

LABOUR: reciprocal exchanges of, 1; shortage of, 41; demands of rice production, 50–67; interdependence, 57; mobilization of, 58, 192; mobilizers, 58; boycott, 62–3; for construction industry, 75; flexibility of fishing, 101; demand in fish processing, 128; resources, 189; comparison between the needs in rice cultivation and fishing, 192–3; *see also* Community labour; Family labour; Hired labour; *Pinjam orang*; *Tolong-menolong*; Wage labour
Land: compared with the sea as a resource, 19; Land Office, 30; ownership of rice land by household, 31; ownership of rice land by tenure status, 32; leasing of rice land, 35, 37–8; long-term rental of land, 40; preparation of, 44, 48–51, 187; availability of land for share-cropping, 138; factors affecting price of rubber land, 154; tenure status of active tapping families, 156; -based economies, 169; scarcity of, 170; increase in price of, 170; as a natural resource, 170, 176; increasing productivity per unit, 173; comparison between rice and rubber land, 177; alienation, 177; limits to sale of rubber land, 180; speculation in, 181; as a secondary economic asset, 181; as a commodity of limited utility, 183; as a finite resource, 185; unequal distribution of rubber land, 198; *see also* Fragmentation; Inheritance; *Gadai*; *Pajak*; Share-cropping
Langkawi Island, 123
Latex: collection stations, 150, 152; quality of, 151; *see also* Hydrometer
Lembaga Padi dan Beras Negara (LPN), 80; *see also* National Rice Board
Livestock: breeding of, 4, 24, 46, 166, 174–5; improved breeds, 24; effect of double-cropping on, 46; *see also* Animal husbandry; *Pawah*; Inheritance
Loans, 72–3, 130; *see also* Credit facilities
Local Credit Centres, 72–3; *see also* Credit facilities
Local leadership, 7, 187, 194, 197–8, 200–1; *see also Ketua kampung*; *Ketua pinjam orang*; Village Development Committees

Logging, 40
Loss of productivity, 5

MAHSURI, 51
Malays: subcultural differences between rural, 9–10; participation in local trade, 9; cultural group cohesion, 10; sense of ethnic identity, 10; preferential treatment of, 11; as producers of primary products, 12; myth of rural, 201; *see also* Partai Islam Sa-Malaysia; United Malays National Organization; Islam; Islamic practices
Malaysian Agricultural Research and Development Institute (MARDI), 21, 60
Malaysian Rubber Development Corporation (MARDEC), 150–1, 160
Managerial skills, 75, 128
Mangkok: location, 4, 82; brief history, 4–5; secondary economic activities in, 5; land use, 5; communications, 83–4
Manufacturing: of construction materials, 167
Marketing: of fresh fish, 5, 109–11, 112, 193; of rice, 79–81; vans, 80; strategies, 127; information, 125–6, 159; of rubber, 157–61; *see also* Exchange of information
Marriage: as a unifying factor, 16; material support for newly-weds, 16; selective alliances, 17–18, 181, 192; *see also Mas kahwin*; Intermarriage
Mas kahwin, 139; *see also* Dowry; Marriage
Mechanization, 48; *see also* Commercialization; Tractors
Merang, 123
Middlemen, 111, 113; *see also* Chinese
Migration, 9, 170
Minangkabau, 9, 16
Ministry of Agriculture, 22, 72
Monsoon, 25, 45, 65, 85, 87–8, 97, 130, 134; *see also* Fishing; Rain
Muda Agricultural Development Authority, 22
Muezzin, 191

NATIONAL FRONT, 11, 15; *see also* Barisan Nasional
National Rice Board, 80; *see also* Lembaga Padi dan Beras Negara
Natural calamity, 197
Natural resources: definition, 2; availability of and access to, 182–5
Negative social sanctions, 63
New Economic Policy, 11
New technology, 169; *see also* Commercialization; Mechanization
Night fishing, 97
Nipah, 5, 90, 122; *see also* Cash crops
Non-farm employment, 74–6, 122, 131, 137, 167; *see also* Women

OPTIMUM YIELD, 42, 70–1; *see also* Rice; Rubber
Osman, 117–18
Owner–operator, 32–3, 156; *see also* Rice; Fishing; Rubber
Owner–tenant, 32–3, 156; *see also* Rice; Fishing; Rubber
Ownership: of rice land, 31; of tractors, 48; of rubber land, 76; of productive resources, 182
Oxen, 44, 47, 49; *see also* Animal husbandry

PADANG TERAP, 10
Padi Pak Saka, 44
Padi Sagupa, 44
Pajak, 37, 173
Pakistanis, 10
Pangkor Island, 123
Pantat potong, 95, 208
Partai Islam Sa-Malaysia (PAS), 10–11
Pasture, 174
Pattani, 134
Pawah, 24, 166, 175, 191, 208
Penarek, 75, 82, 84, 99, 100, 101, 123, 184
Perahu, 94, 99, 208; *see also* Boat designs
Pests, 12, 53, 55; *see also* Birds; Insects
Pesticides, 42, 71, 187
Petty trade, 74, 80; *see also* Chinese; Indians
Pineapple, 142; *see also* Cash crop
Pinjam orang, 80, 188; *see also* Labour
Planting schedule, 51–3
Ploughing: use of tractors, 48; with draught animals, 44, 47, 54

Police Station, 136
Politics, 10–11; *see also* Partai Islam Sa-Malaysia; United Malays National Organization
Population: by ethnic group, 10; of study area, 27
Post Office, 136
Praih moto, 121, 122; *see also* Marketing
Praih van, 121, 122; *see also* Marketing
Preferential relationships, 116
Price cartel, 114, 117
Price fluctuation, 120, 125, 161; *see also* Rice; Rubber; Fishing
Price structure, 109–10
Pricing agreement, 126
Production credit, 72, 167; *see also* Credit Facilities
Progressive farmers, 47, 61
Propitiatory ceremonies, 12; *see also* Islamic practices
Public demonstrations, 177
Pukat dalam, 98, 208
Pukat hanyut, 95–9, 104, 106–7; *see also* Drift net
Pukat hijau, 95–6, 209
Pukat kilat, 100–2, 104, 209
Pukat kokoh, 98–9, 209
Pukat tangkol, 94, 209
Pukat tansi, 97–8, 106–7, 114, 129, 203; *see also* Gill net
Pukat tenggiri, 96, 209
Pukat tiga lapis, 99, 209
Pulau Panjang, 27, 31, 34, 40, 47, 60, 76–8
Purse-seine, 99–100, 123, 124

RAGA, 123, 209
Rain: timing of cultivation, 45; rainfall patterns, 144; *see also* Monsoon
Rambutan, 22
Reciprocal labour obligations, 6, 14, 54, 188–90; *see also Pinjam orang*; Social life; *Tolong-menolong*
Redistribution of wealth, 27–8, 104; *see also* Wealth
Remis, 92, 209
Repayment of production credit, 73; *see also* Credit facilities
Replanting grants, 142–5, 181, 185; *see also* Rubber
Response to innovation, 42
Rice: fertilizer-responsive varieties, 4, 42–4, 52, 55; traditional varieties, 4, 42–4, 56–7; double-cropping, 4, 12, 46–8; surplus, 6; commercialized production, 41, 201; disease, 45; cash input, 47; different maturation rates of, 52; supplementary labour, 54; transplanting, 55–7; cleaning and storing, 66–7; milling, 67; costs of production, 67–9; comparison of costs and yields, 68–9; estimated yields of traditional and new varieties, 69; opportunity costs, 69; average consumption, 70, 164; comparison of different production regimens, 70; optimum yields, 70–1; production constraints, 71; varietal diversification, 72, 202; pests, 91; stored grain as security, 91, 164; subsistence cultivation, 91, 166, 170; land as a source of cash income, 170; sale of land, 170; as a staple food, 178; land as cultural heritage, 178; interdependence of farmers, 187–9; farmers' response to change, 202; *see also* Family labour; Labour; *Rumah padi*; Social life; Women
River: as a natural resource, 91; riverine products, 91
Roads, 118; *see also* Marketing
Root diseases, 167; *see also* Weed control
Ru tree, 91, 209
Rubber: tapping as individual activity, 1; replanting schemes, 5, 141–3; Rubber Research Institute of Malaysia, 5, 141, 144–5; as a cash crop, 6, 178; as an estate crop, 10, 141–6; as a risky enterprise, 12; Rubber Industry Smallholders Development Authority, 141–3, 167; share-cropping of, 77, 143–4, 162; marketing, 140, 150; smallholdings, 141–6; high-yielding varieties, 141; bud-grafted clones, 143; size of holdings, 142, 152–3; land fragmentation, 144, 155; lost production, 145; loss in earnings, 146; yield comparison, 146; processing of, 148–51, 195; price fluctuation of sheet rubber, 150, 197; land-ownership, 152–8; as an exchangeable economic commodity, 154; price differentials of, 159; relationship between local dealers and tappers, 159–61; produc-

tivity of, 162–3; land as investment, 180; life of tapper, 195; *see also* Social life; Labour
Rumah padi, 66, 209
Rural development programmes, 8; *see also* Development programmes

SALE OF FISH BY WEIGHT, 114, 194
Sauk, 92, 210
Schools, 137; *see also* Education
Scrap rubber, 147, 150, 157, 160, 179
Sea, 182
Seasonality of catch, 87
Secondary economic activities, 164
Seed exchange programmes, 42
Seeding, 55, 185, 187
Seine net, 98; *see also Pukat dalam*
Self-sufficiency, 93
Semoh bendang, 12, 210
Settlement patterns, 134
Share-cropping, 31–3, 35–7, 156–8, 170–3, 180; *see also Bagi dua*; *Bagi tiga*
Share-tappers, 197
Short-term tenancy, 38–9
Shrimp, 99; *see also Udang baring*
Siam, 134
Sik: climate, 133–4; population, 134; land use, 134
Singapore, 75–6, 112
Slaughter tapping, 157, 201
Smallholder: definition, 142; management practices, 145; rubber production, 146–52
Smallholders Processing Centre, 77
Smokehouse, 159
Social life, 11–13, 19, 28–9, 40–1, 51, 57, 59, 64, 92–3, 100–3, 139, 188, 200; *see also* Family labour; Marriage; *Pinjam orang*; *Tolong-menolong*; Wealth; Women
Social norms, deviation from, 191–2
Social ostracism, 40
Social security, 2
Socio-cultural diversity, 203
Socio-cultural unity, 12
Soil: Beris, 20; alluvial, 21; Chempaka series, 21; structure, 21; fertility, 144
Spanish mackerel, 85, 109, 113
Specialization of labour, 101
Squatters, 177
Sri Malaysia II, 51
Staggered planting schedules, 55
Standard Malaysian Rubber, 161
State Department of Religious Affairs, 14
Status symbols, 28, 136; *see also* Élite
Subsistence agriculture, 5, 29, 39
Sungai Angga Irrigation Scheme, 21–2
Supplementary income, 122, 142, 167; *see also* Income; Cash crops
Supplementary labour, 57–9, 61–4; *see also* Family labour; *Pinjam orang*; *Tolong-menolong*; Wage labour
Symbiotic relationships, 3

Tajak, 91, 210
Tanah dusun, 25, 171, 210; *see also Dusun*
Tanah kampung, 24–5, 171, 210
Tanah padi, 25, 210
Tea, 58
Technological resources; definition, 2; access to and control over, 185; innovations, 185
Tenaga Baru, 115, 117–18
Tenancy relationships, 30–42
Theft, 176
Third Malaysian Plan, 11, 13
Threshing, 65, 164
Tobacco, 58, 69, 135, 166, 175; *see also* Cash crops
Tolong-menolong, 64, 80, 188, 210; *see also* Labour
Tok Su, 116
Tok Wan, 190–1
Tractors: cost of hire, 48, 69; ploughing with, 50–2; *see also* Ploughing
Trade regulation, 158
Traditional agricultural practices, 42–3
Traditional rice varieties, 56
Trammel net, 99; *see also Pukat tiga lapis*
Transplanting (rice), 55–7, 187; *see also* Rice; Labour
Transport, 26, 63, 82–3, 138; *see also* Communications; Marketing
Trash fish, 124
Trawl net, 98; *see also Pukat kokoh*
Tuesday market, 137
Tuna, 85
Tuntong, 91, 210

Udang Baring, 99–100, 123–30, 210
Unemployment benefits, 2
United Malays National Organization (UMNO), 10–11, 15

Unprocessed liquid latex, 150
Unting, 56–7, 62, 210

VEGETABLES, 134, 166; *see also* Cash crops
Veterinary Department, 24, 49, 191
Village: definition, 14; geographic boundaries, 14; social boundaries, 14; committees, 14; social life, 27
Village Development Committees (*Jawatankuasa Kemajuan Kampung*); functions of, 14–15; membership, 15; elections, 15

WAGE LABOUR, 61–3, 74, 182, 188; *see also* Supplementary labour
Wakaf, 108, 210
Water control, 42, 52, 55, 134, 164, 187; *see also* Rain; Monsoon
Wealth: traditional redistribution, 13, 136, 191; and civil service, 18; traditional functions of, 28; contemporary functions of, 28–9; transmission of, 184; *see also* Gong Tanah Merah; Inheritance
Weaving, 90, 93, 131; *see also* *Nipah*; Women
Weed control, 44, 50, 55–6, 71, 142
Weekly markets, 80, 84–5, 137, 159, 168; *see also* Tuesday market
Wolf herring, 85
Women: reapers, 65; single status of, 92–3; economic dominance of, 131; lack of opportunities for, 131; and family budget, 131–2; in petty trade, 137–8; *see also* Social life; Marriage